TEXAS PARKS AND CAMPGROUNDS

COMPLETELY REVISED 3RD EDITION

TEXAS PARKS AND CAMPGROUNDS

COMPLETELY REVISED 3RD EDITION

BY GEORGE OXFORD MILLER

Gulf Publishing Company
Houston, Texas

Gulf Publishing Company
Book Division
P.O. Box 2608, Houston, Texas 77252-2608

10 9 8 7 6 5 4 3 2

Library of Congress Cataloging-in-Publication Data

Miller, George Oxford, 1943–
    Texas parks and campgrounds/George Oxford Miller.—3rd ed.
        p.   cm. — (The Texas monthly guidebooks)
    Includes bibliographical references (p.) and index.
    ISBN 0-87719-265-0
    1. Campsites, facilities, etc.—Texas—Directories.   2. Campsites, facilities, etc.—Texas—Guidebooks.   3. Parks—Texas—Directories. 4. Parks—Texas—Guidebooks.   I. Title.   II. Series.
    GV191.42.T4M54   1995
    796.54'09764—dc20   94-45017
                                                                            CIP

Printed in the United States of America.

"Blessed is the spot, and the house, and the
place, and the city, and the heart, and the
mountain, and the refuge, and the cave, and the
valley, and the land, and the sea, and the
island, and the meadow where mention of God
hath been made, and His praise glorified."
—Bahá'u'lláh

This book is dedicated to my children, Koda and
Heather, and to those who love the outdoors
and are committed to preserving its natural
condition for future generations.

Texas Parks and Campgrounds

1. Abilene State Park
2. Alabama-Coushatta Indian Reservation
3. Amistad National Recreation Area
4. Andrews:
    Florey Park
    Municipal Trailer Park
5. Angelina National Forest
6. Atlanta State Park
7. Austin: Emma Long Municipal Park
8. Ballenger City Park
    Ballenger Lake Park
9. Balmorhea State Park
10. Bandera: Mansfield Park
11. Bastrop State Park
12. Bensten-Rio Grande Valley State Park
13A. Big Bend National Park
13B. Big Bend Ranch State Park
14. Big Spring:
    Comanche Park
    Moss Lake Park
15. Big Thicket National Preserve
16. Black Kettle National Grassland
17. Blanco State Park
18. Bonham State Park
19. Borger: Huber Park
20. Brady: Lake Brady Park
21. Brazos Bend State Park
22. Bridgeport: Wise County Park
23. Brownsville: Adolph Thomae, Jr. Park
24. Buescher State Park
25. Buffalo Lake National Refuge
26. Caddo Lake State Park
27. Caddo National Grasslands
28. Camp Wood: Lake Nueces Park
29. Canyon Lake
30. Caprock Canyon State Park
31. Castroville Regional Park
32. Cedar Hill State Park
33. Choke Canyon State Park
34. Cleburne State Park
35. Colorado Bend State Park
36. Colorado City:
    Fisher Park
    Ruddick Park
37. Copper Breaks State Park
38. Corpus Christi:
    Nueces River Park
    Padre Bali Park
39. Corsicana: Lake Halbert State Park
40. Daingerfield State Park
41. Dalhart: Rita Blanca Lake Park
42. Davis Mountains State Park
43. Davy Crockett National Forest
44. Devils River State Park
45. Dinosaur Valley State Park
46. Dumas: Texoma Park
47. Eisenhower State Park
48. Enchanted Rock State Natural Area
49. Fairfield State Park
50. Falcon: Starr County Falcon Park
51. Falcon State Park
52. Fort Griffin State Historical Park
53. Fort Parker State Park and Old Fort
    Parker State Historical Park
54. Fort Richardson State Historical Park
55. Fredericksburg: Lady Bird Johnson
    Municipal Park
56. Freeport:
    Quintana Beach County Park
    San Luis County Park
57. Galveston:
    Fort Travis Seashore Park
    Galveston Island State Park
58. Garner State Park
59. Goldthwaite Municipal Park
60. Goliad State Historical Park
61. Gonzales:
    Independence Park
    Lake Wood Recreation Area

62. Goose Island State Park
63. Government Canyon
64. Guadalupe Mountains National Park
65. Guadalupe River State Park
66. Haskell City Park
67. Hill Country State Natural Area
68. Hueco Tanks State Historical Area
69. Huntsville State Park
70. Inks Lake State Park
71. Iraan: Alley Oop Park
72. Joe Pool Lake
73. Kerrville-Schreiner State Park
74. Kickapoo Cavern State Park
75. Kingsville: Kaufer-Hubert Memorial Park
    and SeaWind RV Resort
76. Lake Arrowhead State Park
77. Lake B. A. Steinhagen
78. Lake Bardwell
79. Lake Bastrop
80. Lake Belton
81. Lake Benbrook
82. Lake Bob Sandlin State Park
83. Lake Brownwood State Park
84. Lake Buchanan: Black Rock Park
85. Lake Casa Blanca State Park
86. Lake Colorado City State Park
87. Lake Corpus Christi State Park
88. Lake Cypress Springs
89. Lake Georgetown
90. Lake Granger
91. Lake Grapevine
92. Lake Hords Creek
93. Lake Houston State Park
94. Lake Jacksonville Park
95. Lake Lavon
96. Lake Lewisville
    Hidden Cove Park
97. Lake Livingston State Park
    Wolf Creek Park
98. Lake Meredith National Recreation Area

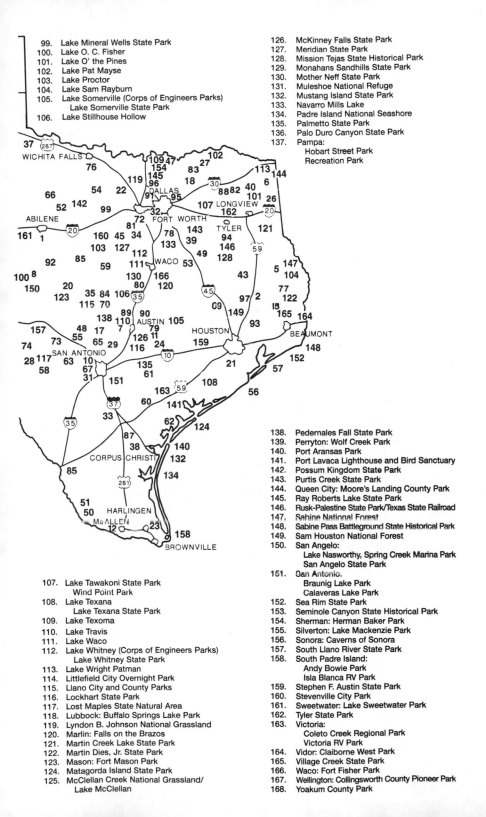

Table of Contents

Introduction

For people who like the great outdoors, Texas has a lot to offer. You can escape the city in 131 state parks, scores of man-made lakes, several national parks, 4 national forests, 400 miles of public seashore, and numerous county and municipal parks. In 1994 23.5 million people visited the state parks alone, and 2.5 million camped overnight. To help you explore the great outdoors in this vast state, this book lists about 415 public parks with campgrounds. In addition, historical parks without camping are listed.

The immense size of Texas gives it more than just impressive numbers, it gives it diversity—there is something for everyone. From the dense pine-hardwood forests of East Texas to the 8,000-foot-high mountains and Chihuahuan Desert west of the Pecos, Texas has a phenomenal diversity of natural habitats. In addition to the flat coastal prairies and a crescent-shaped coastline, this state includes the rocky hill country of Central Texas, the broad prairies of the Panhandle, and a subtropical climate in the lush Rio Grande Valley in the south. The Big Thicket, the most ecologically diverse woodlands in North America, and Big Bend National Park, a million acres of unspoiled wilderness that encompasses an entire mountain range, are two examples of Texas' rich natural heritage.

The diversity of habitats in Texas and its southern locale make camping enjoyable throughout the year, not just in the spring and summer. In the winter, visitors from the north flock to the salubrious climate of South Texas by the tens of thousands. Spring and fall are delightful just about anywhere in the state. The mountains offer a respite from the simmering summer heat, and despite unpredictable weather in the winter, we often find Big Bend National Park warm and sunny in December and January.

Texas encompasses ten distinct vegetational zones, each with its own characteristic plant and animal communities. The Piney Woods, Gulf Coast Prairies and Marshes, Post Oak Savanna, and Blackland Prairies make up the eastern half of the state. South Texas is mostly plains or brush country. Central Texas includes the Edwards Plateau and the Cross Timbers and Prairies. The Panhandle has the Rolling Plains and the High Plains, also called the Llano

Estacado, or Staked Plains. In West Texas, the Trans-Pecos includes mountain ranges and desert flats.

The diversity found in Texas is due, in part, to its size, 276,000 square miles or 7.5 percent of the land area of the United States. To say that Texas is large is an understatement. Anyone traveling across the state, which stretches 830 miles from Beaumont to El Paso and 780 miles between Brownsville and Amarillo, can identify with the old saying, "The sun has riz, the sun has set, and here we is, in Texas yet."

No matter where you go, however, you will be close to some public camping facility. This guidebook provides information to help you decide where to spend your vacation and how to better understand and enjoy the area upon arriving. We explain the ecological and historical significance of each major area and present the facilities available and noteworthy nearby attractions. Our hope is that this book will enhance your outdoor experience and make your vacation, whether a weekend or extended holiday, more meaningful and enjoyable.

WHAT IS INCLUDED IN THIS BOOK

This book includes all state parks, national parks, national forests, and U.S. Army Corps of Engineers parks with public camping facilities. Many of the state parks that do not have campgrounds are mentioned in the relevant descriptions under "Nearby Attractions" and in the section on historical parks.

In addition, we included many noncommercial and concession-operated campgrounds that have decent camping facilities and some recreational interest. As resources, we used a statewide outdoor recreation inventory compiled by the Texas Parks and Wildlife Department, as well as questionnaires mailed to each park. We visited all the state and national parks and forests and the majority of the Corps of Engineers reservoirs, but not all of the county and regional parks. We relied on the questionnaires obtained from the parks not visited to determine whether or not to include them. If the park was very small and had few facilities, we omitted it from the book. However, we did include a few parks that, though they had minimal camping facilities, were interesting places to visit as natural areas or that provided a good overnight stop.

We did not include the hundreds of privately owned campgrounds and RV parks existing cross the state. They are adequately listed in directories published regularly by Woodalls and other commercial directories. Refer to the bibliography for those books.

HOW TO USE THE BOOK

For ease of reference, each campground is designated by number on a map of the state. The campgrounds are listed in the text in alphabetical order. If you desire to visit a specific area, find the campground numbers on the map, and refer to the detailed information found in the text. Alternatively, the vacationer could first read the comprehensive descriptions, decide on an interesting spot, and locate it on the map by its map number. Once you have visited a park and are ready to move on, use the map to select your next stop—attractive and interesting areas are available in every direction.

Besides providing a list of the numbers and types of campsites and recreational facilities, each write-up describes features of special interest to the visitor. The ecological and historical significance of the park is discussed, and nearby attractions are usually noted. This will help you plan your trip around, say, spring dogwood blooms or songbird migration, summer wildflowers, fall hiking, and winter hunting. Knowledge of the camping facilities, recreational opportunities, and natural attractions should greatly enhance vacation planning. Refer to the appendixes for lists of parks with cabins and motels and group facilities.

Before you load up your car or van, we suggest you take advantage of the addresses and phone numbers listed in this book. Write or call the parks for reservations and information about current conditions. Ask the rangers to send maps and brochures to help you make the best use of your precious vacation time.

PRESERVING FOR THE FUTURE

Texas has been tamed. The outdoor experience in Texas has changed vastly in the last two or three generations. Our forefathers, and mothers, saw vast herds of bison ranging across the Texas plains, and piney woods so dense that they repelled Indians and whites alike. Now, the prairies have been converted into farmland, cities, and suburbs. In large areas of West Texas, desert brush now grows on overgrazed land where vast grasslands once held the precious soil in place. The deep piney woods have been logged to such an extent that only 10 percent of the Big Thicket remains. The waterways of Texas have been impounded and channelized, and the underground water reservoirs have almost been pumped dry.

When Texas joined the Union, it retained possession of its vast land resources. Unfortunately, the money-poor but land-rich state gave away practically all of its inherent wealth. The citizens of Texas themselves raised the funds to buy Big Bend National Park and donated it to the federal government. The state park system, since its beginning in 1923, has preserved some of Texas' most scenic areas. Private concerns are racing developers, speculators, and clear-cut forest operations to preserve unique areas, which, once lost, can never be replaced. The Nature Conservancy alone has purchased more than 202,000 acres of the state's pristine natural areas to preserve for future generations, and it has identified over 500 more critical areas that need protection.

Will the outdoor experience of our children and grandchildren be as dramatically different from ours as ours was from our grandparents? We hope that our descendants will know more than vast freeway complexes and crowded picnic parks. As population pressures increase, the preservation of portions of our irreplaceable natural heritage becomes more imperative.

CAMPING ETIQUETTE

With more and more people using our natural areas, each recreationist's actions must reflect a basic consideration for others. This goes beyond simply obeying the rules concerning quiet times in the evening and not littering the campsites and trails. Each of us must consider not only the individual's impact on the natural condition of an area but also our collective impact. For instance, the scenic Twin Falls area in Pedernales Falls State Park had to be closed because overuse was compacting the soil so much that the bald cypress trees were dying.

Common violations of the outdoor ethic include gathering firewood in public parks, chopping off live limbs for firewood, picking flowers, and cutting across switchbacks on mountain trails. Each of those actions may seem harmless when done once, but they are devastating when repeated continually by dozens of park users. The results are denuded trees and unsightly scars caused by erosion along the trails.

The goals of preserving wilderness, scenic beauty, and sensitive ecological areas while providing outdoor recreation for thousands, even millions, of people can be mutually exclusive if we are not aware of our individual responsibilities. Our personal impact on our environment, whether in a neighborhood park or on a remote trail, must be as neutral as possible. Better yet, we can often have a positive impact by picking up litter and assisting in the preservation of natural areas.

PERSONAL COMMENTS

We occasionally have included our own editorial comments on the suitability of some areas for camping. For some of the county and regional parks that we visited, we have added a few words about the quality of the areas. A few of the smaller local parks have exceptionally good facilities, but many have minimally adequate facilities and can be thought of as little more than overnight stopping places.

In general, in our years of camping in Texas, we have found the campgrounds to be pleasant and our fellow campers to be friendly and helpful. However, in an unsupervised park, people driving in for a late-night beer-drinking party can be loud, inconsiderate, and threatening. In parks likely to be a locally popular party spot, it is advisable to camp in a supervised area or in a section of the park where the campers outnumber the day users. More and more of the parks around lakes now lock the gates to the camping areas at night to avoid such problems. The state parks are supposed to be closed to all except campers after 10 P.M., but the gates are usually open all night. We have experienced late-night harassment only in parks that were close to large cities or in the Panhandle where small-town youths presumably have little to do after dark but cruise the parks. After a sleepless night at Lake Meredith, we questioned park personnel the next day to find that the park budget didn't provide for adequate supervision of the grounds. The next night, at Fort Griffin, we were relieved to see the park ranger make his rounds several times before we went to sleep.

RESERVATIONS

The national parks and national forests do not take reservations, except for group facilities and campgrounds leased to concessionaires. The Corps of Engineers now accepts reservations at the toll free number 1-800-284-2267 (CAMP). Reservations are accepted from sixteen to ninety days in advance for developed campgrounds at the following lakes: Bardwell, Belton, Benbrook, Canyon, Granger, Grapevine, Hords Creek, Georgetown, Lake O' the Pines, Lavon, Lewisville, Navarro Mills, O.C. Fisher, Proctor, Sam Rayburn, Somerville, Stillhouse Hollow, Town Bluff Dam and Lake B.A. Steinhagen, Lake Waco, Whitney, and Wright Patman. Credit cards are accepted.

The Texas State Park system has a centralized number for all day-use and overnight facilities, including cabins, screened shelters, and some tours. Call 512-389-8900 (Austin) between 8 A.M. and 5 P.M. (See the listings for the Indian Lodge in the Davis Mountains and the Texas State Railroad, which have separate reservation numbers.) You can expect most parks to fill up on weekends and during the busy season, which is summer for north Texas and winter for south and west Texas. Reservations must be made at least two days prior to arrival, and may be charged on Visa or MasterCard. The centralized reservation system was initiated in March 1994, and may be modified in the future. For general park information, call 1-800-792-1112, or in Austin, 389-8950.

STATE PARKS

The 128 state-owned parks in Texas are classified as state parks, natural areas, historical parks and partnership parks. As of fall 1996, about 10 of the parks were unopened or open only for limited use until funding and/or master plans can be developed, another 5 are undeveloped beaches with no facilities, and 32 are day-use only. So Texas has approximately 80 state-operated parks with developed camping facilities. State parks preserve areas of outstanding ecological or geological importance and offer noteworthy recreational opportunities. Except for a few undeveloped parks and beaches, they all provide tent and RV camping facilities and restrooms with hot-water showers.

The designation "recreation area," used for some state and national facilities, indicates that the main attraction of the park is not as a natural area. In Texas, the term is generally used for parks that are built on man-made reservoirs or on the Gulf coast. Boating and fishing, rather than hiking and exploring nature, are the dominant forms of recreation at those parks.

State historical parks are just what the term implies, areas where a particular aspect of Texas history has been preserved and displayed. Some parks not designated as historic do, nevertheless, have interesting exhibits on Texas' past.

The "natural area" designation indicates that the state is maintaining a biologically unique area in a natural condition, while still allowing camping and hiking in restricted areas. This book describes each park's natural environment, nature trails, and backpacking opportunities, as well as camping and recreation facilities.

Parks in the state system generally have the best camping facilities of any public parks in Texas. In recent years, many of the older parks have upgraded their facilities, installing modern restrooms with hot showers, and many now have recently added sewage hookups to the RV sites.

We were disappointed to discover that few state parks have interpretive exhibits or ranger-led programs. The historical parks, such as Goliad and the forts, have historical structures and displays, but in many of the parks, little information is available on the ecological and historical importance of the area. Some notable exceptions are the wonderful exhibits at Seminole Canyon, Dinosaur Valley, Brazos Bend, Enchanted Rock, and Lost Maples. In our write-ups, we have noted whether the park has interpretive exhibits.

Texas Parks and Wildlife offers a series of professionally led adventure tours. From weekend to week-long outings, the Texas Passport Adventures include meals, lodging, and equipment. You can photograph with a professional, canoe remote canyons, birdwatch, scuba dive, backpack, llama pack, flyfish, and explore outdoor and historical sites. For a tour brochure, call 1-800-792-1112.

Many state parks have free bird lists and trail-guide brochures available. Some do not display their pamphlets; you have to ask for them. Interpretation of the natural habitats of the state parks has a low priority for funding in Texas. In many parks, the supervisor has to act as park manager, security guard, ticket taker, phone answerer, and perform a variety of other time-consuming jobs. Since our first guidebook was published, the state has added more than 30 new parks, but the number of employees has remained about the same. Please, let your state representative know if you would like to see more emphasis on interpretation in your state parks.

Few public parks have adequate facilities for people confined to wheelchairs. However, a few state parks have installed special camping pads and nature trails for wheelchair access. The best facilities are at the state parks. A Texas Parks and Wildlife brochure lists parks with facilities for the handicapped. Inquire at any state park for a copy.

STATE PARK FEES

Beginning May 1, 1996, each person over age 12 will pay an entry fee from $1 to $5, depending on the park. For $50, individuals or families can purchase an annual Gold Texas Conservation Passport that admits all occupants of the vehicle bearing the decal into all state parks and into wildlife management areas at certain times. Additional fees are charged for camping and certain activities and tours. Call the state park information number, 1-800-792-1112, for a four-page, fold-out brochure describing the fees for the various parks.

NATIONAL PARKS

Texas has two national parks, Guadalupe Mountains and Big Bend; Padre Island National Seashore; the Big Thicket National Preserve; two national recreation areas, Amistad and Lake Meredith; and two national historical parks, Missions in San Antonio and Lyndon B. Johnson. The National Park Service operates these facilities. The national recreation areas are impounded reservoirs, which attract those interested in fishing and water sports. In contrast, the national parks, preserve, and national seashore are rare areas of fascinating ecological diversity. They provide superb opportunities to learn about the natural vegetation and wildlife of Texas and to experience the wilderness that once covered this vast state.

The national parks in Texas have few exhibits. Most have pamphlets on the vegetation and wildlife of the areas. Refer to the write-ups on the parks for information about the ecology and history of these unique areas.

STATE FORESTS

Texas have five state forests—Fairchild, near Rusk; Jones, near Conroe; Kirby, near Woodville; Masterson, near Buna; and Siecke, near Kirbyville—all located in the piney woods of East Texas. The forests, varying from 600 to 2,900 acres, are managed by the Texas Forest Service as part of the Texas A&M University System to study modern forestry techniques. Picnicking, hiking, nature study, and limited fishing are allowed. Since camping is prohibited in state forests, they are not included in this book. For information on hiking in the state forests, write to the Texas Forestry Association, 1903 Atkinson Dr., Lufkin, Texas 75902, or call 409-632-8733.

The woodlands of East Texas include longleaf, shortleaf, and loblolly pines; a wide variety of oaks, hickory, magnolia, beech, sweetgum, and American holly; and numerous species of understory trees, shrubs, vines, wildflowers, and mushrooms. Dwarf palmetto, bald cypress, and water tupelo thrive in the lush swamplands. Many birds make their home in the forests, including the large pileated woodpecker, the rare red-cockaded woodpecker, the brown-headed nuthatch, and many warblers and vireos. See the bibliography for field guides to the trees, wildflowers, reptiles, and amphibians of this luxuriant area of the state.

NATIONAL FORESTS

Texas has four national forests operated by the U.S. Forest Service: Angelina, Davy Crockett, Sabine, and Sam Houston. Camping facilities in the national forests are not as well-developed as in the state parks in Texas. Many camping areas have only primitive sites with a water hydrant nearby and pit toilets. Some have flush toilets and cold showers. None of the national forest parks have electric hookups.

The four national forests, each covering more than 150,000 acres, have private land scattered throughout their boundaries. The U.S. Forest Service manages them with a multiple-use philosophy that includes lumbering, grazing, oil production, hunting, and recreation. The timber is managed primarily to maximize pine growth. Portions of the forests are clear-cut and seeded with pine trees; other areas are selectively logged, with the hardwoods culled and mature pines removed for market. Timber is sold to private logging operations, and there is occasional poaching of timber. The trees are considered a cash crop, such as corn, and the land is managed to produce the maximum yield.

The woodlands you see today may have been logged two or three times. Sections thousands of acres in extent are now pine plantations that are as ecologically barren as a wheat field. Fortunately, a few areas have been set aside to preserve the rich diversity of plant and animal life for this and future generations to enjoy.

Deer and squirrel hunting are popular activities in the fall. During deer season in November and December, camping is permitted only in designated campgrounds. At other times, camping is permitted throughout the forests, unless posted otherwise. Hikers are advised to wear regulation orange hunting vests or other highly visible apparel during hunting season.

Logging operations, hunting, and off-road-vehicle use are not conducive to enjoying a quiet walk in the woods. However, the national forests have plenty of areas that allow you to get away from it all. The Lone Star Hiking Trail traverses 140 miles of the Sam Houston National Forest. Developed with the assistance of the Houston Group of the Lone Star Chapter of the Sierra Club, the trail offers hikers a rare opportunity to explore the forest. Refer to the descriptions of individual forests for information on other hiking trails in the Davy Crockett National Forest.

The national forest trails and regulations often are abused by thoughtless users. Policing the forests is difficult, to say the least, because of the vast area and the limited number of rangers.

NATIONAL GRASSLANDS

The U.S. Forest Service operates four national grasslands in Texas: Caddo, Lyndon B. Johnson, Black Kettle, and McClellan Creek. The grasslands are available for public hunting and fishing. The few camping areas available have minimal facilities.

During the thirties, millions of acres of valuable farmland in a vast area, including much of Kansas, Oklahoma, North Texas, and the Panhandle, became a wasteland. Decades of poor soil-conservation practices in the dry central and southwestern prairies left the soil denuded of vegetation. The thirties brought year after year of drought and howling winds. The ravaged area became known as the Dust Bowl. By the end of the decade, more than 20 million acres had lost two to five inches of topsoil, and thousands of farmers in five states had deserted their land.

In the mid-thirties, the federal government began purchasing eroded cropland for rehabilitation. The national grasslands, scattered from Texas to Montana, became a part of the restoration program. At one time the home of bison, prairie dogs, and longhorns, the grasslands today provide pastures for cattle, lakes for fishing, and woods for hunting.

ARMY CORPS OF ENGINEERS RESERVOIRS

Texas has virtually no naturally occurring lakes, but man-made reservoirs abound throughout the state, particularly in the northern and eastern portions. The U.S. Army Corps of Engineers has impounded every major river and stream in the state. Even Caddo Lake, which was originally formed by a natural logjam, has been dammed.

The reservoirs serve the two main functions of flood control and storage for the water normally carried to the Gulf of Mexico by rivers and streams. A reservoir is designed to be filled to a level below its maximum capacity; this extra capacity is necessary for flood protection. Each year, dams on Texas rivers and streams prevent millions of dollars in flood damage. Some of the dams also provide hydroelectric power.

A few of the reservoirs were built adjacent to natural areas that offer interesting habitats for exploration. However, most of the lakes we visited were extensively cleared of natural vegetation and did not offer much of interest to the nature lover. Nonetheless, many of the lakes provide pleasant relief from the hot summer temperatures.

Lakes near large towns may receive as many as five million visitors annually.

Many of the lakes have campgrounds, day-use parks, and wildlife management areas where hunting is allowed. For ease of reference, a matrix itemizing the camping facilities accompanies each write-up. Fishing and water sports are the dominant recreational activities at the reservoirs. All have boat ramps; many have fishing piers and marinas. Campgrounds vary from primitive; with pit toilets and a few water hydrants, to concessionaire-operated parks with full RV hookups, flush toilets, and hot showers.

Parks with high visitation have suffered from vandalism and rude and rowdy visitors. Many of the parks now have full-time gate attendants that lock the gates at 10 P.M. We applaud that security precaution and encourage park users to continue the tradition of politeness that makes camping so enjoyable.

Most of the state has little naturally occurring surface water. Municipalities, agriculture, and industry must depend on ground water or impounded streams and rivers. Surface water is cheaper and easier to obtain than ground water, so many Texas cities rely on reservoirs for their water supply. In West Texas, some towns, such as Coleman, resorted to importing water by train before a local reservoir was built.

Many of the lakes in Texas were built for flood protection and have prevented millions of dollars of damage. However, harnessing a river has many ramifications beyond preventing floods and providing a source of water. Those dependent on the land, both humans and wildlife, must pay the price. While providing downstream flood protection, a reservoir destroys many thousands of acres above the dam. That has resulted in the destruction of entire towns, important archaeological sites, prime farmland, and a major loss of wildlife habitat.

Over the years, silt, which normally would have been deposited in floodplains and deltas, accumulates behind the dam. After several decades, the silt can build up to such high levels that protection from flooding is severely limited. The problem can be particularly acute in shallow lakes, and most Texas reservoirs averaged only 10 to 15 feet deep when formed.

While the trapped water supplies an immediate need for local towns, the lake, by exposing a larger surface area to the sun, increases water loss due to evaporation. In West Texas the rate of evaporation may be ten times greater than the annual rainfall. In addition, the change in the speed of water flow, the increased temperature, and reduced oxygen content of the water makes it an inhospitable habitat for many native fish.

One of the greatest economical and environmental problems created by impounding Texas rivers is the detrimental effect on the bays and estuaries. To the inland user, every drop that reaches the ocean is a wasted drop. To coastal fish and wildlife, fresh water means life. With less fresh water entering the bays, the estuaries and marshes become increasingly saline. The marshes can become more than twice as salty as the ocean, particularly in periods of drought. These delicate areas are some of the most biologically productive habitat in the state and the nursery grounds for fish that support a multimillion-dollar fishing industry. The health of the coastal fisheries depends on the health of the estuaries, which depends on an adequate inflow of fresh water from the rivers.

Texas Parks and Campgrounds

1. ABILENE STATE PARK

LOCATION
Taylor County. 16 miles south of Abilene of FM 89.
Mailing address: 150 Park Road 32, Tuscola, Texas 79562.
Phone: 915-572-3204. For all state park reservations,
call 512-389-8900.

FACILITIES
Camping: 12 campsites with water nearby, 88 campsites with water and electricity, group trailer sites with water, electricity, kitchen, and dining hall. Screened shelters, modern restrooms with showers, trailer dump station. Fees charged.

Recreation: picnic areas and playgrounds, 1.5-mile hiking trail, swimming and wading pools (summer only), fishing and boating in nearby Lake Abilene, dining hall, state longhorn herd, concessions (summer only).

MAIN ATTRACTIONS
The heavily wooded drainage of Elm Creek provides a scenic contrast to the semiarid prairie grasslands of the surrounding area. The dense groves of trees provide a pleasant setting for picnicking and camping. The park swimming pool is open in the summer, and fishing is popular on the 675-acre Lake Abilene, which borders the park. A trail loops around the campgrounds and along Elm Creek. A portion of the state longhorn herd is maintained in the park.

ECOLOGY
The 490-acre park is located in an area known since pioneer times as Buffalo Gap, named for the many bison that moved through the natural pass between two flat-topped buttes northeast of the park.

The hills form the Callahan Divide, separating the headwaters of the Brazos and the Colorado rivers.

The Callahan Divide is characterized by lowlands broken by mesas up to 400 feet high. The hills are capped with Comanchean limestones and underlaid with soft sandstones and shales. The limestones, resistant to weathering in the dry climate of West Texas, have prevented the buttes from eroding away. The red clay soil of the park is the result of the weathering of the shales.

The Permian sedimentary layers beneath the lowlands of the area were deposited in shallow seas 280 million years ago. These same geologic formations are 6,000 feet beneath the surface farther west and have yielded some of the richest oil fields in Texas.

The forested areas of the park are composed of Ashe juniper, live oak, and mesquite trees; yuccas and prickly pear cacti are scattered through the grassy savannas. Groves of pecan trees shade the banks of Elm Creek. Soaptree, elm, Texas oak, and hackberry trees grow in the creek drainage. Poison ivy is common throughout the camping and picnic grounds—arriving in the park late one night, we mistakenly pitched our tent in the midst of a patch!

The most common wildlife in the park are armadillos, squirrels, and rabbits. Deer, raccoons, skunks, and coyotes also occur. Many species of birds are attracted to the groves of trees.

HISTORY

The dense woodlands surrounding Elm Creek have attracted both wildlife and humans since early times. The southern herds of bison passed through the divide, giving the area the name "Buffalo Gap"; today the settlement of Buffalo Gap is popular for its restaurants and its Historical Village, which has a number of original and facsimile pioneer buildings. Tonkawa and Comanche Indians lived in the area, and artifacts are often found in the vicinity of the park.

In the 1870s, in an attempt to eradicate a major food source for the Indians, buffalo hunters were encouraged to eliminate the massive herds of bison, selling their hides for $2 each. Soon cattle dominated the grasslands and great drives passed through the gap. In 1858, the Butterfield State Route from St. Louis to San Francisco passed near the park. When the Texas and Pacific Railroad reached Abilene in 1880, the town became the county seat and the center of activity in the area.

2. ALABAMA-COUSHATTA
INDIAN RESERVATION

LOCATION

Polk County. 17 miles east of Livingston on U.S. 190.
Mailing address: Route 3, Box 640, Livingston, Texas 77351.
Phone: 409-563-4391, Texas only 800-444-3507.

FACILITIES

Camping: 38 campsites with water only, 43 campsites with water and electricity, 42 campsites with water, electricity, and sewage hookups; modern restrooms with showers, trailer dump station. Reservations accepted. Fees charged.

Recreation: picnic areas, swimming in Lake Tombigbee, fishing, canoeing, paddleboat rental, amphitheater, museum, tours, Indian village, gift shop, restaurant, store.

MAIN ATTRACTIONS

Activities on the reservation are designed to provide an entertaining and educational experience. There are interpretive tours of the Big Thicket, an Indian village with demonstrations of crafts and foods, replicas of early Indian homes and camps, and a ride on a miniature train. A museum explains the life and roots of the Alabama and Coushatta tribes, and a gift shop sells crafts. Colorful tribal dances are performed daily in the summer and on weekends during the spring and fall. Write or call for a brochure and a schedule of tours, as they vary seasonally.

At the campgrounds surrounding the 26-acre Lake Tombigbee, fishing, swimming, and canoeing are popular activities. Except on a 2-hour hiking trail, hiking outside the tourist area is not permitted.

The reservation, located in the Big Thicket, encompasses 4,600 acres. The Big Thicket is biologically unique and has the greatest plant and animal diversity of any area in North America. See the write-up of that area for a description.

HISTORY

The first historical record of the Alabama and Coushatta tribes comes from 1541, when they were attacked by Hernando de Soto in what is now Mississippi. These peaceful Indians lived in accord with the French during the French occupation of the area, which ended in

1763. In 1807, a group of Alabama Indians and the Coushatta tribe established a village on the Trinity River in Texas.

The Indians fled into Louisiana rather than side with either Texas or Mexico during the Revolution. When they returned, their lands had been preempted by white settlers. Finally, in 1854, the state legislature purchased 1,280 acres as the initial unit of the reservation, to be held by the Indians "inalienable forever."

3. AMISTAD NATIONAL RECREATION AREA

LOCATION
Val Verde County. Northwest of Del Rio on U.S. 90 and U.S. 277. Headquarters: western edge of Del Rio on U.S. 90, 2 miles west of Plaza del Sol Shopping Center. Mailing address: Box 420367, Del Rio, Texas 78842-0367. Phone: 210-775-7491.

FACILITIES
Camping: Amistad has primitive camping, with no water and accessible only by boat, anywhere along the shore below the 1,144-foot contour line except in restricted areas. Camping is free, on a first-come basis, except in the commercial campgrounds.

There are free primitive campsites with tables, grills, and chemical toilets but no water at San Pedro Flats off U.S. 90 on the south shore, Old 277 North Campground off U.S. 277 on the north shore, Spur 406 Campground off U.S. 90 on the north shore, and Governors Landing off U.S. 90 on the south shore.

Group camping is available at Rock Quarry, Old 277 North, and San Pedro Flats campgrounds. Reservations are accepted for groups.

Commercial campgrounds are at Diablo East off U.S. 90 on the south shore, Rough Canyon off U.S. 277 to RR 2, and the Pecos River off U.S. 90.

There is a trailer dump station at Diablo East service road.

The camping facilities at Amistad are primitive and the terrain rocky and hilly, yet more than a million people a year visit the lake. We recommend the facilities primarily for those interested in fishing and water sports or for winter visitors looking for RV campgrounds with a mild climate.

Recreation: picnicking, nature trails, swimming in Amistad Reservoir, fishing, boating, marinas at Diablo East and Rough Canyon, hunting, pavilion at Rough Canyon, amphitheaters at Governors Landing and Spur 454, stores at Diablo East and Rough Canyon.

AMISTAD NATIONAL RECREATION AREA

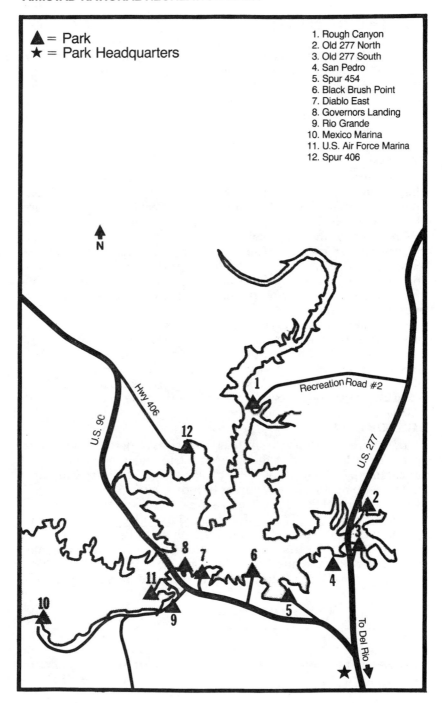

▲ = Park
★ = Park Headquarters

1. Rough Canyon
2. Old 277 North
3. Old 277 South
4. San Pedro
5. Spur 454
6. Black Brush Point
7. Diablo East
8. Governors Landing
9. Rio Grande
10. Mexico Marina
11. U.S. Air Force Marina
12. Spur 406

N

Hwy 406

U.S. 90

Recreation Road #2

U.S. 277

To Del Rio

MAIN ATTRACTIONS

Amistad Reservoir was formed on the Rio Grande by a cooperative effort between Mexico and the United States. The immense lake covers 67,000 acres about half of the year and has 850 miles of shoreline. The reservoir provides water-oriented activities in a semiarid environment. Fishing for channel catfish, yellow catfish, crappie, and sunfish is reportedly best in spring and early summer. Write the park headquarters for information about hunting.

ECOLOGY

The Amistad Dam impounds the Rio Grande just below its confluence with the Devils and Pecos rivers. The reservoir extends 25 miles into Devils Canyon, 14 miles up the Pecos, and 74 miles up the Rio Grande. The lake stands in stark contrast to the semiarid environment of the chaparral-covered hillsides. The vegetation of the dry rocky terrain is mainly thorny blackbrush acacia, guajillo, yucca, mesquite, and sotol. Wildlife adapted to the harsh environment include javelinas, white-tailed deer, jackrabbits, rock squirrels, raccoons, and many reptiles, especially rattlesnakes, king snakes, and lizards.

The temperature in the summer can surpass 100 degrees; sunburn and heat exhaustion can develop rapidly under those conditions. Freezing weather with violent windstorms may occur from December to February. Thunderstorms are common, accounting for the 18 inches of rain received annually. Campers, hikers, and boaters should take adequate precautions to protect themselves from the elements.

HISTORY

Indian artifacts dating back 12,000 years have been found in the area. The rising water of the lake inundated many archaeological sites. However, the nearby Seminole Canyon State Historical Park preserves some excellent examples of Indian pictographs.

The building of the railroad across West Texas, with Irish and Chinese labor, and the activities of the legendary Judge Roy Bean highlighted the colorful period around the turn of the century. The story of the railroad and early ranching is presented at Seminole Canyon State Historical Park, and Judge Roy Bean's role in taming the West is portrayed at the Judge Roy Bean Visitor Center in Langtry.

4. ANDREWS: FLOREY PARK

Andrews County. 65 miles west of Big Spring on TX 176 to Andrews, 10 miles north on U.S. 385. Mailing address: County Courthouse, Room 104, Andrews, Texas 79714. Phone: 915-523-5807.

Camping: 100 campsites with water and electricity, 48 campsites with water, electricity, and sewage hookups; flush toilets, trailer dump station. Fees charged. Recreation: picnic areas and playgrounds, pavilion, recreation hall (must be reserved). Open all year.

ANDREWS: MUNICIPAL TRAILER PARK

Andrews County. Behind Chamber of Commerce building at 700 West Broadway (TX 176 west). Mailing address: Chamber of Commerce, 700 West Broadway, Andrews, TX 79714. Phone: 915-523-2695. Camping: 11 RV sites with tables, water, electricity, sewage hookups, dump station. No restrooms. No fees, no reservations. Open all year.

5. ANGELINA NATIONAL FOREST

LOCATION
Surrounds Sam Rayburn Reservoir, east of Lufkin on U.S. 69 to Zavalla.
Mailing address: Box 756, Lufkin, Texas 75901-0756. Phone: 409-639-8620.

FACILITIES
Angelina National Forest offers six parks with campgrounds. Campsites cannot be reserved. Primitive camping, at no charge, is allowed anywhere in the national forest, except when hunting or logging is in progress. Some campgrounds are free; fees at others vary.

As no map of the forest is included here, the following directions are given to those parks that have campgrounds. Write the headquarters for maps and further details.

Bouton Lake: 8 miles southeast of Zavalla on TX 63, 7.7 miles south on FSR 303.

Boykin Springs: 11 miles southeast of Zavalla on TX 63, 2.5 miles south on FSR 313.

Caney Creek: 4 miles southeast of Zavalla on TX 63, 6.5 miles east on FM 2743. See map for Lake Sam Rayburn.

Harvey Creek: 3.5 miles southeast of Broaddus on FM 83, 5 miles south on FM 2390. See map for Lake Sam Rayburn.

Sandy Creek: 17.5 miles southeast of Zavalla on TX 63, 3 miles north on FSR 333. See map for Lake Sam Rayburn.

Townsend: about 13 miles northeast of Zavalla on TX 147, turn north on FM 1277 about 3 miles to FM 2923, west to park.

Sawmill Hiking Trail: 5.5-mile trail connecting campgrounds at Bouton Lake and Boykin Springs.

Campground	water	fee area	flush toilets	season	dump station	cold-water showers	boating	fishing	swimming	trails
Bouton Lake				all			•	•		•
Boykin Springs	•	•	•	all		•	•	•	•	•
Caney Creek	•	•	•	all	•	•	•	•		•
Harvey Creek		•		all			•	•		
Sandy Creek	•	•	•	Mar.–Sept.		•	•	•		
Townsend	•	•		all		•	•	•		

MAIN ATTRACTIONS

The Angelina National Forest covers 154,916 acres of mixed pine-hardwood forests in Angelina, Jasper, Nacogdoches, and San Augustine counties. Sam Rayburn Reservoir, with the national forest along its shores, is popular for fishing, camping, picnicking, and water sports. At Bouton Lake and Boykin Springs, only boats without motors are allowed.

HIKING

From Bouton Lake, the 5.5-mile Sawmill Hiking Trail follows the winding Neches River, crosses several creeks, passes two abandoned sawmills, and parallels Boykin Creek to Boykin Springs Campground. The bottomlands are filled with a great diversity of hardwoods, including bald cypress, tupelo, oaks, ironwood, and elm. Magnolia and dogwood trees decorate the woods each spring with their fragrant white flowers.

Deer hunting is allowed in the forest during November and December. Hikers as well as hunters should wear regulation orange vests.

6. ATLANTA STATE PARK

LOCATION

Cass County. 20 miles south of Texarkana on U.S. 59 to Queen City, 7 miles west on FM 96, 2 miles north on FM 1154 to PR 42. Mailing address: Route 1, Box 116, Atlanta, Texas 75551. Phone: 903-796-6476. For all state park reservations, call 512-389-8900.

FACILITIES

Camping: 8 campsites with water only, 43 campsites with water and electricity, 8 campsites with water, electricity, and sewage hookups; modern restrooms with showers (wheelchair access), trailer dump station. Fees charged.

Recreation: picnic areas and playgrounds, 3.5 miles of hiking trails, 1.3-mile nature trail, swimming in Wright Patman Lake, fishing, fish-cleaning station, boating, water-skiing, amphitheater.

MAIN ATTRACTIONS

The densely wooded park is located on the 20,300-acre Wright Patman Lake. Water sports and fishing for bass, crappie, and catfish are popular activities. A trail leads through the beautiful oak and pine woodlands and along the shoreline, and high bluffs at the picnic area overlook the lake.

ECOLOGY

The high ridges and stream drainages forming the 1,475-acre park are wooded with a wide variety of trees. Shortleaf and loblolly pines and white oaks are dominant; flowering dogwood, red buckeye, sassafras, sweetgum, viburnum, river birch, and red maple trees are also present.

In the spring, the snow-white blossoms of the dogwoods and the crimson flowers of the buckeyes add color to the campgrounds and the picnic area. Mayapples blanket the forest floor before the deciduous trees are fully leafed out, and delicate purple oxalis flowers are scattered throughout the park.

Many herons, egrets, and waterfowl frequent the large reservoir. Rough-winged swallows and kingfishers make their nest burrows near the picnic area in the eroding bluffs of the old bank of the Sulphur River. The wave action of the lake and variable water levels have caused dangerous undercutting of the once scenic bluffs, and recent cave-ins are evident.

HISTORY

When Europeans first explored East Texas in the 1500s, they encountered the Caddo Indian Confederation, a group of several tribes that were highly developed culturally. The Caddos lived in villages with well-constructed houses and grew corn, five types of beans, sunflowers, and pumpkins. They collected fruit, chestnuts, and pecans and hunted deer, bison, and small animals.

The Smithsonian Institution, conducting archaeological excavations in the park, has uncovered graves, artifacts, and a house or village site. Unfortunately, at the time of writing there was no information available in the park for the visitor regarding either the excavations or the plants and animals common to the park.

7. AUSTIN: EMMA LONG METROPOLITAN PARK

Travis County. 6 miles northwest of Austin on FM 2222, 4 miles west on City Park Rd. to Lake Austin. Mailing address: 1706 City Park Rd., Austin, Texas 78732. Phone: 512-346-1831. Camping: 20 campsites with water and electricity, 50 with tables and water nearby; flush toilets, showers. Fees charged, no reservations. Park gates open 7 A.M. to 10 P.M. Recreation: picnic areas, swimming, fishing, boat ramp. Open all year. This pleasant park is crowded in the summer. Lake Austin is a good bird-watching area—golden-cheeked warblers may be seen on the entrance road in the early summer.

8. BALLINGER CITY PARK

Runnels County. 35 miles northeast of San Angelo on U.S. 67, on the eastern edge of Ballinger. Mailing address: Box 497, Ballinger, Texas 76821-0497. Phone: 915-365-5437. Camping: 4 campsites with water and electricity, flush toilets, cold-water showers. Reservations not accepted. Fees charged. Recreation: picnic areas and playgrounds, swimming pool (summer only), swimming in Elm Creek, fishing, pavilion. Open all year.

BALLINGER LAKE PARK

Runnels County. 5 miles west of Ballinger on eastern shore of 6,050-acre municipal lake. Mailing address: Box 497, Ballinger, Texas 76821-0497. Phone: 915-365-5437. Camping: 16 drive-through campsites with water and electricity, 6 with water only; flush toilets. Fees charged. No reservations. Recreation: boat ramp. The lake is stocked with bass, crappie, walleye, and catfish. Open all year.

9. BALMORHEA STATE PARK

LOCATION
Reeves County. 56 miles west of Fort Stockton on IH-10, south on TX 17, at the head of San Solomon Springs.
Mailing address: Box 15, Toyahvale, Texas 79786. Phone: 915-375-2370. For all state park reservations, call 512-389-8900.

FACILITIES

Camping: 6 campsites with water only, 28 campsites with water and electricity, 18-unit motel, modern restrooms with showers, trailer dump station. Fees charged.

Recreation: picnic areas and playgrounds, swimming pool, concessions (summer only).

MAIN ATTRACTIONS

San Solomon Springs has been the main attraction of the area for centuries—artifacts found indicate that Indian groups relied on the springs long before the Europeans arrived. In the 1930s, the Civilian Conservation Corps constructed the swimming pool around the springs as well as the motel and concession buildings. The pool, at a near constant temperature of 74 degrees, is 1.75 acres in size and 25 feet deep in places; it is one of the largest spring-fed pools in the nation. Its clear water, fed at a rate of 22 million to 26 million gallons daily, and abundant fish life make it ideal for snorkeling and scuba diving.

The nearby Fort Davis National Historic Site, Davis Mountains State Park, and Davis Mountains Skyline Drive, leading to McDonald Observatory, are accessible from the city of Fort Davis, located 30 miles south of the park. Lake Balmorhea, 3 miles southeast of Balmorhea, offers boating and fishing.

ECOLOGY

Very little of the original vegetation remains, because of the use of the surrounding land and modification of the springs. What was once desert grassland has been farmed and grazed and replaced by such thorny shrubs as mesquite, lotebush, catclaw acacia, and native mimosa. The springs and drainages formerly supported cattails, sedges, rushes, reeds, and salt grass. Now the springs and channelized drainages are shaded by large cottonwood, ash, sycamore, and hackberry trees.

The springs are famous for two rare and endangered species of fish. The Comanche Springs pupfish and the Pecos mosquito fish, only a few inches long, can be seen in the drainage canals. Many minnows, perch, and catfish inhabit the cool, clear depths of the pool.

The springs are an oasis surrounded by irrigated farmland and shrubby desert vegetation. Mule deer, white-tailed deer, bobcats, javelinas, skunks, raccoons, porcupines, and coyotes can be seen in and around the park by the alert visitor, primarily at dawn and dusk. Many birds are attracted to the large trees, especially during spring and fall migrations. The colorful vermilion flycatcher, the greater roadrunner, quail, hawks, herons, and ducks frequent the life-supporting springs.

10. BANDERA: MANSFIELD PARK

Bandera County. 2 miles west of Bandera on TX 16. Mailing address: Box 563, Bandera, Texas 78003-0563. Phone: 512-796-3168. Camping: 30 campsites with water and electricity, grills, tables shaded by large oaks, flush toilets, showers, group pavilion, recreation hall with kitchen, ballpark, rodeo arena. Fees charged. Open all year.

11. BASTROP STATE PARK

LOCATION
Bastrop County. 1.5 miles east of Bastrop on TX 21. Also accessible via PR 1 from Buescher State Park.
Mailing address: Box 518, Bastrop, Texas 78602. Phone: 512-321-2101. For all state park reservations, call 512-389-8900.

FACILITIES
Camping: primitive camping on a hiking trail, 18 campsites with water only, 78 campsites with water and electricity, 12 cabins on a small lake with kitchens, bathrooms, and fireplaces; group lodge for 8 people, group facilities—4 bunkhouses with cots and bunk beds, kitchen, and dining hall—for 90 people; modern restrooms with showers, trailer dump station. Fees charged.

Recreation: picnic areas, a series of nature trails and the 8.5-mile loop of the Lost Pines Hiking Trail, swimming pool (summer only), fishing on a small lake, 9-hole golf course and pro shop, kitchen and dining hall for 90 people.

MAIN ATTRACTIONS
Bastrop State Park covers 3,503 acres of the Central Texas loblolly pine forest. This forest is separated from the East Texas Piney Woods by post oak woodlands and by what used to be prairie grasslands but is now ranchland and farmland. Known as the Lost Pines, this remnant forest was probably connected to East Texas forests during the last ice age, about 10,000 years ago, when Texas was wetter and cooler. The area from Bastrop to Buescher state parks preserves 7 percent of the Central Texas pines.

Lake Bastrop is now part of the state park. The south shore is being developed and is expected to open with camping facilities in late 1995. Then the north shore will be developed and incorporated into the park.

HIKING

Nature trails wind through the pines, connecting the campgrounds. The Lost Pine Trail makes an 8.5-mile loop through the woods.

ECOLOGY

The pine forest hosts a wide variety of plants and animals not commonly seen in other parts of Central Texas. Yaupon holly, wax myrtle, farkleberry bushes, and mushrooms thrive in the shade of the towering pines. Alum Creek, with fern-covered banks, winds its way through the park.

More than 200 species of birds have been sighted in the park. Red-shouldered hawks nest in the area, and pileated and red-headed woodpeckers are occasionally seen. The Central Texas population of pine warblers is found in the woods. Some of the birds, plants, mammals, and reptiles are at the western limit of their range. A checklist of birds is available. One of the largest colonies of the endangered Houston toad (*Bufo Houstonensis*) occurs in the park and is the focus of ongoing studies.

The aromatic piney woods of Bastrop seem out of place among the surrounding deciduous woodlands. The pines would not be able to survive on the area's 35 inches of annual rain without the sandstone aquifer underlying the forest. Two sandstone formations, the Carrizo and Recklaw, form the aquifer. Holding water like a giant sponge, they enable the pines to thrive in an otherwise unsuitably dry habitat.

The red stone fence and buildings in the park were built from local sandstone. Iron oxides in the sandstone account for the red and yellow colors of the rocks and sandy soil. Rain leaches the iron out of the soil into the creeks and discolors the water.

Just outside the park entrance, an abrupt change from pines and oaks to mesquite trees indicates the contact between the Carrizo sandstone, which forms sandy soil, and the Sabinetown shale, which weathers into a clay soil.

HISTORY

The town of Bastrop, one of the earliest settlements in Texas, is 1.5 miles west of the park on TX 21. The town was settled by William Barton, Josiah Wilbarger, and Reuben Hornsby in 1829. Originally called Mina, the town was renamed in 1837 in honor of the Baron de Bastrop, who helped Stephen Austin in his negotiations with the Mexican government to allow colonists into the area.

Early industry in Bastrop included lignite mining, lumbering, and brick making. As the cost of other fuels has risen in recent years, plans for strip-mining the lignite near Bastrop to fuel an electrical power plant are being considered.

The cabins, swimming pool, bathhouse, roads, and golf course in the park were constructed in the thirties by the Civilian Conservation Corps.

12. BENTSEN-RIO GRANDE VALLEY STATE PARK

LOCATION
Hidalgo County. 7 miles west of McAllen on U.S. 83 to Mission, 6 miles southwest via U.S. 83, Loop 374, south on FM 2062. Mailing address: Box 988, Mission, Texas 78572-0988. Phone: 210-585-1107. For all state park reservations, call 512-389-8900.

FACILITIES
Camping: 65 campsites with water nearby, 77 campsites with water, electricity, and sewage hookups; modern restrooms with showers, trailer dump station. Fees charged.

Recreation: picnic areas and playgrounds, nature trails with trail guide booklets, bird-watching, fishing, boating, pavilion.

MAIN ATTRACTIONS
The park, donated by the Bentsen family in 1944, borders the Rio Grande and includes two resacas, or oxbow lakes. The subtropical climate of the lower Rio Grande Valley makes the park a favorite winter vacation spot. Bird-watching and fishing and boating in the large resacas are popular.

Santa Ana National Wildlife Refuge, another popular spot for bird-watchers, is 30 miles southeast of the park via U.S. 83 to Alamo, FM 907, and U.S. 281. The refuge, which is open for walk-in visits from dawn to dusk, has an excellent nature trail system; cars are not allowed on days when tram tours are offered. Many unusual South Texas birds, such as the red-billed pigeon, hook-billed kite, and Altamira oriole, may be sighted here. Two photography blinds located at morning feeding stations offer excellent photo opportunities.

Nearby Mission is the home of the Texas Citrus Festival, held during the last week of January. The colorful Poinsettia Show and the annual meeting of the American Poinsettia Society, whose national headquarters is in Mission, are held every December.

HIKING
There are two nature trails leading through the park. The Singing Chaparral Nature Trail makes a 1.5-mile loop through brush and woodlands. The River Trail, 1.8 miles long, leads hikers through

riparian woodlands to the Rio Grande. Both are excellent for seeing birds, other wildlife, and the subtropical vegetation typical of the lower Valley.

ECOLOGY

Like a biological island, the park is surrounded by cultivated farmland. Except in a few protected sanctuaries, the plants and animals once native to the deep alluvial soil of the lower Rio Grande plains have been displaced by cabbage patches, onion fields, and citrus groves—today, the fertile Rio Grande Valley is one of the most productive farming areas in North America. To step into the park is to step into a bygone era of lush, subtropical vegetation and abundant wildlife.

The rich soil formed by the Rio Grande's deposits of sand and clay supports a wide variety of plants. Subtropical vegetation thrives in the mild climate, where freezing temperatures are very rare. The two dominant plant communities native to the area are the dry brushlands and the rich riparian woodlands.

The Valley's moderate rainfall, high temperatures, and rapidly draining soils create arid conditions favoring drought-resistant species. Thorny shrubs form an impenetrable brush woodland. Examples of the plant and animal communities found in this habitat are identified along the Singing Chaparral Nature Trail. The small thorny bushes include lotebush, guayacan with its feathery foliage, catclaw acacia, brazilwood or bluewood, and the aromatic lime prickly ash.

Woodlands parallel the river and surround the resacas, where moisture is more abundant. Cedar elms and hackberry trees are common, as are the anaqua with its sandpapery leaves and the Texas ebony with its thick black seedpods. Rio Grande ash and willow trees prosper along the waterways.

Bentsen-Rio Grande Valley is famous among bird-watchers from across the nation; more than 200 species of birds have been recorded in the limited confines of the park. Nineteen species, including the green jay and the chachalaca, can be seen in the United States only in South Texas. Ask for a checklist of the birds and other wildlife at the park entrance. A large number and variety of migrating birds spend their winters along the Rio Grande Delta, and occasionally a rare Mexican species will unexpectedly appear in the park. However, the most common winter birds throughout the Valley are the snow-birds, retirees who flee the northern chill and flock to the warm climate here.

Mammals common to the park include raccoons, opossums, coyotes, striped skunks, and armadillos. Bobcats are frequently sighted at dawn and dusk, and the tropical jaguarundi and ocelot occur, but rarely.

HISTORY

The lower Rio Grande Valley abounds with historical significance. The city of Mission was named after the small mission, La Lomita Chapel, located 3 miles south on FM 1016. The chapel was established in 1824 by priests of the oblate order.

The early priests may have been the first to plant citrus trees in the Valley. Now Mission, considered the home of the famous ruby red grapefruit, is the location of more than 30 citrus-processing plants.

13A. BIG BEND NATIONAL PARK

LOCATION

Brewster County. Headquarters: 70 miles south of Marathon on U.S. 385 or 100 miles south of Alpine on TX 118.
Mailing address: Headquarters, P.O. Box 129, Big Bend National Park, Texas 79834. Phone: 915-477-2251. Mailing address: Chisos Mountains Lodge, Basin Rural Station, Big Bend National Park, Texas 79834. Phone: 915-477-2291.

FACILITIES

Camping: Big Bend has free primitive camping, with no water, at designated areas only. A permit is required. Fees are charged at the campgrounds listed below. No reservations are accepted except for group campgrounds at Rio Grande Village. Privately owned RV parks operate near Study Butte, outside the park's western edge.

The Chisos Basin Campground has 63 campsites with water nearby, modern restrooms but no showers, and a trailer dump station. Trailers over 20 feet long are not recommended. The Chisos Mountains Lodge has motel rooms, cabins, and a restaurant; reservations are recommended.

Cottonwood Campground, near Santa Elena Canyon, has 31 campsites with water nearby and chemical toilets.

Rio Grande Village has 100 campsites with water nearby; 24 trailer sites with water, electricity, and sewage hookups; group campgrounds with water nearby; modern restrooms with pay showers, a laundromat, and a trailer dump station.

Recreation: picnicking, hiking and nature trails, interpretive exhibits with trail-guide booklets and animal checklists, swimming in the Rio Grande, fishing in the Rio Grande, canoeing and rafting in the Rio Grande (permit required), amphitheaters at the Basin and Rio Grande Village, restaurant and coffee shop at the Basin, park headquarters and service station at Panther Junction, gasoline at Rio Grande Village, stores at the Basin, Rio Grande Village, and Castolon.

MAIN ATTRACTIONS

Big Bend National Park is large—1,256 square miles—so large that the visitor should begin by touring the park headquarters at Panther Junction. Exhibits and ranger-led programs help explain the park's unique geology, cacti and other plants, wildlife, and history. Guidebooks are essential to understanding and enjoying the park: particularly helpful are the "Road Guide," "Backcountry Road Guide," and "Hiker's Guide." Books on the wildflowers and cacti and guides to various nature trails are also sold. After visiting the park more than twenty times in as many years, I still find that Big Bend is one of my favorite spots.

Big Bend is situated in a large crook, or bend, in the Rio Grande, which forms the 107-mile southern boundary of the park and occupies 801,163 acres of the Chihuahuan Desert. But the park offers more than desert scenery. The Chisos Mountains, with mile-high peaks, are completely surrounded by the park. The rugged mountains provide the visitor unparalleled vistas both of the desert below and of distant peaks in Mexico. There are many hiking trails—varying from easy to strenuous—in the mountains. When conditions are right, the evenings provide some of the most beautiful sunsets in the West.

The desert has its own special charm, especially in the cooler months of the year. Secluded canyons offer surprises to the explorer, and springs often provide glimpses of desert wildlife. In the early spring, wildflowers are scattered across the seemingly barren desert floor, if there has been ample rainfall. By April, the cacti begin to bloom. Many of the delicate blossoms may last only one day.

The third scenic wonder in the park, after the desert and the mountains, is the Rio Grande. The river has cut three spectacular canyons, with sheer walls up to 1,500 feet high. Santa Elena, to the west, is the most impressive. Here, the river has sliced a snakelike gorge across a mesa that towers above the desert basin. Boquillas Canyon is near Rio Grande Village on the eastern side of the park. Mariscal Canyon, midway between the other canyons, is accessible only by boat or four-wheel-drive vehicle.

Big Bend and the surrounding area are rich in legends and lore of the Indians, the Spanish, and the early settlers. Numerous books have been written about the rugged pioneers who mined, ranched, farmed, and hid out in this remote section of Texas. Many of the place-names in the park are reminders of heroes and events of past days.

HIKING

The "Hiker's Guide" lists 41 trails, varying from easy day hikes to strenuous backpacking hikes. Several of the most popular trails will be mentioned here.

The Lost Mine, Window, and South Rim trails have trailheads in the Basin. The trail to Lost Mine Peak is 4.8 miles round trip, ascends 1,250 feet, and is rated medium difficulty. The view from the top is breathtaking, though some say the climb is more so! The Window Trail, another medium-difficulty hike of 5.2 miles round trip, leads down an oak-lined canyon to the point where Oak Creek plunges over a cliff to the desert below. The South Rim Trail is a strenuous 14-mile hike suitable only for those in good physical shape. There are other trails branching from the South Rim Trail, including ones to Emory Peak, Boot Canyon, Juniper Canyon, and Blue Creek.

Eight self-guided trails have signs and pamphlets explaining significant ecological and historical facts. These trails are suitable for almost everyone, and the easy walking provides an excellent opportunity for exploring the park. Also, pullouts along the roadsides have interpretive exhibits relating interesting geological and historical events.

ECOLOGY

The park has a wide variety of ecosystems, including desert, mountain, and riparian environments. In addition, desert springs, mountain slopes, and protected canyons provide specialized habitats for rare plants and animals. The mountains are a biological island surrounded by inhospitable desert. A small grove of aspen trees, a rarity in Texas, grows near the top of Emory Peak, while just a few miles away, creosote bushes cover the parched desert floor.

Water is the limiting factor in the desert—the river is like a green ribbon stretched through the arid land. Trees, cane, and an often impenetrable shrubby growth parallel the life-giving river. Desert springs also support rich vegetation. Cottonwood trees and rare columbine flowers find a home around pools and streams formed by runoff from the mountains.

Mule deer, javelinas, coyotes, desert cottontails, and blacktail jackrabbits are commonly seen in the desert. Foxes, bobcats, and mountain lions are occasionally reported, especially near the springs. Beavers live along the river, white-tailed deer are seen in the mountains, and skunks are common camp guests throughout the park. Nocturnal ringtails and badgers may be seen on the back roads at night.

Birdlife is abundant, with several species occurring in the United States only in the park. The Colima warbler can be seen only in Boot Canyon in the Chisos Mountains, and the Lucifer hummingbird builds its delicate nests on ocotillos in the desert. Thirteen other hummers have been sighted in the park, making one of the largest concentrations of hummingbirds in the state. Other rare birds include the golden eagle, peregrine falcon, painted redstart, and varied bunting.

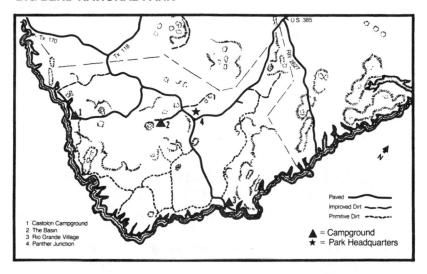

1 Castolon Campground
2 The Basin
3 Rio Grande Village
4 Panther Junction

▲ = Campground
★ = Park Headquarters

The vegetation in much of the park is different from that of a hundred years ago. When ranchers moved into the area around the turn of the century, what is now rocky soil supporting only scrub brush was a desert grassland. Old photographs show horses and cattle standing in deep grass. Even the driest part of the park, Tornillo Flat, was covered with grass. But, as in most of Texas, many ranches were stocked with too many cattle and sheep and the land was overgrazed. When the park was acquired in 1944, more than 40,000 head of stock were removed from the area.

Insufficient vegetation allowed wind and rain to strip away the topsoil, leaving the barren, rocky slopes as we see them today. With the scanty rain running off into the washes and rivers instead of soaking into the ground, springs dried up and creeks stopped flowing. Large cottonwood stumps can still be seen along the dry wash that was once Terlingua Creek. The beavers are gone, and so are the farmers. Terlingua Abaja, once a farming community, is now a cluster of tumbling adobe ruins on a gravelly hillside.

The weather at Big Bend can be, and often is, quite rugged. Desert temperatures in the summer exceed 100 degrees, and in the mountains gusts of wind will rock RVs and test the durability of a tent. From late fall to early spring, blue northers may drop temperatures 20 to 30 degrees in less than an hour, causing misery for those caught on the trail. However, except in the summer, the climate is generally pleasant, and many retirees journey to the park for their winter vacation. Even in the summer, hiking and camping are pleasant at higher elevations of the Chisos Mountains. Peak visitation occurs during March and April, college spring break, and Thanksgiving. At these times, expect the park and private campgrounds and motels to be filled to capacity.

Big Bend is a textbook example of geological processes—many universities from across the nation annually bring classes to the park during spring break. The mountains, canyons, and desert provide classic examples of igneous, metamorphic, and sedimentary rocks, of faulting and folding, weathering and erosion. Fossils are common in some strata, varying from tiny sea organisms to crocodilelike creatures with six-foot skulls to the world's largest flying reptile. Guidebooks are available for those with specific interests in geology.

13B. BIG BEND RANCH STATE NATURAL AREA

LOCATION

Brewster and Presidio counties. Extends 60 miles along Rio Grande and north of TX 170 between Lajitas and Fort Leaton State Historical Park.
Mailing address: Access south of TX 170—Barton Warnock Environmental Education Center, HC 70, Box 365, Terlingua, TX 79852. Phone: 915-424-3327.
Access north of TX 170—P.O. Box 1180, Presidio, TX 79845. Phone: 915-229-3416. For bus tour reservations, call the statewide reservation number 512-389-8900.

FACILITIES

Camping: Primitive camping is permitted at unimproved sites on the sandy, grassy, and gravel riverbanks of the Rio Grande at Colorado Canyon, Madera Canyon, and Grassy Banks. Composting toilets and trash receptacles are available. Backpackers can camp on the Rancherías Loop Trail. Ten primitive sites, some accessible only by high-clearance vehicles, are located along roads within the park. Campsites may not be reserved.

Ranch Headquarters Sauceda Complex: Individuals can rent the three bedrooms at the Big House or bunks in the bunkhouse. The bunkhouse sleeps fifteen people each in the segregated men's and women's sections. Call the Presidio headquarters for reservations. A limited selection of motels are available at Lajitas, Study Butte, and Presidio.

Barton Warnock Environmental Education Center: Located east of Lajitas on TX 170, the center offers geological, ecological, and historical displays of the area. The botanical gardens provide an opportunity to learn the desert vegetation and see cacti in bloom. A book store sells guidebooks, trail maps, and other related materials. Admission is charged to the museum sections.

MAIN ATTRACTIONS

With one purchase, the state doubled the total acreage in the state park system. This 268,495-acre park covers some of the most remote, rugged, and beautiful country in west Texas. It includes the Solitario, a crater-like geological uplift more than 5 miles in diameter. The unusual formation reveals a concentric sequence of rock strata spanning 500 million years. The park borders the Rio Grande and harbors scenic waterfalls, Indian pictographs, rare plants, mesas, mountains, scenic vistas, hidden canyons, caves, and volcanic formations. The trails and river corridor provide excellent opportunities for bird watching (390 species), wildlife observations (cougars, javelina, deer), scenic photography, and studying the cacti and other plants adapted to the rugged Chihuahuan Desert. Several developed landings on the river provided access for boating and fishing.

A 27-mile dirt road passable to all vehicles provides access to the interior of the park and the Sauceda Ranch headquarters. The road continues another eight miles to the Solitario overlook.

The 60-mile drive on TX 170 through the park between Presidio and Lajitas can be an adventure in itself. The road parallels the Rio Grande, climbs steep, winding grades to dramatic viewpoints above the river, and traverses numerous low-water crossings prone to flooding after thunderstorms. In addition to the frequent pullouts, you can stop for photography, or to soak up the vistas, or to eat a leisurely lunch at the Tepee roadside park at Madera Canyon.

HIKING

Old stock, wagon, and jeep trails crisscross the ridges and canyons of the park, which was a cattle and goat ranch after the Indians were driven out in the 1870s. Hiking on the old roads offers an exciting way to experience the rugged beauty of the desert mountains and canyons, but cross-country hiking is prohibited. Two hiking trails have been opened north of the river: the 19-mile Rancherías Loop Trail and the Rancherías Canyon Trail, a 4-mile one-way trip. The Canyon Trail at the west trailhead on TX 170 leads up the drainage to an 80-foot pour-off. Water and trees along the creek provide a shady and cool respite and an opportunity to see some of the desert wildlife. Hikers must pay a daily use fee and an activity fee, but are required to purchase the annual conservation passport only for the Rancherías Loop Trail.

The Rancherías Loop Trail also begins at the west trailhead and climbs out of the canyon. It meanders along low mesas and ridges past historic ruins, springs, incredible examples of volcanism, and scenic vistas of the surrounding desert and mountain ranges, including 8,000-foot peaks across the river in Mexico. About 2¾ miles of TX 170 separate the east and west trailheads of the "loop."

A short trail (about one-mile round trip) leads from a roadside parking lot to Closed Canyon. This easy, one-way trail enters a canyon so narrow that you can almost touch the sides at places. Erosion has sliced through the walls of compacted ash (tuff) creating a winding corridor that leads you on a shadowy adventure.

Hiking in the desert presents many potentially dangerous situations. Overheating even in mild temperatures can occur rapidly, so always take plenty of water, a gallon per day in the summer. Steep trails with sharp, loose rocks, thorny vegetation, and poisonous snakes can cause injury in an area where the closest hospital is more than a hundred miles away in Alpine.

RAFTING

One of the most popular rafting trips in the Big Bend area is through Colorado Canyon. The nine-mile float is an easy day trip and can be arranged through several outfitters in Lajitas and Terlingua. The river, with Class II and III rapids, is not considered dangerous during normal flow. Obtain permits for private trips and check on river conditions at the Barton Warnock Center.

TOURS

The park provides two bus tours weekly into the heart of the park to a viewpoint overlooking the Solitario crater. The all-day tour on an air-conditioned bus with a restroom includes lunch. The tour leaves from Fort Leaton on the first Saturday of the month and from the Barton Warnock Education Center on the third Saturday. Make reservations at the statewide reservations number in Austin. A fee is charged.

14. BIG SPRING: COMANCHE TRAIL PARK

Howard County. In Big Spring, 4 miles south of IH-20 on U.S. 87. Mailing address: City Parks Department, Box 3190, Big Spring, Texas 79721. Phone: 915-263-7641. Camping: 9 campsites with water, flush toilets, trailer dump station. Recreation: picnic areas and playgrounds, hiking, bicycle path, swimming pool, fishing, golf course, tennis courts, pavilion. Fees charged. Open all year.

BIG SPRING: MOSS LAKE PARK

Howard County. 7.5 miles east of Big Spring on IH-20, 5 miles south on Moss Lake Rd. Mailing address: City Parks Department,

Box 3910, Big Spring, Texas 79720. Phone: 915-393-5246. Camping: primitive camping only. Fees charged. Recreation: swimming, fishing, boat ramp, store.

15. BIG THICKET NATIONAL PRESERVE

LOCATION
Mailing address, south district office: P.O. Box 7408, 8185 Easttex Freeway, Beaumont, Texas 77706. Phone: 409-839-2689. Visitor information station: 7 miles north of Kountze on U.S. 69/287, 3 miles east on FM 420. In the winter, closed Tuesdays and Wednesdays. For program information and reservations, call 409-246-2337.

FACILITIES
Camping: Only primitive backcountry camping in designated areas is allowed. Write for maps and permits. Public campgrounds in the area include the Alabama-Coushatta Indian Reservation, Lake B. A. Steinhagen, Martin Dies, Jr., State Park, Village Creek State Park, and Lake Livingston State Park.

Recreation: ranger programs, a self-guided auto tour, hiking, bird-watching, photography, nature study, canoeing.

Note: Mosquitoes can be serious any time of the year, so unless you enjoy donating blood, take repellent on your outings.

MAIN ATTRACTIONS
The Big Thicket National Preserve is composed of 15 separate units and river corridors for a total of more than 100,000 acres. Begin your exploration of this wilderness at the visitor station in the Turkey Creek Unit north of Kountze. The small building has a few exhibits, maps and information, and a ranger on duty. A self-guided nature trail leads through the deep woods, along scenic Village Creek, by sloughs with waist-high cypress knees, and across pine-covered ridges. You can take a 1.7-mile , 2.4-mile, or 5-mile loop on the 15-mile-long Turkey Creek Trail. The trail follows the creek and lets the hiker sample the wildness of the deep woods that makes the Big Thicket so special. The quarter-mile Pitcher Plant Trail, on the northeast side of the Turkey Creek Unit, shows visitors rare carnivorous plants. The Pitcher Plant and Sundew trails are wheelchair accessible.

The Sundew Trail, a 1-mile, self-guided trail, leads through the Hickory Creek Savanna Unit. The hard-topped trail passes through a longleaf pine wetland savanna with a large variety of flowers. Another 1-mile loop trail winds through the Beech Woods Unit. This trail gives you the majestic experience of hiking through a mature beech-magnolia-loblolly forest with trees towering into the sky. The

5.4-mile Woodland Trail winds through the Big Sandy Creek Unit. Shorter loops of 3.3 and 4.5 miles are possible.

If you have ever floated down one of the peaceful, primeval waterways of the Big Thicket, you know why canoeing is one of the most popular activities in the preserve. The river corridor units preserve beautiful wilderness stretches of Village Creek, Pine Island Bayou, and the Neches River. Canoers can float 93 miles on the Neches River between Lake B. A. Steinhagen and Beaumont, 49 miles on Pine Island Bayou, and 37 miles on Village Creek. Camping is permitted on the sandbars and within preserve boundaries with a permit. A canoe trip planner and maps are available. Park rangers often lead canoe outings. Several canoe liveries operate in the area.

A 75-mile auto tour takes you through seven different plant communities and shows you why the Big Thicket is considered the biological crossroads of North America. At the stops, you can explore deep mature forests, a sandhill plant community, a wet baygall community with acid-loving plants, a cypress slough, a pitcher plant savanna, a climax pine forest with a thick carpet of pine needles, and wetlands abounding with carnivorous sundews.

ECOLOGY

The first settlers discovered three million acres of dense forests, swamps, marshes, bogs, and sloughs laced with meandering streams and bayous. They bypassed the trackless region, leaving it to bears, beavers, panthers, and outlaws. Later, businessmen saw money in the giant pines and hardwoods and began chipping away at the seemingly endless acres of woodlands. Now powerful tree-crushing machines level thousands of acres of forest annually. Less than a tenth of the original Big Thicket remains. Monocultures of pine trees now grow where the richest diversity of plant life in North America once existed. Each of the scattered units of the national preserve represents examples of the diverse plant communities that make this area special.

Four major plant provinces converge in the Big Thicket, making it one of the richest biological regions on the continent. Cacti typical of the Southwest deserts grow on xeric sandhills, while bog-loving plants also found in Florida swamps grow a few yards away. In the dense woodlands of the Thicket, one finds a majestic interplay of tree species from northern, eastern, and southern forests. Grasses, mushrooms, vines, shrubs, and herbs mingle like an intricately composed symphony, as do mammals, reptiles, amphibians, and birds. Forty kinds of orchids grow in the Big Thicket, and 1,000 kinds of fungi. Three hundred species of birds make their way through the canopy of trees. Beavers cut a silent v across the slow-moving sloughs, the drumming of pileated woodpeckers resounds through the pine-oak forests, and mosquitoes remind visitors that the idyllic forest exacts a price from those with romantic visions of Walden Pond.

Concerned citizens organized the Big Thicket Association a number of years ago to raise funds and influence legislation for the

BIG THICKET NATIONAL PRESERVE

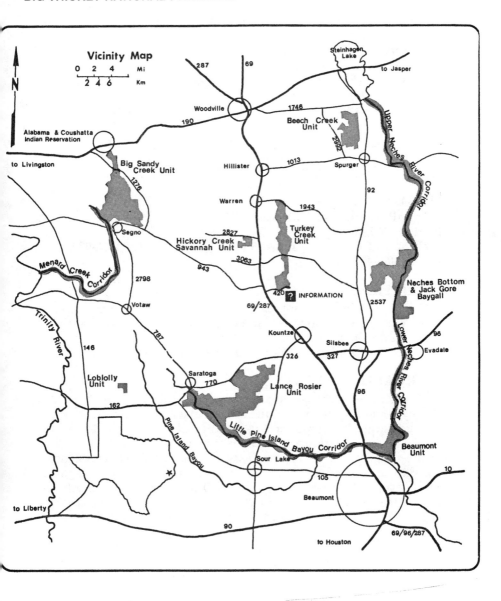

preservation of the rapidly diminishing mixed pine-hardwood forests in East Texas. The result was the establishment of the national preserve. The association still is active in preserving lands not included in the national preserve. The Big Thicket Museum is operated by the association as part of its program of educating the public about this significant natural area. The museum, closed on Mondays, is in Saratoga and has plant and animal exhibits and information.

16. BLACK KETTLE NATIONAL GRASSLAND/LAKE MARVIN

LOCATION
Hemphill County. 12 miles east of Canadian on FM 2266 (Formby Rd.).
Mailing address: Route 1, Box 55-B, Cheyenne, OK 73628-9725.
Phone: 405-497-2143.

FACILITIES
Camping: primitive campsites with water nearby, group camping area with water nearby, 3 cabins, chemical toilets. Reservations accepted for cabins. Fees charged. Open all year.
Recreation: picnicking, hiking trails, fishing, boating, store.

MAIN ATTRACTIONS
The 575-acre national grasslands were purchased by the U.S. Department of the Interior in the thirties in an effort to restore eroded, agriculturally abused land to productivity. Fishing and boating on 63-acre Lake Marvin are the main attractions of this park, located in the farthest reaches of the Texas Panhandle. Open grasslands, marshes, and woodlands provide homes for deer, turkeys, rabbits, and beavers. The quarter-mile Big Tree Trail leads to a large cottonwood tree used by early pioneers as a landmark. A Watchable Wildlife Trail leads to a lakeside viewing platform, where ducks and waterfowl are abundant in the winter.

Many eastern species of birds reach their western breeding limit along the lake and the adjoining Canadian River. Nesting birds at this park include the northern oriole, wood duck, barred owl, and least tern.

17. BLANCO STATE PARK

LOCATION
Blanco County. 42 miles west of Austin on U.S. 290, 8 miles south on U.S. 281 to Blanco, on the Blanco River.

Mailing address: Box 493, Blanco, Texas 78606. Phone: 210-833-4333. For all state park reservations, call 512-389-8900.

FACILITIES

Camping: 21 campsites with water and electricity, 10 campsites with water, electricity, and sewage hookups; 7 screened shelters, modern restrooms with showers, trailer dump station. Fees charged.

Recreation: picnic areas and playgrounds, swimming in the Blanco River, fishing, boating (electric motors only), pavilion with kitchen.

MAIN ATTRACTIONS

The shaded banks of the Blanco River provide the perfect setting for picnicking, camping, and family recreation. There is swimming in the river, and a three-foot-deep wading pool is filled as the water cascades over a small picturesque spillway. This park, as are all parks in and near cities, is heavily used by local inhabitants.

The 105-acre park, located in the city of Blanco, consists of a narrow corridor along the Blanco River. A small dam impounds the river in the park, and much of the well-kept shore is shaded with large oaks. Because of modifications of the natural environment, the native vegetation is not especially representative of Hill Country rivers.

Lyndon B. Johnson National Historical Park, with a reconstructed 1880-period ranch and exhibits, is 14 miles north in Johnson City. And Lyndon B. Johnson State Historical Park is 15 miles northwest near Stonewall. The park features bus tours of the LBJ Ranch, a working pioneer farm, bison and longhorns, and a swimming pool.

18. BONHAM STATE PARK

LOCATION

Fannin County. 28 miles east of Sherman on U.S. 82 to Bonham, 1 mile south on TX 78, 2 miles east on FM 271.

Mailing address: Route 1, Box 337, Bonham, Texas 75418. Phone: 903-583-5022. For all state park reservations, call 512-389-8900.

FACILITIES

Camping: 10 campsites with water nearby, 11 campsites with water and electricity, group barracks for 96 people with kitchen and dining hall, modern restrooms with showers, trailer dump station. Fees charged.

Recreation: picnic areas and playgrounds, swimming in lake, fishing, with lighted pier, boat dock and launch (5-mph speed limit), pavilion.

MAIN ATTRACTIONS

This 261-acre park, with its gently rolling hills, is located on the edge of the blackland prairies and the post oak savanna vegetation regions of Texas. The rocky slopes are dominated by eastern red cedars and oaks. Grasslands of little bluestem and bushy bluestem are interspersed throughout the woodlands. The shore of the 65-acre lake and the creek drainages are covered with black willow, hackberry, cottonwood, osage orange, and shagbark hickory trees.

Wildlife in the park is mainly centered around the small lake. Beavers were once so numerous that they undermined the earthen dam with their excavations and controlled the level of the lake. Raccoons, skunks, and opossums are often seen, especially in the evening hours.

Nearby attractions include the Sam Rayburn Library and Home in Bonham and the Eisenhower Birthplace State Historic Site in Denison.

19. BORGER: HUBER PARK

County: Hutchinson. Located in city at 104 Pine St. Mailing address: Park Department, P.O. Box 5250, Borger, Texas 79008-5250. Phone: 806-273-2881. Camping: 5 sites with water only, 5 RV sites with water, electricity; chemical toilets, dump station. This 17-acre city park has picnic areas, playgrounds, swimming pool, tennis. No fees, no reservations. Open all year.

20. BRADY: LAKE BRADY PARK

McCulloch County. 4 miles west of Brady on FM 2028, 1 mile north on FM 3022. Mailing address: Route 1, Box 75, FM 3022, Brady, Texas 76825. Phone: 915-597-1823. Camping: 12 campsites with water and electricity, 20 campsites with water, electricity, and sewage hookups; 20 screened shelters, flush toilets, showers, trailer dump station, and primitive camping area. Fees charged. Reservations accepted. Open all year. Recreation: picnic area, playground, boat ramp, boat rental, designated swimming area, group pavilion, store.

BRADY: RICHARDS PARK

McCulloch County. Located west of town off U.S. 87 on Memory Lane. Mailing Address: P.O. Box 351, Brady, Texas 76825. Phone: 915-597-2152; fax: 915-597-2068. Camping: 20 sites with water and electricity, 10 sites with water, electricity, sewage, 15 screened shelters, restrooms, dump station. Recreation: picnicking, group pavilion, playgrounds; fishing, swimming, and boating on Brady Creek. Fees charged, reservations accepted. Open all year.

21. BRAZOS BEND STATE PARK

LOCATION
Fort Bend County. 30 miles south of Houston on TX 288 to Rosharon, 11 miles west on FM 1462, 1 mile north on FM 762. Mailing address: 21901 FM 762, Needville, Texas 77461. Phone: 409-553-5101. For all state park reservations, call 512-389-8900.

FACILITIES
Camping: primitive camping area with composting toilet 1.1 miles from road on hiking trail, 35 campsites with water only, 42 campsites with water and electricity, 14 screened shelters, late-arrival camping area, modern restrooms with showers, trailer dump station. Fees charged.

Recreation: picnic areas and playgrounds, 15 miles of hike and bike trails, bird-watching, interpretive exhibits, observation tower, observation platforms on lakes, fishing, with 2 lighted piers and cleaning stations, 2 screened pavilions, screened dining hall with equipped kitchen, amphitheater, observatory.

MAIN ATTRACTIONS
The overnight and day-use facilities, the extensive hiking trails, six lakes offering fishing and wildlife observation, and the abundant wildlife make Brazos Bend one of the most exciting state parks in Texas. The eastern park boundary is the Brazos River, accessible only by trails. Other trails lead around the lakes, which host a large population of alligators, waterfowl, and wading birds. There are six observation platforms on Elm Lake and an observation tower over-looking Forty-Acre and Pilant lakes. The observation stations provide good spots for bird-watching and photography.

Fishing in the small lakes is excellent: bass, catfish, perch, and crappie are the main catches. The Houston Museum of Natural Science operates an observatory in the park; it is open to the public from 3 P.M. to 10 P.M. Saturdays.

HIKING
The 15 miles of hike and bike trails circle the six lakes, parallel Big Creek, and lead visitors along the Brazos River. The trails are surfaced with small pebbles and are easy to follow. There are approximately 20 miles of other trails that were once cow paths or roads. They are not regularly maintained and may or may not lead to anywhere in particular. However, they do offer opportunities for exploring.

ECOLOGY

The 4,897-acre park is situated in the Brazos River floodplain in the Gulf Coast region of prairies and marshes. About 450 acres are upland prairies; the remainder consists of marshes and riparian woodlands. Pecans, live oaks and other oak species, hackberries, and elms form the hardwood forest. Yaupon holly, dwarf palmettos, and numerous shrubs and vines grow under the forest canopy. Weeping willow and Chinese tallow trees are common around the lakes.

Two of the small lakes are natural oxbow lakes formed from Big Creek, which meanders throughout the park. Three other oxbow lakes were formed when the creek was channelized, and Pilant Lake is a 450-acre marsh. The lakes are congested with aquatic vegetation, especially water hyacinths and cattails.

The lakes, marshes, and woodlands provide excellent habitats for a diverse wildlife population. Waterfowl winter by the thousands on the lakes. Herons, egrets, anhingas, and other wading birds and shorebirds frequent the shallow lakes; gallinules tiptoe across the lotus pads; and alligators tumble off logs into the water like turtles. More than 300 species of birds have been seen in the park—ask at the entrance for a checklist.

Hundreds of white-tailed deer live in the forest. Other common mammals in the park include armadillos, raccoons, opossums, squirrels, bobcats, gray foxes, and coyotes. Feral hogs and Russian boars are occasionally seen but should be avoided. Poisonous snakes in the park include the cottonmouth, copperhead, coral snake, and rattlesnake.

22. BRIDGEPORT: WISE COUNTY PARK

Wise County. 35 miles northwest of Fort Worth on U.S. 287 to Decatur, 13 miles west on FM 1810 through Chico, on Lake Bridgeport. Mailing address: Box 899, Decatur, Texas 76234. Phone: 817-627-6655. Camping: primitive camping area, 14 campsites with electricity, 8 campsites with water, electricity, and sewage hookups; cabins, group camping area, flush toilets, showers, trailer dump station. Reservations accepted. Fees charged. Recreation: picnic areas and playgrounds, nature trail, bicycle path, swimming in Lake Bridgeport, fishing, boat ramps, pavilion, restaurant, store. Open all year.

23. BROWNSVILLE: ADOLPH THOMAE, JR., PARK

Cameron County. North of Brownsville on FM 1847 to Arroyo City, 6 miles east on FM 2925. Mailing address: Route 2, Box 499, San

Benito, Texas 78586. Phone: 512-748-2044. Camping: 35 campsites with water, electricity, and sewage hookups; 10 sites with water, flush toilets, showers. Recreation: 2 lighted fishing piers, boat ramp, playground, wildlife observation tower. This wooded 57-acre park is surrounded by Laguna Atascosa National Wildlife Refuge and has 1.7 miles of shoreline on Arroyo Colorado. Fishing, boating, and wildlife observations are the main attractions. Fees charged, reservations accepted. Open all year.

24. BUESCHER STATE PARK

LOCATION
Bastrop County. 10 miles southeast of Bastrop on TX 71, northeast on FM 153.
Mailing address: Box 75, Smithville, Texas 78957-0075. Phone: 512-237-2241. For all state park reservations, call 512-389-8900.

FACILITIES
Camping: 25 campsites with water only, 40 campsites with water and electricity, 4 screened shelters, modern restrooms with showers, trailer dump station. Fees charged.

Recreation: picnic areas and playgrounds, fishing on a 30-acre lake, pavilion, recreation hall with kitchen.

MAIN ATTRACTIONS
Buescher State Park has 1,016 acres of mixed hardwoods, brushy shrubs, and loblolly pines; the park encompasses a small lake. Visitors can explore the lake edge or hike on the 7.5-mile round-trip trail. A hiking trail is planned to connect Buescher and Bastrop state parks.

ECOLOGY
The different soil types in Bastrop County each produce a characteristic plant community. In Buescher, gummy, reddish clay soils support post oak, blackjack oak, eastern red cedar, and brush shrubs dominated by yaupon holly. Sparta sandstone weathers into a light-colored sandy soil on which grow loblolly pine, oak, and hickory. A gravelly substratum supports pine, oak, farkleberry, and American beauty-berry. The pines, which dominate most of Park Road 1 between Buescher and Bastrop, thrive in Buescher only in those few areas where porous sandy or gravelly soils allow drainage while trapping enough water to support the trees.

The diverse vegetation provides a variety of wildlife habitats. More than 200 species of birds have been recorded in the area. Ducks, geese, warblers, and hawks are a few of the migratory birds that complement the large population of resident species in the spring and fall.

Some species of animals, such as the flying squirrel, reach the western limit of their distribution in Bastrop County. The patchy vegetation results in small local populations of animals that have become separated from the main body of their species. For example, the largest remnant population of the endangered Houston toad occurs in Buescher and Bastrop state parks, with the remaining population in Houston's Memorial Park. Such correlations between animal populations and zones of vegetation provide dramatic examples of the complex environmental interactions between soils, plants, and animals.

25. BUFFALO LAKE NATIONAL WILDLIFE REFUGE

LOCATION
Randall County. 10 miles west of Canyon on U.S. 60 to Umbarger, 3 miles south on FM 168.
Mailing address: Box 228, Umbarger, Texas 79091. Phone: 806-499-3382.

FACILITIES
Camping: 25 campsites with water only, group camping area, flush and chemical toilets. Group reservations accepted. Fees charged.
Recreation: picnicking, auto tour, wildlife photography, nature trail, bird-watching. Hours, 8 A.M. to 10 P.M.

MAIN ATTRACTIONS
This refuge in the Texas Panhandle consists of 7,667 acres of water, marshes, shortgrass prairie, and croplands. An auto tour road, with various observation points, winds through the refuge. Plan your tour in the early morning or evening when the wildlife are most active and easier to see. Many migrating songbirds, wading birds, eagles, and other raptors stop over in the refuge during the year. Though the bird checklist documents 274 species, the main attraction is the thousands of ducks and geese that overwinter in the refuge. In addition to birds, visitors may catch a glimpse of deer, bobcats, prairie dogs, porcupines, and coyotes. An interpretive trail leads to a prairie dog town off TX 168 on the east side of the refuge. Hikers and birders will enjoy the half-mile trail into Cottonwood Canyon. Restrooms are located at the end of the trail.

In the mid-sixties, 800,000 ducks and 40,000 Canada geese from the Central Flyway spent their winter in Buffalo Lake. Then the lake began to dry up. Today, with no regular inflow, the lake is dry, and the future value of the refuge as a sanctuary for waterfowl is uncertain. Each year, about 1,000 acres of forage crops are planted in the dry lake bed to provide food for the ducks and geese. Efforts are under way to create a marshy area for the wildlife.

26. CADDO LAKE STATE PARK

LOCATION
Harrison County. 15 miles northeast of Marshall on TX 43, 1 mile east on FM 2198.
Mailing address: Route 2, Box 15, Karnack, Texas 75661. Phone: 903-679-3351. For all state park reservations, call 512-389-8900.

FACILITIES
Camping: 20 campsites with water only, 20 campsites with water and electricity, 8 campsites with water, electricity, and sewage hookups; 8 screened shelters, 9 cabins, modern restrooms with showers, trailer dump station. Fees charged.

Recreation: picnic areas and playgrounds, 3.75 miles of hiking and nature trails with trail guide pamphlet, interpretive exhibits, fishing, pier, boat ramp, canoe rentals (summer and weekends only), recreation hall.

MAIN ATTRACTIONS
The park is situated on Big Cypress Bayou near its confluence with Caddo Lake. Though not on the lake proper, the park offers access to its maze of winding waterways. Bald cypress trees draped with Spanish moss line the shore and grow into the shallow portions of the lake. They create a ghostly atmosphere, especially in early-morning fog or against the darkening sky at dusk. Boating and fishing for bass, crappie, bream, and catfish are popular activities.

HIKING
A nature trail and several miles of hiking trails lead the visitor through the dense vegetation, with birds and other creatures calling in the distance. A guide to the trees along the three-quarter-mile interpretive trail is available at the entrance to the park.

ECOLOGY
Its 32,500 acres make Caddo Lake the largest naturally formed lake in the South. Originally, it was created by a massive logjam, which caused a widening of Big Cypress Bayou near its confluence with the Red River. In 1874, the Army Corps of Engineers cleared the jam, and in 1914 it constructed a dam, which maintains the present lake.

The soil in this area is composed of poorly draining clays with outcroppings of sandy deposits. Pine trees, post oaks, and blackjack oaks occur on the sandy, faster-draining soils; the moist bottomlands are filled with various species of oaks, hickory, flowering dogwood, basswood, sweetgum, American hornbeam, prickly ash, honey locust, walnut, and many other hardwoods. The swampy lake is surrounded and invaded by bald cypress trees, their knees protruding up through the shallow, placid water.

Each spring, the woods come alive with flowering trees. Tiny crimson blossoms cover the leafless limbs of the redbuds, and the snowy flowers of the dogwoods decorate the forest. The white fringe tree, with its delicate flowers, blooms beneath the towering oaks and pines. Many wildflowers, common and rare, as well as ferns, vines, and mushrooms can be seen along the trails.

Wildlife is abundant in the woodlands and along the lakeshore. Deer, raccoons, opossums, squirrels, foxes, and skunks live in the forest. Alligators, turtles, and waterfowl may be seen if one explores the picturesque channels of the lake. Many birds, both resident and migratory, occur in the differing habitats of the park.

HISTORY

Caddo Lake, named after the Indians who once inhabited East Texas, played a significant role in the early history of the state. Before railroads, Port Caddo—second only to Galveston in the amount of cargo shipped—was the port of entry for Northeast Texas. Sidewheeler steamships carried cotton and other freight from Jefferson via Big Cypress Bayou, the Red River, and the Mississippi to New Orleans.

The first locomotive in Texas was used to transport freight 14 miles inland from Swanson's Landing to Jonesville. After the locomotive was melted down during the Civil War, mules were used to pull the railroad cars. Freshwater pearls were discovered in mussels in the lake around the turn of the century, attracting many people to the area for the next decade.

Jefferson, 15 miles northwest on FM 134, was once the most prosperous city in Northeast Texas. Until the 1870s, it was the major river port and manufacturing center in the area—in 1867, Jefferson was the first Texas town to use gas to light its streets, and it boasted the first commercially manufactured ice in 1868. Jefferson had a population over 30,000 before its decline after the railroad was established in nearby Marshall. Much of the splendor of those early years is still preserved, with more than thirty buildings designated as state historic structures. The Jefferson Historic Pilgrimage, held on the first weekend in May, relives the Old South traditions with costumes and festivities.

27. CADDO NATIONAL GRASSLANDS

LOCATION
Fannin County. 43 miles east of Sherman on U.S. 82 to Honey Grove, 11 miles north on FM 100.
Mailing address: Box 507, Decatur, Texas 76234. Phone: 817-627-5475.

FACILITIES
Camping: Lake Coffeemill, 1.5 miles south of Telephone on FM 2029, east on FM 409, has 13 free campsites with water only and pit toilets. Lake Davy Crockett, 11 miles north of Honey Grove on FM 100, half mile west on FM 409, has 9 campsites with water only, and chemical and pit toilets. Fee charged.

Recreation: Lake Coffeemill has picnic areas, hiking (no designated trails), fishing, boating, a boat ramp, and hunting. Lake Davy Crockett has picnic areas, hiking (no designated trails), fishing, hunting.

MAIN ATTRACTIONS
The Caddo National Grasslands cover 17,830 acres of post oak and blackjack oak savannas and grasslands. The grasslands, scattered throughout Fannin County, are managed for fishing and hunting and leased for cattle grazing. Bobwhite quail, mourning doves, and deer are hunted, and the lakes are stocked with bass, bream, and catfish. Boats on the lakes are restricted to less than 10 horsepower motors.

ECOLOGY
These oak savannas and grasslands are located in the Cross Timbers vegetation zone. Severely eroded by poor agricultural practices in the late 1800s and early 1900s, they were purchased by the federal government in the 1930s. To prevent further erosion, the cattle that are now grazed here are periodically rotated between native grasslands and areas planted in Bermuda grass.

The bison and the prairie dog are two native mammals that once called this part of Texas home. The bison were systematically slaughtered in the late 1800s in an attempt to eliminate a major food source for the Indians. Later, in the 1930s, because they competed with ranchers for range vegetation, millions of prairie dogs were poisoned with strychnine-treated grain.

28. CAMP WOOD: LAKE NUECES PARK

Uvalde County. 35 miles northwest of Uvalde on TX 55, on Lake Nueces. Mailing address: Uvalde County Courthouse, Uvalde, Texas 78801. Phone: 210-597-3223. Camping: 42 campsites with water only, 25 campsites with water and electricity, flush toilets, showers, trailer dump station. Fees charged. Recreation: picnic areas, swimming, fishing, boat ramp. Open all year.

29. CANYON LAKE

LOCATION
U.S. Army Corps of Engineers. Comal County. Project office: 16 miles north of New Braunfels on FM 306.
Mailing address: HC 4, Box 400, Canyon Lake, Texas 78133-4112. Phone 210-964-3341.

Campground	water	fee area	flush toilets	season	dump station	warm-water showers	electricity
Canyon	•	•		all year	•		
Comal	•	•		all year	•		
Cranes Mill	•	•		all year	•	•	
Jacobs Creek	•		•	all year	•	•	
Potters Creek	•	•		all year	•	•	•
North	•			all year			

FACILITIES
Camping: 6 parks with campgrounds, primitive group campsites at Canyon Park and Potters Creek Park. Fees vary. Group campgrounds and electric sites at Potters Creek may be reserved. Parks not listed on the matrix do not have camping.

Recreation: swimming, fishing, boat ramps, marina, boat rentals.

MAIN ATTRACTIONS
Built for flood control and water storage on the Guadalupe River, Canyon Lake covers 8,231 surface acres at its normal level and has 80 miles of shoreline. It is one of the deepest reservoirs in Texas, with

an average depth of 47 feet. Walleye, hybrid striped bass, and small-mouth bass are stocked in the lake, and there is a trout fishery below the dam. There is no hunting on the property. Natural Bridge Caverns, one of the largest and most interesting caves in Texas, is west of New Braunfels off TX 46 on FM 1863. Tubing and white water recreation is popular on the Guadalupe River between the dam and New Braunfels.

CANYON LAKE

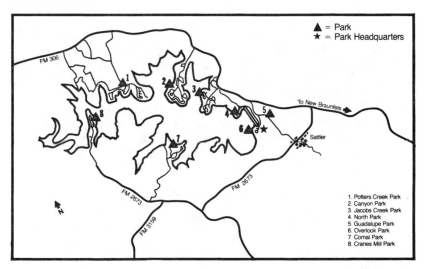

1. Potters Creek Park
2. Canyon Park
3. Jacobs Creek Park
4. North Park
5. Guadalupe Park
6. Overlook Park
7. Comal Park
8. Cranes Mill Park

30. CAPROCK CANYONS STATE PARK

LOCATION
Briscoe County. 50 miles south of Amarillo on IH-27, 45 miles east on TX 86 to Quitaque, 3 miles north on FM 1065.
Mailing address: Box 204, Quitaque, Texas 79255.
Phone: 806-455-1492. For all state park reservations, call 512-389-8900.

FACILITIES
Camping: 20 primitive campsites with no water at trailhead, 2 primitive camping areas with no water 1 mile from trailhead, equestrian primitive camping area with no water, three-quarter mile from trailhead, 10 campsites with water only, 25 campsites with water and electricity, modern restrooms with showers, trailer dump station. Fees charged.

Recreation: picnic areas and playgrounds, 97 miles of multi-use trails (hiking, biking, equestrian) nature trails under development, equestrian trail over 74 miles long, interpretive exhibits, swimming in Lake Theo, fishing with a lighted pier, boating, amphitheater.

MAIN ATTRACTIONS

The park preserves an area of rugged beauty in the deeply eroded canyons that border the Caprock Escarpment in the Panhandle. Scenic views of the canyons, carved through brick-red sediments laced with snow-white veins of gypsum, and picturesque formations await the visitor. Wildlife is abundant and often seen on the hiking trails and roads in the park. Caprock Canyons, a newly developed park, is one of the most beautiful state parks in Texas. Its location, far from any large population centers, ensures visitors a wilderness that city dwellers often forget exists.

The park has a small lake of 120 acres when filled to capacity. During the summer the lake is quite low, and the fishing pier may be well out of the water. The lake is stocked, and catches of channel catfish, largemouth bass, sunfish, and crappie are common. There is also a shaded picnic area and a swimming beach.

HIKING AND HORSEBACK RIDING

Hiking trails ideal for day hikes or backpacking lead through the picturesque canyons, along streambeds at the foot of castlelike formations, and atop ridges overlooking the maze of canyons and the colorful badlands extending eastward. The Upper and Lower Canyon trails form a figure 8, and each has a campground with a composting toilet. The 2-mile Eagles Point Trail connects two day-use areas. The equestrian camping area, three-quarter mile from the equestrian trailhead, has a composting toilet and connects with a 10-mile loop trail and a 1.5-mile trail to a county road. In a "rails to trails" acquisition, a three-county network of old railroad beds has been converted to trails. The trails, easy grades of 1 percent or less, take hikers and riders through a cross section of West Texas ecology from mesquite and sand sage, over the caprock escarpment, and on to the High Plains.

ECOLOGY

The park, comprising 15,177 acres, is located at the juncture of the High Plains, which extend into New Mexico, and the Rolling Plains to the east. Deep canyons have been cut by streams, exposing the caprock of the erosion-resistant caliche and gravel of the Ogallala formation of the Tertiary period, 3 million to 11 million years old. Palo Duro Canyon and Caprock Canyons state parks, with similar geologic histories, are examples of the erosive force of small seasonal streams on the softer underlying rocks. The Ogallala overlies red sandstones and shales approximately 200 million years old. The oldest layers exposed in the park are the red sandstones, siltstones, and shales of the Permian, more than 230 million years old, interlaced with crumbling white gypsum layers.

Plants characteristic of both the Rolling and the High Plains grow in the park. In the moist North and South Prong canyons, Rocky Mountain junipers are common, while Mohr shinnery oaks grow on the drier slopes. Cottonwoods grow along wet drainages. The prairies consist of buffalo, grama, and beard grasses as well as yucca and prickly pear and tasajillo cacti. Many of the prairies were overgrazed and have been invaded by mesquite and red-berry juniper trees.

The park is rich in wildlife. An evening drive or hike will often reveal scaled and bobwhite quail, jackrabbits, mule deer, and the impressive aoudad sheep. Introduced in 1957, the sheep increased so rapidly that the park allowed some hunting in the past to reduce the population to a number compatible with the available food supply. Coyotes can be heard serenading the moon, while raccoons, badgers, and the secretive ringtail prowl through the night. Bison, once kings of the prairies, were exterminated in the late 1800s.

More than 175 species of birds have been seen in the park. Golden eagles nest in the canyons, and such rare birds as the red-necked grebe and the red-throated loon have used the lake during migrations. The steep red cliffs are the home of a ledge-nesting bird familiar to us all but unexpected in this rugged setting: the domestic pigeon. A bird checklist is available.

HISTORY

The north plains of Texas are rich in historic lore of the Comanches, frontier forts, and early cattle barons. After the Comanches were finally driven onto reservations in Oklahoma and the bison were eliminated, ranchers moved onto the plains, herded the longhorns, and later introduced improved breeds of cattle. George Baker established the Quitaque Ranch in what is now the park with 2,000 heads of cattle in 1878.

The famous Panhandle rancher Charles Goodnight, whose two million-acre spread included Palo Duro Canyon, bought Baker's ranch for 22 cents an acre in 1880. The parkland passed through many hands until 1936, when it was purchased by Theo Geisler, who lived there in a dugout house until 1940. The state acquired the land in 1973.

31. CASTROVILLE REGIONAL PARK

Medina County. 20 miles west of San Antonio on U.S. 90, 6 blocks south on Athens St., in Castroville on the Medina River. Mailing address: 1209 Fiorella, Castroville, Texas 78009. Phone: 210-538-2224. Camping: 35 campsites with water, electricity, and sewage hookups; flush toilets, showers, trailer dump station. Reservations accepted. Fees charged. Recreation: picnic areas and playgrounds, swimming pool, fishing, tennis courts, volleyball, pavilion. Open all year.

32. CEDAR HILL STATE PARK

LOCATION
Dallas County. West of Dallas on IH-20, exit FM 1382, 4 miles south. Mailing address: P.O. Box 941, Cedar Hill, Texas 75104. Phone: 214-291-3900. For all state park reservations, call 512-389-8900.

FACILITIES
Camping: 355 sites with water and electricity, shaded tables, 30 primitive sites, restrooms, showers, dump station. Campsites vary in size of parking pads and some are multi-level with steps, so specify any special requirements when making reservations. Fees charged. Open 8 A.M. to 10 P.M. for day use, overnight for fishing and camping.

Recreation: 210 picnic tables, 4 playgrounds, 2 boat ramps, 2 lighted fishing jetties, 5 miles of hiking trails, 7 miles of mountain bike trails, swimming beach, volleyball court, historic Penn Farm.

MAIN ATTRACTIONS
This 1,826-acre wooded park is on the southeast shore of Joe Pool Lake and serves the recreational needs of the Dallas-Fort Worth metroplex. In the spring and fall, a colorful array of wildflowers covers the rugged hills, once known as the Cedar Mountains. Juniper, mesquite, cedar, and elm trees vegetate the limestone hills, while rich bottomland soils support remnant prairie stands of little and big bluestem and Indian grass. The forest and prairies, surrounded by urban growth, provide shelter for a variety of small mammals, including bobcats and coyotes. The endangered black-capped vireo, as well as other migrating and nesting songbirds, frequents the park.

The rocky hills of Cedar Mountain escarpment drop steeply into the bottomlands of Mountain Creek. Early pioneers farmed the rich blackland soils, grazed livestock on the slopes, and cut the prairie grasses for hay. The 1,100-acre homestead farm of William Penn exists within the park boundaries. The Penn family lived on the farm, built in 1860, and ranched the area until 1970. The hand-hewn structures and period artifacts provide a glimpse into the daily lifestyle of the founders of the state. Many of the original stacked rail fences survive the years. At the time of this writing, the demonstration farm, an example of the small farms that once typified the rural area, was closed for restoration.

NEARBY ATTRACTIONS

The Trinity River Authority operates two parks on Joe Pool Lake, including Loyd Park with camping (see listing #73) and Lynn Creek Park for day use. The 360-acre Dallas Nature Center (7171 Mountain Creek Parkway, 214-296-1955) offers seven miles of trails, picnicking, and plant and wildlife observation.

33. CHOKE CANYON STATE PARK

LOCATION
McMullen and Live Oak counties.
South Shore Unit: 4 miles west of Three Rivers on TX 72.
Mailing address: Box 1548, Three Rivers, Texas 78071. Phone: 512-786-3538.
Calliham Unit: 11 miles west of Three Rivers on TX 72. Mailing address: Box 2, Calliham, Texas 78007. Phone: 512-786-3868. For all state park reservations, call 512-389-8900.

FACILITIES
South Shore Unit
Camping: 2 walk-in camping areas with 14 and 21 campsites, 20 campsites with electricity and water, trailer dump station, modern restrooms with showers. Fees charged.
Recreation: picnic area, 2 group picnic shelters, fishing, playgrounds, 2 fish-cleaning shelters, 2 boat ramps, swimming but no designated area, rinse showers, snack bar, convenience store.

Calliham Unit
Camping: 40 campsites with water and electricity, 20 screened shelters, trailer dump station. Fees charged.
Recreation: picnic sites with shade shelters, 6 group picnic shelters, tennis, basketball, baseball, swimming pool, swimming beach, bathhouse, park store, fish-cleaning area, boat ramp, nature trails, birdwatching, and hunting in the nearby Daugherty Wildlife Management Area.

MAIN ATTRACTIONS

Water sports, wildlife, and a day away from the city attract visitors to this park. Fishermen troll the waters for largemouth, striped, and white bass, crappie, sunfish, and flathead, channel, and blue catfish. Swimmers, boaters, and skiers play in the lake while picnickers enjoy the shoreline and game courts. Bird-watchers look for crested caracaras, or Mexican eagles, turkeys, herons, egrets, ducks, and other wading and water birds and migrants attracted to the reservoir. A wooded camping and picnicking area exists along the river below the dam in the South Unit. Brushy scrub growth typical of South Texas covers the shoreline and most of the park.

Choke Canyon was named for the "choking" of floodwaters by the steep banks of the Frio River. An earthen dam impounds the river just upstream from Three Rivers, where the Frio, Atascosa, and Nueces rivers join. The 26,000-acre lake supplies water for Corpus Christi. In addition to the 1,485 acres set aside for the two state park units, the James Daugherty Wildlife Management Area preserves 8,700 acres for hunting.

ECOLOGY

Choke Canyon lies in the northern portion of the Rio Grande Plains vegetational region of Texas. Thorny chaparral and mesquite-grassland savannas characterize this area. Huisache, black brush, guajillo, prickly pear, mesquite, and other shrubby, thorny plants cover the rocky, rolling hills and alluvial plains. As early as February, bluebonnets, paintbrushes, huisache daisies, and firewheels blanket the countryside with a myriad of colors.

This area has been ranching country since the first longhorn was roped and branded. Though overgrazing has allowed mesquite and chaparral to invade the grasslands, most of the area retains its wild character. As a result, wildlife abounds. White-tailed deer, Rio Grande turkeys, javelinas, and coyotes claim the brushlands as their home and often roam through the state park, and alligators live in the reservoir.

HISTORY

This area of Texas gave birth to the legend of the cowboy and the cattle drive. After the Civil War, the state of Texas was bankrupt, many of the men had been killed in action, and millions of wild longhorns roamed the chaparral thickets of South Texas. But the only profit from the ornery cows came from skinning them and shipping their hides to New Orleans. When the railroads brought the eastern markets as close as Kansas, Texans saw a fortune in the wild cattle and began the longest and largest human-influenced migration ever. Within twenty years, railroads reached Texas and a colorful era of American history ended, but the indomitable spirit of the cowboy had forever burned its brand into the American psyche. Folk historian and author J. Frank Dobie grew up in nearby Tilden. His numerous books on the ranching, wildlife, and folklore of South Texas bring that rich era alive for modern generations.

34. CLEBURNE STATE PARK

LOCATION
Johnson County. 7 miles west of Cleburne on U.S. 67, 6 miles south on PR 21.
Mailing address: Route 2, Box 90, Cleburne, Texas 76031. Phone: 817-645-4215. For all state park reservations, call 512-389-8900.

FACILITIES
Camping: 31 campsites with water and electricity, 27 campsites with water, electricity, and sewage hookups; 6 screened shelters, group facility—2 bunkhouses, kitchen, and dining hall—for 48 people, modern restrooms with showers, trailer dump station. Fees charged.

Recreation: picnic areas and playgrounds, hiking/nature trail, swimming in Cedar Lake, fishing, boating (5-mph speed limit), boat rentals, store (summer only).

MAIN ATTRACTIONS
Fishing, canoeing, and sailing on the spring-fed lake are the primary attractions in this 528-acre park. The crystal springs, now under Cedar Lake, have attracted many to their clear waters. The springs were well known to Indians, and Comanches are said to have made frequent encampments nearby. Over a hundred years ago, wild horses are thought to have been corralled in the area—look for the barbed wire still embedded in the trees. In more recent times, bootleggers used the springwater for their brew.

ECOLOGY
The dominant tree in the park is the Ashe juniper, which forms dense cedar brakes on the thin soil overlying the Edwards and Comanche Peak limestones. Around and below the lake grow Texas and bur oaks, hackberry, elm, and Texas ash. Smaller trees and shrubs include flame-leaf sumac, catclaw acacia, redbud, and Mexican buckeye.

The spring-fed lake attracts many species of birds, including the endangered golden-cheeked warbler. Large numbers of black and turkey vultures roost in the trees surrounding the lake. In the early-morning hours, white-tailed deer are commonly seen grazing in the open meadows. Dawn and dusk are the best times to look for raccoons, opossums, and skunks, and occasionally a mountain lion may be sighted.

The still of the evening may be accented by the serenade of coyotes or the hooting of owls. In the fall, an early-morning fog sometimes hangs over the lake, creating an eerie mood, while in the spring bluebonnets and other wildflowers bloom profusely.

35. COLORADO BEND STATE PARK

LOCATION
San Saba County. West of Lampasas on FM 580 to Bend, south on gravel road at sign for state park for 4 miles.
Mailing address: Box 118, Bend, Texas 76824. Phone: 915-628-3240.

FACILITIES
Camping: primitive camping area with tables and water nearby, chemical toilets. Entrance fees charged, no reservations.

Recreation: picnicking, swimming in river, fishing, boat ramp, mountain biking, hiking, backpacking. Weekend tours of Gorman Falls and the wild caves are offered; fee charged. Visitation limited to 300 cars.

MAIN ATTRACTIONS
This 5,328-acre park preserves a section of the Colorado River long known for good fishing and splendid scenery. The cypress-lined river winds past high cut banks, a picturesque waterfall, and floodplains forested with giant pecans, sycamores, and oaks. The park has two developed hiking trails, each about four miles long with designated camping areas for backpackers.

One of the most scenic attractions in the park, Gorman Falls and the undeveloped wild caves, can be visited only on a weekend guided tour. Gorman Creek, a spring-fed stream, flows through the park and plummets over a high cliff to the river below. Travertine formations border the rim and decorate the cliffside of this spectacular waterfall, and fern and mosses thrive in the splash zones. Such delicate formations and plant life could easily be destroyed by overuse by park visitors. Visitors on the cave tour can expect crawling through small and sometimes difficult passages. Hard hats are supplied, but you must bring flashlights.

Mountain bikers can use the Gorman Creek and river trails, which are old dirt roads.

36. COLORADO CITY: FISHER PARK

Mitchell County. 9 miles south of town on TX 208, 3 miles west on local road. Mailing address: P.O. Box 912, Colorado City, Texas 79512. Phone: 915-728-3464. Camping: 18 RV sites with electricity only, restrooms, cold water showers, dump station. Recreation: fishing on Champion Lake, fishing barge, boating, park store with groceries, fishing supplies. Fees charged, no reservations. Open year round.

COLORADO CITY: RUDDICK PARK

Mitchell County. In Colorado City at the intersection of E. Seventh and Houston streets. Mailing address: 180 W. 3rd St., Colorado City, Texas 79512. Phone: 915-728-5331. Camping: 5 primitive campsites with tables and water, pit toilets. Recreation: playground, swimming pool. This 30-acre park along a small creek is suitable for an overnight stop.

37. COPPER BREAKS STATE PARK

LOCATION
Hardeman County. 30 miles east of Childress on U.S. 287 to Quanah, 12 miles south on TX 6.
Mailing address: Route 2, Box 480, Quanah, Texas 79252. Phone: 817-839-4331. For all state park reservations, call 512-389-8900.

FACILITIES
Camping: 11 campsites with water only, 25 campsites with water and electricity, primitive campsites, 10 campsites with water only for equestrian use, group campground with water only, modern restrooms with showers, trailer dump station. Fees charged.

Recreation: picnic areas and playgrounds, half-mile nature trail with trail guide pamphlet, 2-mile hiking trail, 6-mile equestrian trail, excellent interpretive exhibits, swimming in Lake Copper Breaks, fishing with fishing pier, boating (5-mph speed limit), paddleboat rentals, state longhorn herd, amphitheater with theatrical productions in June.

MAIN ATTRACTIONS
Fishing and swimming are popular activities at Lake Copper Breaks, a 60-acre impoundment of Devils Creek. The lake is stocked with catfish, bass, and perch. A self-guided nature trail identifies many of the plants and explains the ecology of the area. An excellent museum, located in the headquarters building, explains the history

of the Indians in the region, ranching, and early pioneer life. Also featured are taxidermy and paintings of the wildlife and exhibits of the plants of the North Texas plains. Part of the state longhorn herd is kept in the park.

ECOLOGY

The terrain of the park consists of rolling plains broken by hills and canyons. The red shales and clays forming the colorful hills were deposited 230 million years ago during the Permian age. Low-grade copper deposits give a greenish tint to strata scattered through the area. Mining was once attempted but proved unsuccessful.

This part of North Texas was once covered with grasslands of grama, bluestem, Indiangrass, cottontop, and other species. Large herds of bison grazed the rolling hills, and pronghorn antelope bounded across the prairies unimpeded by fences. After the bison were eliminated by buffalo hunters, cattle were introduced and allowed to severely overgraze the land.

Without the grasses to protect the fragile land, erosion stripped away much of the topsoil, and brushy plants became established. Today, mesquite trees and red-berry junipers dominate. Originally, grasslands covered 60 to 70 percent of the land; now they occupy less than 30 percent.

HISTORY

The history of the park, and of all of North Texas, is deeply involved with the Comanche and Kiowa Indians, the efforts to drive the Indians onto Oklahoma reservations, and the development of ranching.

Of particular historical interest is the capture of Cynthia Ann Parker in 1860 by Texas Ranger Captain Sul Ross on the banks of the Pease River near the park. Cynthia Ann had been kidnapped by the Comanches in 1836, when she was 9 years old. After living 24 years as an Indian, she was unable to acclimate to Anglo life—she died in 1864, soon after the death of her daughter. The book, *Quanah,* by Paul Foreman, is an interesting historical novel about that period of Texas history.

38. CORPUS CHRISTI: NUECES RIVER PARK

Nueces County. Northwest of Corpus Christi at the intersection of U.S. 77 with the Nueces River. Mailing address: Corpus Christi Parks and Recreation Department, Box 9277, Corpus Christi, Texas 78408. Phone: 512-880-3460. Camping: free primitive campsites with three-day permit, chemical toilets. Recreation: fishing in the Nueces River, boating. Open all year. This is a 40-acre fishing park with minimal facilities.

CORPUS CHRISTI: PADRE BALLI PARK

Nueces County. On the north end of Padre Island, from Corpus Christi, southeast on PR 22. Mailing address: Nueces County Parks Dept., P.O. Box 18608, Corpus Christi, Texas 78480. Phone: 512-949-8121. Camping: primitive camping on beach, camping on hardtop area without hookups, 66 RV sites with water and electricity, flush toilets, showers, trailer dump station. Fees charged. Recreation: swimming in the Gulf of Mexico, 1,240-foot lighted fishing pier, boating, concessions. Open all year.

39. CORSICANA: LAKE HALBERT PARK

Navarro County. South of Corsicana, 1 mile east of IH-45 on U.S. 287. Mailing address: City Hall, 200 N. 12th, Corsicana, Texas 75110. Phone: 903-654-4840. Camping: 3 campsites with water and electricity, 3 campsites with water, flush toilets. No reservations. Fees charged. Recreation: picnicking, playground, group pavilion, boat ramp, fishing, softball, soccer; 145 acres. Open all year.

40. DAINGERFIELD STATE PARK

LOCATION
Morris County. 40 miles north of Longview on U.S. 259 to Daingerfield, 2 miles east on TX 49.
Mailing address: Route 1, Box 286B, Daingerfield, Texas 75638.
Phone: 903-645-2921. For all state park reservations, call 512-389-8900.

FACILITIES
Camping: 15 campsites with water only, 17 campsites with water and electricity, 8 campsites with water, electricity, and sewage hookups; 3 cabins, group lodge for 20 people, modern restrooms with showers, trailer dump station. Fees charged.

Recreation: picnic areas and playgrounds, 2.5-mile hiking trail, swimming in Lake Daingerfield, bathhouse, fishing pier, boat ramp, boat rentals, store (summer only), wheelchair access to some facilities.

MAIN ATTRACTIONS
The park preserves 551 acres of beautiful mixed pine-hardwood forest and includes a picturesque 80-acre lake. A scenic hiking trail circles the lake, which is stocked for fishing. Swimming, canoeing, and paddleboating are popular. In early April, the park roads, camp-grounds, and picnic areas are covered with a canopy of snow-white dogwood blossoms, and in the fall, brilliant colors decorate the park.

ECOLOGY

The forest surrounding the small reservoir is an excellent example of East Texas woodland dominated by loblolly pines and a variety of oak species. Seepages along the porous hillsides support a rich growth of woodland herbs, including luxuriant cinnamon ferns.

Lake Daingerfield is the home of domesticated ducks eager to accept food from park visitors. More interesting to bird-watchers are the rare red-cockaded woodpeckers and the large, red-crested pileated woodpeckers that can be heard drumming against dead pine trees in the forest; a checklist of birds is available at the park headquarters. Squirrels, rabbits, deer, and armadillos are commonly seen in the park.

HISTORY

The first iron plant in Texas was built near the park in 1855. Other plants were soon constructed in the area, including one operated by the Confederate government to manufacture gun barrels. Production had virtually ceased by 1910 but was renewed during World War II, when the government built the plant now owned by the Lone Star Steel Company.

Today, Daingerfield State Park is located in the center of the iron-smelting industry in East Texas. Morris and the three surrounding counties have the only iron ore deposits that presently can be mined economically in Texas. The deposits of brown ore occur as nodules or thin strata near the tops of the sand-covered hills.

41. DALHART: RITA BLANCA LAKE PARK

Hartley County. Operated by Dallam and Hartley counties. 1 mile south of Dalhart on FM 281. Mailing address: Box 9395, Dalhart, Texas 79022. Phone: 806-249-2450. Camping: tent sites, RV sites with water, electricity, and sewage hookups; flush toilets, trailer dump station. Fees charged. Recreation: picnic areas and playgrounds, exercise trail. Poor camping facilities. Home of the XIT Rodeo, this park offers free barbecue with the rodeo in early August.

42. DAVIS MOUNTAINS STATE PARK

LOCATION

Jeff Davis County. 30 miles northwest of Alpine on TX 118 through Fort Davis.
Mailing address: Box 786, Fort Davis, Texas 79734. Phone: headquarters 915-426-3337, Indian Lodge 915-426-3254. For all state park reservations, call 512-389-8900.

FACILITIES

Camping: 43 campsites with water only, 20 campsites with water and electricity, 27 campsites with water, electricity, and sewage hookups. Modern restrooms with showers, trailer dump station. Indian Lodge hotel with 39 rooms. Fees charged.

Recreation: picnic areas and playgrounds, hiking trails, interpretive exhibits (summer only), swimming pool for Indian Lodge guests, amphitheater with summer programs, restaurant.

MAIN ATTRACTIONS

Davis Mountains State Park, 1,869 acres of rolling foothills, includes the most scenic portions of Keesey Creek and Keesey Canyon. The area is renowned for its scenic vistas, its expansive ranches, McDonald Observatory, and the reconstructed Fort Davis. This is one of the most beautiful state parks in Texas.

The 74-mile Davis Mountains Skyline Drive is one of the most impressive and highest roads in the state. The drive passes through wooded canyons, past the state park and observatory, and along beautiful Limpia Creek; the loop returns through the town of Fort Davis.

The University of Texas' McDonald Observatory is located on Mount Locke. Public viewing on the 82-inch telescope is allowed on the last Wednesday of each month. Reservations must be made six months in advance; a self-addressed, stamped envelope should be enclosed. The visitors' center provides a slide show and a self-guided tour of the observatory. Write Box 1337, Fort Davis, Texas 79734.

The park's interpretive center provides information about the geology, plants, and animals of the Davis Mountains. The center overlooks a wildlife watering station that attracts many birds, squirrels, and other animals. Interpretive programs are scheduled throughout the summer.

HIKING

There are two hiking trails in the park. A short loop trail begins behind the interpretive center. This rugged trail continues, traversing the four miles across a beautiful mountain ridge and descending to historic Fort Davis. A shorter hike is possible by intercepting the trail at the scenic overlook at the end of the park's Skyline Drive, which parallels the trail along the mountain ridge.

ECOLOGY

The park encompasses both the desert plains grasslands, which surround the mountains, and the oak-pinyon-juniper woodlands common to the intermediate elevations. Emory and gray oaks and one-seed juniper are the dominant trees in the park. Conspicuous shrubs include the yellow trumpet flower, evergreen sumac, little-leaf leadtree, Apache plume, little walnut, and catclaw acacia. In the

61

spring and summer, the grasslands and slopes abound with evening primrose, red penstemon, scarlet gilia, and blue flax. Bluebonnets cover the slopes at the lower elevations and provide breathtaking scenes.

Birds representative of both the desert grasslands and the mountain woodlands are found in the park. More than 140 species have been recorded, including the rare Montezuma quail, which has been eliminated from most of its original range. Scrub jays are common camp visitors, and barn swallows can be seen in the spring nesting under the eaves of Indian Lodge. A checklist is available.

The Davis Mountains, the most extensive mountain complex in the state, are a series of large, irregularly shaped peaks capped with flat layers of volcanic rock. Within the park, reddish brown and gray lava flows and crumbling, soft to glassy volcanic material called tuff are prevalent.

The rocks exposed in Keesey Canyon, in the heart of the park, and behind the parade grounds of Fort Davis are a type of lava called rhyolite. The volcanic rocks of the Davis Mountains are believed to have oozed up to the surface through multiple fractures in the earth's crust. More recent faulting in the area has split the volcanic rock layers, with as much as 200 feet of vertical displacement in some sections. Prominent faulting is evident near the Barrel Springs State Route sign on the scenic loop.

Outside the park, several peaks formed by intrusive igneous material are found. Mount Livermore and Sawtooth Mountain were formed by pluglike intrusions of molten rock that pushed upward through the earth, cooled before reaching the surface, and were later exposed by erosion. Mount Livermore, 8,381 feet high, is the dominant feature of the range. Blue Mountain, at 7,331 feet, rises southwest of Indian Lodge; Sawtooth Mountain is visible from the scenic loop drive; and Mount Locke, at 6,809 feet and topped by McDonald Observatory, is northwest of the park.

The boulders at the Rock Pile Roadside Park, along the scenic loop drive, came from small intrusions forming a rock called syenite. The famous polished boulders are believed to have been used by the Indians for defleshing animal skins.

HISTORY

The Davis Mountains are rich in historic lore. In the mid 1800s, Mescalero Apaches lived in the mountains and had a farming village near the present site of Fort Davis. They irrigated their fields with water diverted from Limpia Creek. The Comanches camped in the area on their migrations from Oklahoma to Mexico.

In 1849, an overland route for the stage from San Antonio to San Diego was surveyed through the Davis Mountains. Henry Skillman established three stage stations in the mountains to allow drivers to change horses and to provide accommodation for the passengers.

The Indians resisted the encroachment of the Anglos with repeated attacks on the mail coaches and wagon trains. In 1854, Fort Davis, named after Jefferson Davis, the U.S. secretary of war and later president of the Confederacy, was established to combat the hostile Indians. The fort was abandoned during the Civil War and reoccupied in 1867. By 1885, the Indians had been driven from the area, and the fort was decommissioned in 1891.

Partially rebuilt by concerned citizens in the 1940s, Fort Davis was purchased by the U.S. Congress in 1963 and became a national historic site. The remaining adobe and stone buildings were reconstructed. The eighteen residences on Officers' Row, two troop barracks, a warehouse, and the hospital now stand as they did originally; there is also a museum. The fort, which broadcasts a recorded military parade and mounted review across the parade grounds, provides a vivid perspective on a bygone era. Fort Davis is the most impressive example in the nation of the frontier forts that once stretched across the West to protect early settlers.

43. DAVY CROCKETT NATIONAL FOREST

LOCATION
West of Lufkin, east of Crockett.
Mailing address, Neches Ranger District: 1240 E. Loop 304, Crockett, Texas 75835. Phone: 409-544-2046. Mailing address, Trinity Ranger District: Box 130, Apple Springs, Texas 75926. Phone: 409-831-2246.

FACILITIES
Camping: There is free primitive camping in the forest and along the Four C National Recreation Trail and the Big Slough Canoe Trail. Check with the ranger headquarters about primitive camping during hunting season in November and December.

Ratcliff Lake, 20 miles east of Crockett on TX 7, is the only park with camping facilities. It has the following: 76 campsites with water nearby, flush toilets with showers, picnic area with two shelters, hiking trails. Reservations can be made for the picnic shelters only. Fees charged for camping and swimming in lake.

MAIN ATTRACTIONS
Davy Crockett National Forest, covering 161,497 acres in Houston and Trinity counties, is bordered on the northeast by the Neches River. The forest includes Ratcliff Lake, a 45-acre lake offering fishing, swimming, and boating—electric motors, paddleboats, and canoes only. Concessions, a bathhouse, and two day-use picnic pavilions are available. In the summer months, park rangers present

programs at the amphitheater and conduct guided walks on a 1.5-mile forest trail.

HIKING AND CANOEING

The Four C National Recreation Trail begins at Ratcliff Lake and travels through 20 miles of forest to the Neches Overlook. Primitive campgrounds are available along the trail, but there is no potable water. The hiking trail passes through the 4,000-acre Big Slough Wilderness Area. The Big Slough Canoe Trail, within the wilderness, is not maintained and is difficult to traverse. For maps and other information, contact the district headquarters.

44. DEVILS RIVER STATE NATURAL AREA

LOCATION
Val Verde County. From Del Rio, U.S. 277 north 43 miles to Dolan Creek Rd., west 22 miles to park headquarters.
Mailing address: HCR-1, Box 513, Del Rio, Texas 78840. Phone: 210-395-2133.

FACILITIES

This 21,000-acre natural area is open to the public Wednesday through Sundays by reservation only. A maximum of ten overnight visitors are allowed in the primitive camping area and ten in the bunkhouse. The bunkhouse has restrooms, showers, and five bedrooms, two bunks per room, but you must bring your own linens and pillows. A dining hall has gas and electric stoves, refrigerators, and a large conference room. The tent camping area with no water or facilities is located 200 yards from the bunkhouse. Fees charged.

MAIN ACTIVITIES

The park preserves many archaeological and pictograph sites, some more than 8,000 years old. All areas of the park are off-limits except developed trails to prevent vandalism of rock art and disturbance of the endangered black-capped vireo. The black-capped vireo nests in the park from March to August. A 13-mile loop trail takes hikers through the broken canyon country with half the length traversing the rim and half in the canyons. A five-mile road leads to the river. The park ranger offers guided hikes and tours in state vehicles (fee charged), usually on Saturdays.

HISTORY

Deep canyons with rock shelters dissect this area of Texas. As the last Ice Age receded, leaving a cooler, moister climate, humans lived in the rock shelters and hunted bison and other big game now extinct. Nearby Seminole Canyon State Park, with similar topography, has beautiful exhibits and daily tours of some of the most outstanding rock art in the state.

45. DINOSAUR VALLEY STATE PARK

LOCATION
Somervell County. 24 miles west of Cleburne on U.S. 67 through Glen Rose, 3 miles north on FM 205.
Mailing address: Box 396, Glen Rose, Texas 76043. Phone: 817-897-4588. For all state park reservations, call 512-389-8900.

FACILITIES
Camping: primitive campsites along hiking trails, 40 campsites with water and electricity, modern restrooms with showers, trailer dump station. Fees charged.

Recreation: picnic areas and playgrounds, several miles of hiking trails, dinosaur exhibits, state longhorn herd, swimming in the Paluxy River, fishing, pavilion, amphitheater with summer programs.

MAIN ATTRACTIONS
More than a hundred dinosaur tracks are visible in the flat limestone bed of the scenic Paluxy River. Life-size dinosaur models and summer interpretive programs explain the significance of the tracks and how they were discovered. Be sure to view the exhibits in the visitor center. The Paluxy River, whose meanderings helped uncover the dinosaur tracks hidden in the rock, winds through the wooded hills and offers campers swimming and fishing. A portion of the official Texas longhorn herd, in an enclosure above the river, can be viewed from a trail.

HIKING
A system of trails leads through the hills, across picturesque tributaries, and along ridges with scenic views. Primitive camping is allowed in designated areas along one trail. Obtain a trail map and permits at the park entrance.

ECOLOGY
The park preserves evidence of plant and animal life that existed more than 100 million years ago. At the time of the dinosaurs, Texas was moist and warm, with vast swamps, mud flats, and shallow

bays. For more than 100 million years, dinosaurs, the "terrible lizards," were the dominant creatures. Some were as small as a dog, while the 40-ton, 70-foot-long *Brontosaurus* was a giant.

The dinosaurs waded through the shallow water and across mud flats, leaving deep imprints in the soft mud. The impressions were gradually covered with hundreds of feet of sediment, which preserved the tracks. By modern times, the river had cut through to the original layer containing the tracks, exposing more than a hundred prints of the large plant-eating *Pleurocelus* and the smaller meat-eating *Acrocanthosaurus*.

Besides the dinosaur tracks, the park includes a beautiful section of the Paluxy River. The camping and picnic grounds are located in the wooded river bottomland. Elms and a variety of oaks grow along the river, and juniper trees dominate the rocky, dry uplands. Alongside the dinosaur tracks, more recent footprints of deer, raccoons, opossums, skunks, and foxes can be seen in the sand.

46. DUMAS: TEXOMA PARK

Moore County. Western edge of Dumas on U.S. 87. Mailing address: City Park Dept., Box 438, Dumas, Texas 79029. Phone: 806-935-4101. Camping: 24 free RV sites with water nearby and electricity, flush toilets, trailer dump station; 24-hour parking limit. Recreation: picnic areas and playgrounds. Closed in winter. Minimal facilities but okay for an overnight stay.

47. EISENHOWER STATE PARK

LOCATION
Grayson County. 3.5 miles north of Denison on TX 75A to FM 1310, 2 miles west to PR 20.
Mailing address: Route 2, Box 50K, Denison, Texas 75020. Phone: 903-465-1956. For all state park reservations, call 512-389-8900.

FACILITIES
Camping: 48 campsites with water only, 45 campsites with water and electricity, 50 campsites with water, electricity, and sewage hookups; 35 screened shelters, group trailer campgrounds with electricity, group facility with kitchen and dining hall for 48 people, modern restrooms with showers, trailer dump station. Fees charged.

Recreation: picnic areas and playgrounds, multi-use hiking trail approximately 7 miles long, minibike trail, swimming in Lake Texoma, fishing with piers and cleaning stations, boating, marina, store.

MAIN ATTRACTIONS

Eisenhower State Park is on the 40-mile-long Lake Texoma, formed in 1944 by damming the Red River in Texas below its confluence with the Washita River in Oklahoma. Lake Texoma, with white, striped, and black bass as well as other game fish, has long been a favorite among fishermen. Water sports of all types are popular on the lake. Some camping and fishing supplies may be purchased at the marina. A boat launch, boat shelters, and facilities for boat repairs are available.

Nearby attractions include the Eisenhower Birthplace State Historic Site in Denison. Hagerman National Wildlife Refuge, with 11,300 acres, is 15 miles west of Denison on Lake Texoma.

HIKING

A hiking trail extends the length of the park. Visitors can drive to all campsites, but backpackers may choose to use the trail to reach their campgrounds and explore the park. Also, the Army Corps of Engineers maintains the 14-mile-long Cross Timbers Hiking Trail on Lake Texoma, west of the state park. Obtain a map from the Corps headquarters at the dam site. The Corps operates various parks on Lake Texoma and offers tours of the dam and hydroelectric facilities.

ECOLOGY

The Red River cuts through an area of rolling hills dissected by deep canyons. Woodlands of cedar elm, oaks, osage orange, and Texas ash thrive in the canyon drainages. In the spring, the shrubby rough-leaf dogwood, with its clusters of tiny, fragrant white flowers, and beautiful redbud trees add color to the woods. Prairie grasses and a wide variety of wildflowers dominate the uplands.

The 457-acre park is on a part of the lake typified by steep cliffs rising abruptly out of the water. The cliffs are formed by a limestone cap covering a thick layer of clay and sandstone. The weathering of the exposed clay under the limestone ledges causes large sections of the cliffs to cave into the lake. Many unfortunate homeowners with houses perched on the scenic cliffs across from the park are fighting a losing battle trying to stabilize the crumbling cliff edges.

Waterfowl, shorebirds, and many migrants, including the osprey, are attracted to the large lake. Deer, raccoons, squirrels, and gray foxes frequent the park. Fossils, the remains of a rich marine life of 100 million years ago, are abundant in the limestone outcrops. The rounded imprints of large ammonites and fossilized oysters can be found along the limestone ledges overlooking the lake.

48. ENCHANTED ROCK STATE NATURAL AREA

LOCATION
Gillespie County. 18 miles north of Fredericksburg on FM 965. Mailing address: Route 4, Box 170, Fredericksburg, Texas 78624. Phone: 915-247-3903. For all state park reservations, call 512-389-8900.

FACILITIES
Camping: 60 primitive campsites with composting toilets, 46 walk-in tent campsites with water only, modern restrooms with showers. No vehicle camping or overnight parking of RVs allowed. Fees charged.

Recreation: picnicking, hiking trails, rock climbing throughout the park and at 48 sites rated according to difficulty, pavilion with 10 tables.

MAIN ATTRACTIONS
Enchanted Rock is in the heart of the Texas Hill Country. Its 1,643 acres encompass a massive granite dome rising 325 feet above the surrounding terrain. The dome, the tip of an extensive underground block called a batholith, is surpassed in size only by the famous Stone Mountain in Georgia. Enchanted Rock was purchased by the Texas Parks and Wildlife Department with the assistance of the Nature Conservancy in 1978. This unique site has been designated a state natural area. The designation indicates that to preserve its natural beauty, much of the area will be protected from overuse by visitors. Enchanted Rock is one of my favorite parks.

The awe-inspiring dome has long been the source of superstitions and legends. The Indians believed it to be inhabited by spirits because of the strange creaking noises often heard on cool nights. The surface of the rock contracts as the temperature drops after a hot day, causing the eerie sounds. Tales and superstitions involving the dome grew among early settlers, who considered the rock enchanted or bewitched.

South of Enchanted Rock, the picturesque German settlement of Fredericksburg is famous for its period architecture, German restaurants, and bakeries. Also in Fredericksburg is the Admiral Nimitz Museum and Historical Center, with many mementos of World War II.

HIKING

A trail from the campgrounds leads to the top of the dome and down again. The hike is fairly strenuous and slippery in wet weather, but it is well worth the effort to gain a true appreciation of the size and beauty of the dome. The park is a favorite for rock climbers. A small rock crevice cave is near the top on the far side of the dome.

ECOLOGY

Enchanted Rock is part of the Llano uplift, or the Central Texas mineral region, an area with granite bedrock surrounded by the limestone of the Edwards Plateau. Nearly a billion years ago, during the Precambrian era, a massive plug of molten lava was forced toward the earth's surface. As the lava cooled beneath the earth, it hardened into a dome of granite. The granite remained unexposed for millions of years while oceans deposited thousands of feet of limestone above it. Uplifts during the late Paleozoic era, approximately 275 million years ago, caused erosion of this overlying limestone, eventually exposing the granite dome to the surface.

The surface of the granite dome weathers by a process called exfoliation. Joints and fractures develop, which cause the surface of the rock to peel away in layers like the skin of an onion, leaving a smooth, rounded dome. Wind, rain, and frost weather the granite into sand, which is washed into creeks and rivers. The sandy banks and shores of the rivers that flow across the Hill Country to the Gulf are formed from the eroded granite of the Llano uplift.

Many of the plants found in the sandy soil around the granite dome do not occur on the adjacent alkaline soil formed from the Edwards Plateau limestone. Texas hickory, blackjack oak, and post oak are abundant in the park, where the dominant tree of the Edwards Plateau, Ashe juniper, is rare. The red sandy soil and the composition of the woodlands give Enchanted Rock a decidedly different appearance from the white chalky soil and vegetation typical of the Edwards Plateau.

Enchanted Rock is a textbook example of the changes bare rock undergoes during the process of soil building. The development of the plant community as soil accumulates is very evident. Beautiful multicolored lichens cover the red granite like splattered paint. Lichens are composed of fungi and algae growing together in a symbiotic relationship: a fungus cannot produce its own food but provides the substrate, or house, for the alga, which manufactures enough food to support both of them. Over time, lichens and the effects of weather slowly break down the rock to form soil.

Ferns and mosses are the next plants to get a toehold in the scant soil hidden in the cracks and depressions of the rock. Like miniature forests, rock ferns thrive around the sheltered bases of dislodged boulders. As more soil accumulates, the seeds of annuals find a home and decorate the depressions and irregularities with a colorful display of blooms. In deeper soil, perennials set their roots and become firmly established.

The deeper depressions, or soil islands, support a healthy growth of grasses, prickly pear cacti, and rain lilies, which magically appear soon after a thunderstorm. Surprisingly, oaks, buckeyes, and other trees flourish in the deep cracks and crevasses on top of Enchanted Rock. The mountain is far from being a bare, lifeless dome of exposed granite—it beckons those with the spirit of discovery to explore its every crack and crevice.

After a rain, the surface of the dome takes on an ephemeral appearance. Shallow depressions fill with water and, like mirages, seem to dance in the reflected sunlight. Ghost shrimp, hatching from long-dormant eggs, scurry through the temporary ponds to hurriedly mate and lay drought-resistant eggs before the sun can reclaim the water of their transitory homes.

The animals seen at Enchanted Rock are typical of the Hill Country. White-tailed deer are common, as are rock squirrels, jackrabbits, raccoons, and skunks. Lizards scamper across the sun-baked rocks and dive into shaded crevices for shelter. Vultures and an occasional migrating eagle circle on the columns of warm air rising from the massive dome. In the spring, vermilion flycatchers flit through the trees along the creeks like tiny balls of fire. Chickadees and titmice noisily forage for insects, and by night diminutive screech owls patrol the open savannas at the base of the rock.

HISTORY

Enchanted Rock is rich in Indian artifacts up to 8,000 years old. Projectile points indicate that prehistoric groups hunted deer, birds, and fish and gathered plants in the area. Bedrock metates, round holes in the rock used to grind nuts and seeds, can be seen in the park, and archaeological sites are scattered along the spring-fed creeks flowing around the dome.

When Europeans arrived in the 1700s, Tonkawa and other Indians inhabited the region. By the 1800s, Comanches and Apaches had been forced out of the Great Plains and into Texas. In 1841, Texas Ranger Captain John Hays, who had been separated from his company, repulsed a band of Comanches from a vantage point near the summit of the dome. A plaque commemorates the location of the battle.

70

49. FAIRFIELD LAKE STATE PARK

LOCATION
Freestone County. 6 miles northeast of Fairfield via FM 488 to FM 2570 to PR 64.
Mailing address: Route 2, Box 912, Fairfield, Texas 75840. Phone: 903-389-4514. For all state park reservations, call 512-389-8900.

FACILITIES
Camping: primitive group camping area at the end of a 4.5-mile trail, 36 campsites with water only, 99 campsites with water and electricity, modern restrooms with showers, trailer dump station. Fees charged.

Recreation: picnic areas and playgrounds, 4.5-mile nature trail with trail guide booklet, swimming in Fairfield Reservoir, fishing with lighted pier and cleaning stations, amphitheater, dining hall.

MAIN ATTRACTIONS
The state park is located on the 2,400-acre Fairfield Reservoir, an impoundment of Big Brown Creek. The reservoir—formed to provide cooling water for a lignite-fueled power plant, visible on the shore opposite the park—is one of the top three bass-producing lakes in the state. A survey in 1979 showed that the lake supported 112 pounds of largemouth bass per acre, with the record bass weighing over 10 pounds. Channel catfish, redfish, and hybrid striped bass are also year-round favorites for fishermen.

HIKING
A 4.5-mile hiking trail leads to the Big Brown Creek primitive camping area. An interpretive trail booklet, available at the park entrance, identifies the plants on the first 1.5 miles of the trail. The trail leads through native grasslands and oak woodlands to a primitive campsite.

ECOLOGY
The 1,460-acre park is in the post oak savanna vegetation zone of Texas. The heavy forest is composed of a wide variety of oaks, interspersed with hickory and eastern red cedar. Yaupon holly and other small bushes make up the understory or shrub layer of the forest. Scattered through the woodlands are open grasslands with tallgrass prairie species, including Indian grass, switchgrass, little bluestem, and eastern gama grass. In the spring, flowering dogwoods and red-

buds decorate the woods, and wildflowers cover the prairies with a blanket of colors.

Wildlife thrive throughout the park but are most numerous at the edges of prairies and woodlands, where the grassland and forest habitats overlap. Acorns from the many oaks provide an excellent food source for white-tailed deer, squirrels, and other animals.

Many habitats for birds occur within the park. Woodpeckers, crows, and other woodland species live in the forest; juncos, sparrows, and prairie species inhabit the grasslands. Bald eagles, geese, ducks, terns, kingfishers, cormorants, and wading birds are attracted to the reservoir.

A massive strip-mining operation west of the reservoir supplies the power plant with lignite, a low-grade fuel with a carbon content less than that of true coal. The decimated land is a painful reminder of the cost we must pay for our increasing demand for energy.

50. FALCON: STARR COUNTY FALCON PARK

Starr County. 65 miles northwest of McAllen on U.S. 83, southwest on FM 2098 to PR 46. Mailing address: County Commissioner's Precinct 2, Box 103, Roma, Texas 78584. Phone: 210-849-3788. Camping: campsites with water nearby, flush toilets (but you might need to bring your own paper). Fees charged. Recreation: This primitive site is in an area popular with bird-watchers because of the uncommon species from Mexico and with fishermen and water-sports enthusiasts because of its proximity to Falcon Lake. The dam and a port of entry to the Mexican town of Nuevo Guerrero are 1 mile south of the park.

51. FALCON STATE PARK

LOCATION
Zapata and Starr counties. 80 miles southeast of Laredo on U.S. 83 past Falcon, 2.5 miles southwest on FM 2098, north on PR 46. Mailing address: Box 2, Falcon Heights, Texas 78545. Phone: 210-848-5327. For all state park reservations, call 512-389-8900.

FACILITIES
Camping: 55 campsites with water only, 31 campsites with water and electricity, 31 campsites with water, electricity, and sewage hookups; 24 screened shelters, modern restrooms with showers, trailer dump station. Fees charged.

Recreation: picnic areas and playgrounds, swimming in Falcon Lake, bird-watching, fishing and fish-cleaning stations, boating, recreation hall.

MAIN ATTRACTIONS

Falcon State Park is located on the eastern shore of Falcon Reservoir. In 1953, the Rio Grande was dammed to form the 60-mile-long, 87,000-acre lake. The dam is owned by the United States and Mexico. A hydroelectric power plant at the dam can produce 30 megawatts of electricity on the U.S. side. The state park, opened in 1965, has become a paradise for fishermen, bird-watchers, and snowbirds—retirees spending the winter in the warm climate of South Texas. Travelers may cross the bridge over Falcon Dam into Mexico and visit the towns of Nuevo Guerrero, Mier, and Miguel Alemán.

ECOLOGY

The park consists of rolling brushlands, lakeshore woodlands, and the large reservoir, an unusual habitat in semiarid South Texas. The upland brush country, or chaparral, is characterized by desert-like vegetation. Head-high thorny shrubs, mesquite, blackbrush, catclaw acacia, guayacan, and allthorn form an impenetrable thicket. Prickly pear and yucca are common.

When there has been ample spring rain, the desertlike environment abounds with a medley of wildflowers. Desert mallows surround the cacti, and fleabanes cover the clearings. Indian blankets decorate the roadsides with white, yellow, and red and prickly poppies crowding the fence lines. The thickets resound with the buzz of bees attracted to the dense yellow flowers of the thorny shrubs, which seem to set the brushland ablaze with their bright flashes of color.

Many subtropical species of birds frequent the park and the woodlands below Falcon Dam; ask for a checklist at the park entrance. Birds seen in the park that are near the northern limit of their distribution include the plain chachalaca, white-tipped dove, red-billed pigeon, great kiskadee, tropical kingbird, groove-billed ani, green jay, common pauraque, Audubon's and Altamira orioles, and olive sparrow.

Large and boisterous ringed kingfishers and brown jays, as well as the gray hawk, can be found in the undisturbed woodlands along the river below the dam. Other subtropical birds seen in the United States primarily in South Texas include the clay-colored robin, yellow-throated vireo, long-billed thrasher, common black hawk, bronzed cowbird, and varied bunting.

The large body of water, an anomaly in South Texas, attracts many water birds and shorebirds and, occasionally, rare seabirds. The least grebe, olivaceous cormorant, least tern, and black-bellied whistling duck are commonly seen, as well as loons, herons, egrets, and many species of gulls, terns, ducks, and wading birds.

HISTORY

Many significant historical events have occurred along the lower Rio Grande. The Spanish, who first explored the area in 1638, established missions and settlements in the 1700s. After Texas won its independence, border disputes and invasions by Mexican troops were frequent until Texas joined the United States. Forts were established in Brownsville (Fort Brown), Rio Grande City (Fort Ringgold), and Laredo (Fort McIntosh). Fort Ringgold, 30 miles south of Falcon State Park, is one of Texas' best-preserved forts; it includes the house occupied by Robert E. Lee, who was stationed in Texas before he assumed command of the Confederate forces.

The Mexican towns of Guerrero and Mier, just across Falcon Dam, were sites of a historic confrontation between Texas forces and the Mexican army. In 1842, six years after Texas gained independence from Mexico, General Adrian Woll attacked and captured San Antonio, the second time the city had been occupied by Mexican troops within one year. Many Texans, outraged by the invasion, marched to join forces with Colonel Matthew Caldwell. A group of 54 volunteers from La Grange was intercepted by Mexican forces and forced to surrender. All but 15, three of whom escaped, were massacred.

General Woll retreated to Mexico, pursued by Texans intent on revenge. General Alexander Somervell led the Texas forces against the town of Guerrero, now under the reservoir, but found it deserted. He elected to turn back, but 308 men pressed on—determined to plunder the town of Mier, where the Mexican army was bivouacked. After heavy fighting, the Texans were tricked into surrendering. The men were marched to Mexico City and, after an attempted escape en route, received the order that one in ten be executed: they were forced to select the victims themselves by drawing from a jar containing 159 white beans and 17 black beans, the black beans signifying death. The survivors were imprisoned until after the Mexican War. A statue honoring the men of Mier was erected in 1936 in La Grange.

52. FORT GRIFFIN STATE HISTORICAL PARK

LOCATION
Shackelford County. 35 miles northeast of Abilene on TX 351 and U.S. 180 to Albany, 15 miles north on U.S. 283.
Mailing address: Route 1, Box 125, Albany, Texas 76430. Phone: 915-762-3592, Fax: 915-762-2492. For all state park reservations, call 512-389-8900.

FACILITIES
Camping: 5 campsites with water nearby, 16 campsites with water and electricity, 1 site with water, electricity, sewage, 1 overnight shelter; 50 primitive campsites; modern restrooms with showers, trailer dump station. Fees charged.

Recreation: picnic areas and playgrounds, interpretive exhibits, historic buildings, state longhorn herd, amphitheater with weekend programs in the summer, group shelter.

MAIN ATTRACTIONS
The park preserves the ruins of Fort Griffin, one of the frontier forts established after the Civil War to rid North Texas of the Indians. The stone walls of several of the structures remain, along with two small rebuilt wooden barracks and mess hall and the original stone bakery. An added attraction is the official state longhorn herd, which can be seen grazing in pastures in the park. The visitors' center has displays on the old fort, the Indians, and the longhorns.

The 506-acre park is situated on a hill overlooking the Clear Fork of the Brazos River. Mesquite trees, live oaks, prickly pear cacti, and grasses dominate the rocky higher grounds, while elm, hackberry, and pecan trees grow along the river bottom and shade the picnic and camping area.

HISTORY
Fort Griffin, established in 1867, played a major role in driving the Kiowa and Comanche Indians from North Texas. The Indians, who courageously defended their homeland from the advancing wave of white settlers, often sought refuge in Indian Territory, Oklahoma, an area that was supposedly off limits for the army. In 1871, a raiding party nearly captured General William Sherman, the commander who ravaged the South during the Civil War; the Indians succeeded in stealing all of the general's horses. Sherman immediately ordered his troops to follow the Indians into Oklahoma and subdue them.

By 1874, more than half of the Comanches had died from war, smallpox, and cholera. Buffalo hunters had nearly eliminated the bison, a chief source of food for the Indians. Finally, in 1874, Colonel Ranald Mackenzie defeated the Comanches in Palo Duro Canyon and slaughtered 1,500 of their horses in Tule Canyon, south of Palo Duro Canyon State Park. Without horses, the Indians were unable to acquire food for the approaching winter and were forced to remain on the reservations in Oklahoma. The following year, under the leadership of the great war chief Quanah Parker, the Comanches surrendered.

With the Indian hostilities over, buffalo hunters completed the extermination of the bison from the Texas plains, and the era of the cowboy began. Millions of longhorn cattle—the descendants of Spanish cattle introduced into Texas in the 1600s—freely roamed the rich grasslands of South Texas. Two hundred years of surviving in a harsh environment had created a breed of rugged cattle that would become a symbol of the Old West.

The 1870s saw the birth of the trail drive, and during the next two decades some 10 million longhorns were driven to northern markets. When railroads reached Texas in the 1880s, the laborious and financially risky drives were no longer necessary. Soon barbed-wire fences dominated the range, and selective breeding was producing cattle with more beef and less brawn than the longhorns. The very traits that had guaranteed its survival on the open range almost doomed the longhorn to extinction.

The western author J. Frank Dobie gathered a small herd of longhorns in the 1920s, which eventually became the state herd. Today the herd of about 125 animals is selectively bred for all the longhorn characteristics, not just impressive horns. The breeding herd is maintained at Fort Griffin, while the steers, which have the longest horns, are also displayed in several other state parks.

53. FORT PARKER STATE PARK AND OLD FORT PARKER STATE HISTORICAL PARK

LOCATION
Limestone County. 38 miles east of Waco on TX 164 to Groesbeck, 3 miles north on TX 14 to the Old Fort, 4 miles north from town to the state park.
Mailing address, state park: Route 3, Box 95, Mexia, Texas 76667. Phone: 817-562-5751. Mailing address, Old Fort: Route 3, Box 746, Groesbeck, Texas 76642. Phone: 817-729-5253. For all state park reservations, call 512-389-8900.

FACILITIES

Camping: 25 campsites with water and electricity, 10 sites with water, 10 screened shelters, group primitive camping area for organized youth groups only, group barracks for 96 people with kitchen and dining hall, modern restrooms with showers, trailer dump station. Fees charged.

Recreation: picnic areas and playgrounds, short hiking trail, reconstructed fort, swimming in lake, fishing, boating, pavilion, store (summer only).

MAIN ATTRACTIONS

The state park is situated on a 750-acre impoundment of the Navasota River. Fishing is popular; catches of sunfish, catfish, crappie, and largemouth bass are typical. The heavily wooded shoreline is a good place for nature study, bird-watching, and photography.

Old Fort Parker State Historic Park, one mile south of the state park, is a reconstructed family fort, built for the protection of a small group of pioneer families in 1834. The site is open from 10 A.M. to 6 P.M. A small entrance fee is charged. Teachers can obtain a packet of information on the fort for classroom use. The Confederate Reunion Grounds State Historical Park is 6 miles south of Mexia on TX 14, west on FM 2705. The historic gathering place has picnicking, fishing in the Navasota River, and nature trails.

ECOLOGY

The 1,485-acre state park is located in the gently rolling deciduous woodlands of the post oak savanna of Texas. The dense forest surrounding the lake consists of post oak, cedar elm, eastern red cedar, pecan, hickory, and yaupon. The undisturbed woods and the lake provide a variety of wildlife habitats.

Great blue herons and great egrets wade in the shallows of the numerous inlets, while kingfishers perch poised on overhanging limbs, ready to dive for small fish. Ducks, geese, and cormorants overwinter on the lake, and many species of warblers migrate through the park each spring and fall. Ask for a bird checklist at the park headquarters.

Raccoons, opossums, and gray foxes leave their tracks in the moist soil along the shore. Cottontail rabbits, gray squirrels, and white-tailed deer are commonly seen in the early morning and evening.

HISTORY

The settlers of the early 1800s were attracted to the rich blackland prairies of the area, the abundance of timber in the woodlands, and the ample water supplied by the river. In 1833, the Parker family, with several other families, moved to the region from Illinois and built a stockade fort, reconstructed at the state historic site south of present-day Mexia. They constructed a split-cedar stockade with blockhouses on opposite ends and cabins along the inside walls.

There were no Indian hostilities until 1836, when a band of Comanches attacked the fort. Several people were killed, and five captives were taken. Nine-year-old Cynthia Ann Parker and her five-year-old brother, John, were raised by the Indians. John, who grew to be a skillful Comanche raider, eventually lived in Mexico as a rancher. Cynthia Ann became a legend in her own time: she married Chief Peta Nocona and had three children, two sons and a daughter.

In 1860, Cynthia Ann and her two-year-old daughter were captured by Captain Sul Ross of the Texas Rangers at the Battle of Pease River, near present-day Copper Breaks State Park. Cynthia Ann was forced to live with her white family again but could not adjust to white society; she was very unhappy and tried to escape several times. She died in 1864, shortly after the death of her daughter.

Cynthia Ann's oldest son, Quanah, became a famous Comanche war chief. He led the last Indian battles in Texas, fought in Palo Duro Canyon and Adobe Walls in 1874. In 1875, the Quohodi Comanches, worn down by disease and starvation, surrendered. A leader in peace as well as in war, Quanah helped his people adjust to the white citizens' ways. He settled in Oklahoma and, in 1910, had the grave of his mother moved to the Indian reservation. He was admired by Teddy Roosevelt, who appointed him judge of the Court of Indian Offenses. The historical novel *Quanah,* by Paul Foreman, depicts the life of this intriguing character.

54. FORT RICHARDSON STATE HISTORICAL PARK

LOCATION
Jack County. 60 miles northwest of Fort Worth on TX 199, in Jacksboro.
Mailing address: Box 4, Jacksboro, Texas 76458. Phone: 817-567-3506.
For all state park reservations, call 512-389-8900.

FACILITIES
Camping: 23 campsites with water and electricity, 11 screened shelters with RV hook-ups. Modern restrooms with showers, trailer dump station. Fees charged.

Recreation: picnic areas, nature trail, interpretive exhibits, reconstructed fort, museum, and fishing in Quarry Lake, stocked with catfish and rainbow trout.

MAIN ATTRACTIONS

The 389-acre park preserves seven original buildings and two reconstructed barracks. The fort protected settlers from raiding Comanches, Kiowas, and Kiowa-Apaches between 1867 and 1878. The large stone building housing the hospital and morgue, refurnished to a frontier hospital, dominates one end of the parade ground. On either side of the parade ground are the original officers' quarters, which were built with cottonwood timber, and the barracks. A reconstructed officers' barrack serves as an interpretive center. The bakery, which produced 600 loaves of bread daily, the commissary, the guardhouse, and the magazine are clustered near the hospital.

ECOLOGY

The fort was situated on the south bank of the small but beautiful Lost Creek. The creek drainage is heavily wooded with elm, hackberry, and oak trees. Large expanses of prairie surround the creek. Prickly pear cacti and mesquite trees have invaded portions of the prairie, especially around the old hospital. A short nature trail, beginning at the campgrounds, leads through a wooded area along the creek.

The wooded stream attracts many birds, while grassland species such as bobwhite quail and meadowlarks inhabit the meadows. Waterfowl are occasionally seen on the small quarry lake near the entrance. Buffalo were once common to the area, and buffalo wallows can be seen south of the parade ground.

HISTORY

With no protection from the U.S. Army during the Civil War, the white settlements in North Texas were under continual threat of Indian attack. After the war, a series of frontier forts was reestablished to rout the Indians.

Fort Richardson, named in honor of General Israel B. Richardson, was strategically located only 70 miles from Indian Territory in Oklahoma. The Indian raiding parties would swoop down from Oklahoma, attack a settlement or supply train, and hastily retreat to the protection of their own territory.

In 1874, an expedition from Fort Richardson led by Colonel Ranald Mackenzie, of the famed Mackenzie's Raiders, destroyed a large Comanche village in Palo Duro Canyon and defeated the famous war chief Quanah Parker. With no provisions, shelter, or horses, the Indians were unable to continue their raids and were at last forced out of Texas.

55. FREDERICKSBURG: LADY BIRD JOHNSON MUNICIPAL PARK

Gillespie County. 3 miles southwest of Fredericksburg on TX 16. Mailing address: Box 111, Fredericksburg, Texas 78624. Phone: 210-997-4202. Camping: 65 campsites with water and electricity, 48 campsites with water, electricity, and sewage hookups, 10 tent sites; flush toilets, showers, trailer dump station. Reservations accepted. Fees charged, monthly rates available in winter. Recreation: picnic areas and playgrounds, swimming in pool and small lake, fishing, boat ramp (no motorboats), golf course, tennis courts, volleyball, recreation hall. Open all year. This park has excellent and diverse facilities; it may be crowded in the summer.

56. FREEPORT: QUINTANA BEACH COUNTY PARK

LOCATION
Brazoria County. 5 miles south of Freeport on FM 1495 across the Intracoastal Canal, 3 miles north on County Rd. 723 to Quintana, east on Fifth St.
Mailing address: 320 5th Street, Quintana, Texas 77541. Phone: 409-233-1461 (Brazoria County Park Commission) or 1-800-872-7578.

FACILITIES
Camping: 39 sites with water, electricity, and sewage hookups; 17 sites with water and electricity. Screened shelter, 2 group RV sites, group pavilion, restrooms, showers, trailer dump station. Reservations accepted. Fees charged. Primitive camping on beach. Open all year.

Recreation: picnicking on and off the beach, half mile of beach, swimming; jetty, surf, and pier fishing; 2 historic houses with nature exhibits; shelling, hiking trails, playgrounds. Open daily dawn to dusk.

MAIN ATTRACTIONS
The beautiful beaches and rolling surf of the Gulf of Mexico attract visitors to this park for a day, or longer, of fun in the sun. Two historic houses from the 1880s have been moved to the park and

restored. One has displays of seashells, beach ecology, area history, and a touch-and-feel table for the youngsters. Fishermen catch speckled trout and redfish, and beachcombers collect interesting shells washed ashore. Hiking trails lead to a World War II gun emplacement and through wetlands and dunes bordering the beach.

FREEPORT: SAN LUIS COUNTY PARK

LOCATION
Brazoria County. Take FM 332 southeast of Lake Jackson to Surfside beach, then 13 miles northeast on County Rd. 257, before the San Luis Pass toll bridge. Also referred to as Brazoria County Access Point.
Mailing address: 14001 CR 257, Freeport, Texas 77541. Phone: 409-233-6026 or 1-800-372-7578 (Brazoria County Park Commission).

FACILITIES
Camping: 89 campsites with water, electricity, sewage hookups, primitive camping, flush toilets, showers, trailer dump station. Reservations accepted. Fees charged. Open all year.
Recreation: quarter-mile bay front for fishing and sailing; picnicking area, park store, group pavilion, playground, recreation hall, boat ramp.

MAIN ATTRACTIONS
At the northern end of Follets Island at San Luis Pass, this 17-acre park is an ideal spot for fishing and sailing in the bay. The colorful sails of windsurfers dot the water, and shell collectors stroll the beach. Bird-watchers enjoy the many shorebirds and wading birds attracted to the surf and wetlands, and photographers find a picturesque setting for sunset and sunrise pictures.

57. GALVESTON: FORT TRAVIS SEASHORE PARK

Galveston County. 1.5 miles northeast of Bolivar Ferry on TX 87, on Bolivar Peninsula. 59 acres on the Gulf of Mexico. Mailing address: Galveston County Beach Park Board, 613 Nineteenth St., Galveston, Texas 77550. Phone: 409-766-2411. Camping: 16 primitive campsites, 6 screened shelters, flush toilets, showers. Reservations accepted. Fees charged. Recreation: picnic areas and playgrounds, fishing. Historical interpretation of fort. All facilities are within the confines of the old fort, with access to the beach for swimming and fishing. Open all year. Reservations accepted.

GALVESTON ISLAND STATE PARK

LOCATION
Galveston County. 6 miles southwest of the Galveston City Seawall on FM 3005.
Mailing address: Route 4, Box 156A, Galveston, Texas 77554.
Phone: 409-737-1222. For all state park reservations, call 512-389-8900.

FACILITIES
Camping: 150 campsites with water and electricity on beachside; bayside group trailer area with 20 sites with water and electricity, 10 screened shelters, modern restrooms with showers, trailer dump station. Fees charged.

Recreation: picnic areas, 4 miles of nature trails with observation platforms and bird blinds, swimming in the Gulf of Mexico, fishing, amphitheater with summer drama performances.

MAIN ATTRACTIONS
Spanning the width of Galveston Island from rolling surf to protected bayfront, the park encompasses 1,952 acres of sand dunes, marshes, bayous, mud flats, and coastal prairies. More than 1,000 acres of ecologically important wetlands are preserved on an island rapidly being developed into resort property.

The wide, 1.6-mile-long beach attracts swimmers, surfers, sunbathers, and beachcombers. Bayou fishing and wade fishing in the marshes are popular activities, as is surf fishing for flounder, drum, and trout. Four miles of nature trails wind through the salt marshes, with observation platforms, bird-viewing blinds, and boardwalks over bayous.

The Mary Moody Northern Amphitheater features outdoor dramas every evening except Mondays throughout the summer. Past performances include *The Sound of Music* and *Showboat*.

ECOLOGY
The vegetation of the park is characteristic of a barrier island continually swept by the wind, pounded by the surf, and periodically stricken by tropical storms and hurricanes. The soil is sand and silt deposited by the Gulf currents and washed onto the island. The marshes vary in salinity from 3 parts salt per thousand parts water,

nearly fresh, to salty, with 33 parts salt per thousand parts water. The vegetation must adapt to the varying salinity, as well as to the salty soil and the wind.

Dominant grasses are marshhay cordgrass, smooth cordgrass, and seashore saltgrass. In high areas with deeper soil, vines and shrubby plants produce thick tangles. Wildflowers grace the park almost year-round. Evening primroses and composites decorate the dunes, and gaillardias, asters, and goldenrods, among others, bloom on higher ground.

The wetlands are rich in wildlife. Hundreds of species of waterfowl and wading birds winter here in the marshes. In the early spring, the thousands of birds that have migrated across the Gulf of Mexico reach land on or near Galveston Island, and as spring progresses, the marshes are alive with breeding activity of the resident species. Throughout most of the year, the wet areas abound with hordes of mosquitoes that covet the blood of warm-blooded creatures, especially humans.

HISTORY

When discovered by Europeans, Galveston Island was the home of the Karankawa Indians, and there are several archaeological sites on the island today. The first European settlement came in 1817, when the colorful Jean Lafitte established a center for his smuggling and pirating activities on the island.

The city of Galveston is famous for its resort facilities and its many historic buildings. The Bishop's Palace, open daily except Tuesdays, is the city's most celebrated landmark. The Galveston Historic Foundation is restoring to period specifications many buildings, especially those along the historic Strand Street. Galveston is resplendent with parks, museums, festivals, and fine seafood restaurants.

58. GARNER STATE PARK

LOCATION
Uvalde County. 31 miles north of Uvalde on U.S. 83.
Mailing address: HCR #70, Box 599, Concan, Texas 78838. Phone: 210-232-6132. For all state park reservations, call 512-389-8900.

FACILITIES
Camping: 211 campsites with water only, 146 campsites with water and electricity, 40 screened shelters, 18 cabins with kitchens, group shelter with bunkhouses, kitchen, and dining hall for 40 peo-

ple, late-arrival area with 40 pull-in spaces, modern restrooms with showers, trailer dump station. Fees charged.

Recreation: picnic areas and playgrounds, nature trails, paved bicycle trail, swimming in the Frio River, fishing, paddleboat rentals (summer only), miniature-golf course (summer only), nightly dance (summer only), group shelter with kitchen for 75 people, store (summer only).

MAIN ATTRACTIONS

Recreation in the park is centered around the broad, wooded bottomlands and the spring-fed Frio River. The variety of summer activities and the large number of camping and day-use facilities make Garner one of the most popular parks in the state. There are short trails along the river and a paved trail along portions of the road. This park is suitable for a quiet outdoor experience only during the fall and winter months.

The 1,420-acre park is named after John Nance Garner, who was vice president under Franklin Roosevelt. The Garner home and museum in Uvalde is open daily.

The park is situated along open grasslands and wooded bottomlands bordering the scenic Frio River. The flat meadows end abruptly with steep, rocky hillsides and sheer cliffs typical of the rough terrain of Central Texas. The bottomlands are shaded with numerous pecan trees, and live oak and mesquite trees grow in the grassland savannas. Much of the grassland has been invaded by brush and trees, which provide good habitat for the deer, turkeys, and rabbits common to the park. The hills are covered with juniper, live oak, mountain laurel, and evergreen sumac.

59. GOLDTHWAITE MUNICIPAL PARK

Mills County. In Goldthwaite at the intersection of South U.S. 183 and TX 16. Mailing address: Box 450, Goldthwaite, Texas 76844. Phone: 915-648-3186. Camping: 6 campsites with water and electricity, flush toilets, group camp area. Recreation: playground, swimming pool. No reservations, no fees. Open all year.

60. GOLIAD STATE HISTORICAL PARK

LOCATION
Goliad County. 25 miles southwest of Victoria on U.S. 59 to Goliad, one mile south on U.S. 183.

Mailing address: Box 727, Goliad, Texas 77963. Phone: 512-645-3405. For all state park reservations, call 512-389-8900.

FACILITIES

Camping: 10 primitive campsites with water nearby, 20 campsites with water, electricity, and sewage hookups; group site for 24 trailers with water and electricity, 5 screened shelters, modern restrooms with showers, trailer dump station. Fees charged.

Recreation: picnic areas and playgrounds, nature trail with trail guide booklet, interpretive exhibits, swimming pool (summer only), fishing and boating on the San Antonio River, historical buildings and museum, dining hall with kitchen.

MAIN ATTRACTIONS

The Spanish mission Nuestra Señora del Espíritu Santo de Zuñiga is the dominant feature in the park. The mission, built in 1749 for the purpose of converting the Aranama and Tamique Indians to Christianity, operated for 110 years—longer than any other Spanish mission in Texas. The church has been restored, as have the adjoining granary and workshop. The granary now serves as a museum of Indian and Spanish colonial exhibits and artifacts. The original foundation and floors of the priests' quarters and the ruins of the living quarters are immediately behind the granary.

Ruins of the mission Nuestra Señora del Rosario, founded in 1754 by Franciscan missionaries, are 6 miles southwest of Goliad on U.S. 59. The mission, which attempted to convert the Karankawa, Cujane, and Coapite Indians, was abandoned and reoccupied periodically; it achieved only limited success.

The park also includes General Ignacio Zaragosa's birthplace. Zaragosa is one of Mexico's most famous military heroes. He commanded the Mexican army that defeated the invading French at the Battle of Puebla on May 5, 1862. That victory is celebrated as a national holiday in Mexico, Cinco de Mayo, and is observed throughout South Texas.

The Presidio La Bahía, is just south of the park on U.S. 183; it has been restored to its original condition. The presidio—built near Mission Espíritu Santo to protect it from hostile Indians—grew into one of the most important Spanish frontier forts. Today it is the finest example in Texas of a Spanish fort.

In March 1836, Colonel James Fannin and his men were forced to surrender to the Mexican army at the Battle of Coleto Creek. They were marched to the Presidio La Bahía at Goliad. By order of Santa Anna, 342 of the prisoners were executed on March 27. The graves and a memorial to those heroic Texans are located near the presidio. Fannin Battleground State Historic Site, 9 miles east of Goliad on U.S. 59, marks the location of the battle of Coleto Creek.

HIKING

The self-guided Aranama Nature Trail, only one-third of a mile long, provides an excellent introduction to the plant and animal communities of the area. A guidebook to the trail, explaining the plants and the ways the Indians used them, is available from the park headquarters, along with a comprehensive bird list.

ECOLOGY

Goliad State Park contains 184 acres of gently rolling plains at the crossroads of three major ecological regions in Texas. The plant and animal life is characteristic of the Gulf Coast prairies and marshes, South Texas plains, and post oak savannas. Much of the park lies along the San Antonio River; Goliad's dense riparian woodland is composed of live oak, cedar elm, hackberry, and anaqua trees.

A majority of the original grassland of the South Texas plains, which spawned the great Texas cattle empire, is now covered with impenetrable thorny brush. After a hundred years of overgrazing, the land has been irreparably altered. Prairie that once stretched from horizon to horizon is now a tangle of brushy, thorny plants. Snakewood, lotebush, blackbrush, bluewood, and mesquite have invaded the grassland that was once common around Goliad.

Located at the juncture of three biotic zones, the park contains a rich diversity of plants and animals. The natural area is an important landfall for migratory birds. More than 300 species have been recorded in the park, including the subtropical groove-billed ani, olivaceous cormorant, brown-crested flycatcher, long-billed thrasher, and olive sparrow.

62. GONZALES: INDEPENDENCE PARK

Gonzales County. In Gonzales where U.S. 183 crosses the Guadalupe River. Mailing address: P.O. Box 547, Gonzales, Texas 78629. Phone: 210-672-2520. Camping: 21 RV sites with water, electricity, sewage hookups, 1 with water, electricity; tent camping area; dump station. With swimming pool, golf course, rodeo arena, softball and volleyball fields, and picnic pavilions, expect this 169 acres city park to be heavily used by locals, but it would be suitable for an en route overnight stay. Fees charged, reservations accepted, open all year.

Nearby attraction: The Gonzales Pioneer Village, with ten reconstructed log houses from the 1800s, is one-half mile north of town on U.S. 183. Open weekends only.

GONZALES: LAKE WOOD RECREATION AREA

Gonzales County. On Lake Wood and Guadalupe River; 48 acres. 3 miles west of Gonzales on U.S. 90A, 3 miles south on FM 2091. Mailing address: Route 2, Box 158-A, Gonzales, Texas 78629. Phone: 210-672-2779. Camping: 12 tent sites with water, 16 campsites with water, electricity, and sewage hookups; restrooms with showers, trailer dump station. Fees charged. Reservations accepted. Recreation: picnic area, park store, swimming in lake, boat ramp, fishing. Open all year.

63. GOOSE ISLAND STATE PARK

LOCATION
Aransas County. 8 miles north of Rockport on TX 35 to PR 13, at the north side of Copano Bay.
Mailing address: HCO 1, Box 105, Rockport, Texas 78382. Phone: 512-729-2858. For all state park reservations, call 512-389-8900.

FACILITIES
Camping: 25 tent sites with water nearby, 57 campsites with water and electricity, 45 unscreened shelters with water and electricity on Copano Bay, modern restrooms with showers, trailer dump station. Fees charged.

Recreation: picnic areas and playgrounds, bird-watching, fishing on a 1,620-foot lighted pier, boating, pavilion, hiking.

MAIN ATTRACTIONS
Goose Island State Park—at the confluence of Aransas, Saint Charles, and Copano bays—offers the visitor excellent fishing and bird-watching. The shallow bay teems with fish and attracts a large

variety of birds. Saltwater fishermen catch trout, flounder, sheepshead, and redfish from the shore, pier, and boats.

Aransas National Wildlife Refuge, 30 miles north by car, has a number of nature trails, a loop drive, an observation tower, and an excellent interpretive center with displays, media presentations, and literature. Whooping cranes live in the refuge from October through April and occasionally can be seen from the tower.

The best way to see the whoopers is to take one of the commercial tour boats that operate from Fulton Beach, the Sea Gun Inn Marina, Rockport, and Port Aransas. Captain Ted Appel, from the Sand Dollar Pavilion Marina on Fulton Beach Road, also offers birding tours in the spring to see rookery islands in the bay with thousands of nesting shorebirds. Call 1-800-338-4551 for schedule and reservations. The state park has a listing of currently operating tours.

Nearby Rockport has a ski basin, a beach, the Texas Maritime Museum, and fine seafood restaurants. Fulton Mansion State Historic Structure is on Fulton Beach Road. It was built in 1872 and has been restored by the Parks and Wildlife Department.

ECOLOGY

The 314 acres of Goose Island State Park encompass two distinct ecosystems: the bay and the uplands. Gulls, pelicans, oystercatchers, egrets, herons, shorebirds, and many species of ducks feast on fish and other small creatures in the bays and marshes.

Millions of migrating shorebirds and waterfowl winter along the Texas coast, making Goose Island a favorite for bird-watchers. Situated on the Central Flyway, the park attracts many birds on their way to and from the tropics. More species of birds have been sighted in the Rockport area during the annual Audubon Christmas Bird Count than in any other place in the country.

Live oaks, red bay trees, and yaupon hollies form dense thickets in the sandy coastal uplands. The thickets are an excellent habitat for raccoons, skunks, squirrels, and opossums.

One of the national champion coastal live oaks, *Quercus virginiana*, is near the park. The tree measures 35 feet in circumference, is 44 feet high, and has a crown spread of 89 feet. This ancient tree, at least a thousand years old, is located north of the main park entrance and overlooks the bay.

64. GOVERNMENT CANYON STATE PARK

Access by special request only.

LOCATION
Bexar County. San Antonio, Loop 1604 near Seaworld.
Mailing address: P.O. Box 669, Helotes, Texas 78023.
Phone: 210-219-8821 (mobile phone).

MAIN ATTRACTIONS
Parks and Wildlife recently acquired 4,700 acres almost within the city limits of San Antonio. The former ranch contains the historic Government Springs, a rich archaeological site from prehistoric and historic times. A stone house, believed from the Civil War era, still stands near the springs, which were a stop-over on the old San Antonio to Fredericksburg road and an outpost for an Indian fort.

The park includes portions of blackland prairie, but 96 percent lies within the recharge zone of the Edwards Plateau. Rugged limestone hills dissected by deep canyons typify the park. The oak-juniper forest provides habitat for the endangered golden-cheeked warbler, which breeds only in old-growth juniper woodlands of central Texas.

At the time of publishing, the feasibility study was complete, but no master plan was envisioned for another year. The nearest opening date for day-use was projected as 1996, probably later. The primary recreational focus will be hiking, wildlife viewing, and picnicking, with minimal camping and development due to the ecologically sensitive nature of the recharge zone and endangered species.

65. GUADALUPE MOUNTAINS NATIONAL PARK

LOCATION
Culberson and Hudspeth counties. Headquarters Visitors Center and Pine Springs Campground: 110 miles east of El Paso or 55 miles southwest of Carlsbad, New Mexico, on U.S. 62/180. Dog Canyon Ranger Station: 12 miles north of Carlsbad on U.S. 285, 57 miles south on NM Highway 137, or 5 miles south of Carlsbad on U.S. 62/180, then take County Road 408 for 60 miles to NM 137. Mailing address: HC 60, Box 400, Salt Flat, Texas 79847-9400. Phone: 915-828-3251.

FACILITIES

Camping: free primitive camping in designated areas in the high country (permit required), tent sites with water nearby at Pine Springs and Dog Canyon campgrounds, trailer camping area with no hookups at Pine Springs Campground, modern restrooms with no showers at Pine Springs Campground. Fees charged.

Recreation: picnicking, more than 80 miles of hiking and nature trails, interpretive exhibits with trail guide pamphlets and animal checklists.

MAIN ATTRACTIONS

Towering 5,000 feet above the desert basin, the sheer cliffs of the Guadalupe Mountains can be seen from a distance of 50 miles. The park encompasses the southern edge of the range, deep canyons that cut into the rugged mountains, and the surrounding desert. A crystal clear stream flows through the heavily wooded McKittrick Canyon, described as the most beautiful spot in Texas. Each fall, the bigtooth maple trees turn breathtaking hues of crimson, burgundy, and orange. We have trouble deciding between Big Bend and the Guadalupe Mountains as our favorite Texas vacation spot.

Nearby attractions include Carlsbad Caverns National Park, 45 miles northeast of the Headquarters Visitors Center. Camping and lodging are available in commercial facilities at Whites City. The Living Desert Zoological and Botanical State Park is in Carlsbad. Plant and animal life of the Chihuahuan Desert is displayed in natural settings. There is no camping in the park.

HIKING

Major access to the park is by hiking. There are more than 80 miles of improved trails, leading to the top of Guadalupe Peak, the highest spot in Texas, into picturesque McKittrick Canyon, and into the pine- and fir-covered high country. There are short day hikes and many opportunities for backpacking. A topographic map is essential for mountain hiking. Maps and backcountry camping permits are available at the Headquarters Visitors Center.

The trails in the park vary from paths on relatively level terrain to rugged, steep trails only for well-conditioned, experienced hikers. Water is available only at the trailheads in Pine Springs Campground and in McKittrick Canyon, at the Visitors Center and at the Dog Canyon Ranger Station and trailhead. During the summer, a gallon of water per day per person is required for overnight camping, half a gallon for day hikes. Park regulations prohibit the use of surface water for drinking or washing.

GUADALUPE MOUNTAINS NATIONAL PARK

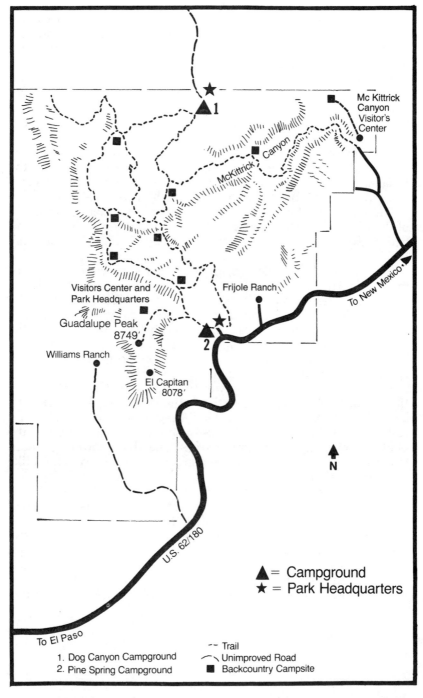

Mc Kittrick Canyon Visitor's Center

McKittrick Canyon

Visitors Center and Park Headquarters

Guadalupe Peak 8749'

Williams Ranch

El Capitan 8078'

Frijole Ranch

To New Mexico

N

▲ = Campground
★ = Park Headquarters

U.S. 62/180

To El Paso

1. Dog Canyon Campground
2. Pine Spring Campground

-- Trail
⌒ Unimproved Road
■ Backcountry Campsite

Smith Spring and Manzanita Spring are reached by a one-mile hike from the Frijole Ranch Museum. Smith Spring is in a luxuriant small canyon tucked away between the mountain ridges. Manzanita Spring magically appears below the dry mountain slopes and forms a circular pond attracting much wildlife. From the trail, the mirror surface of the water reflects the blue West Texas sky and an unusual nipple-shaped peak in the distance.

From the Pine Springs trailhead, trails lead atop Guadalupe Peak, 8,749 feet above sea level, and to a series of loop trails in the high country. The well-maintained Guadalupe Peak Trail climbs over 3,000 feet in 4.5 miles. The view from the top of Texas encompasses vast salt basins and gypsum sand dunes to the west and the Delaware Mountains to the south. The Guadalupe Mountains and Lincoln National Forest stretch to the north in New Mexico.

The Tejas Trail climbs to the ridge along the southern escarpment of the mountains. The Bear Canyon Trail to the summit is steep and badly eroded, causing hazardous footing. The Bush Mountain, Bowl, and Juniper trails intersect a short distance from the summit of the Tejas Trail and connect with others to form a variety of mountain loops. There are three designated campsites along the trails.

Two trails lead from the McKittrick Canyon Visitors' Center. The Permian Reef Geology Trail climbs the steep ridge out of the park into Lincoln National Forest. It passes through the heart of the gigantic fossilized sponge and algae reef that forms the Guadalupe Mountains. Some of the best examples of more than 500 fossil species found in the park are exposed along the trail.

The trail into McKittrick Canyon provides a walk along the fairly flat terrain of the shaded streambed. The Pratt Lodge Historic Site, 2.4 miles into the canyon, is an ideal picnic spot with tables and restrooms in the summer. The trail continues another mile to the Grotto picnic area. The canopy of trees beneath the towering mountain peaks and the gently babbling stream produce a cathedral-like atmosphere along the trail.

McKittrick Trail ascends McKittrick Ridge and connects with the Tejas and other mountain trails. A primitive campsite is located half a mile below the ridgetop or 7.6 miles from the visitors' center.

The Dog Canyon Campground and trailhead are in a remote section of the park, reached by a 2-hour drive from Carlsbad. The Tejas and Marcus trails traverse Dog Canyon and West Dog Canyon and connect with the high-country trail system. The trails, not as steep as the trail from Pine Springs, lead to spectacular views of the park.

ECOLOGY

Because the Guadalupe Mountains are at the southern tip of the Rockies, the northern edge of the Chihuahuan Desert, and the western extension of the Central Plains, the park contains a diverse mixture of plants and animals. The northern range of many Mexican species merges with the southern limit of Rocky Mountain species.

The park includes plants adapted to the Chihuahuan Desert, the sheltered canyons cut into the mountain slopes, and the high country. Creosote bush, lechuguilla, white-thorn acacia, and snakeweed dominate the desert basin surrounding the southern end of the mountain range. Yucca, sotol, agave, prickly pear cactus, and oneseed juniper grow on the lower mountain slopes.

The heads of the canyons are wooded with pinyon pine, alligator juniper, gray oak, Texas madrone, agarita, and sumac. Farther up the watersheds, deciduous trees, maples and oaks, dominate. A coniferous forest of ponderosa and limber pines and Douglas firs grows on the upper slopes and mountaintops. The Bowl, a protected depression north of Hunter Peak, is heavily wooded with conifers and is a favorite destination for hikers.

Millions of years of erosion have dissected the slopes with deep canyons which harbor delicate ecosystems in their protected interiors. McKittrick Canyon is the most spectacular and accessible of such canyons. Bigtooth maples, Texas madrones, pines, and a variety of oaks and other hardwoods shade the perennial stream as it cascades through the scenic canyon. Quiet pools bordered with sawgrass reflect the rugged mountains and blue sky above. The sawgrass, with its long serrated blades, is as much at home in this mountain setting as it is on the Gulf Coast, where it is common.

Animals such as the pronghorn antelope, kit fox, peccary, and kangaroo rat live in the desert and on the drier lower slopes. Mule deer, elk, mountain lions, coyotes, and gray foxes range from the lower slopes into the protected canyons and wooded high country. Mountain species include the rare black bear, gray-footed chipmunk, and an introduced species of elk. The mountain bighorn sheep and Meriam's elk, which used to roam the high country, have been extirpated by human activities.

More than 270 species of birds have been recorded in the park. The endangered peregrine falcon nests in the park, and golden eagles may be seen soaring along the escarpment edge. Seven species of owls occur in the various habitats of the park, and six species of hummingbirds have been sighted among the many cacti and wildflowers that bloom from the desert floor to the mountain ridges.

From 230 million to 280 million years ago, a shallow sea covered West Texas. A massive reef, formed mainly by lime-secreting algae, developed along its southern shore. The horseshoe-shaped reef, the largest known, stretched for 350 miles and was more than a mile wide and several hundred feet high. Eventually, the outlet to the sea was closed off, and the briny water evaporated, forming thick deposits of salt and gypsum. Then the area was covered with thousands of feet of stream-deposited sediments. Each of those complex processes occurred over millions of years.

Uplifts, tilting, and block faulting began 10 million to 12 million years ago and gradually elevated the area far above sea level. Erosion began the slow process of removing the overlying rock, finally exposing portions of the fossilized reef and carving the rugged canyons we see today. The Guadalupe Mountains, rich in fossil marine organisms, have many caverns created as groundwater dissolved the limestone bedrock.

The weather in the Guadalupe Mountains is known for two characteristics: changeability and high winds. Thunderstorms can build over the mountains in hours, and windstorms can sweep the ridges and down the canyons with hurricane velocity. Semitrailers have been blown off the highway through Guadalupe Pass, and the trailer once serving as the ranger station in McKittrick Canyon was blown down the canyon like a tumbleweed.

In the lower elevations, temperatures average in the eighties in the summer and in the low thirties during the winter. Mountain temperatures will be 10 to 15 degrees lower, and wind can reduce effective temperatures even more.

The area averages about 20 inches of precipitation a year, with the high country being wetter. In contrast, the surrounding desert averages 8 to 10 inches per year. The rainy months extend from June to September, but campers should be prepared for rain during any season. Wool clothing, which retains body heat even when wet, is advisable for winter hiking and backpacking.

HISTORY

Pictographs (rock paintings in red, yellow, and black) and petroglyphs (designs carved into the rock) have been discovered in and around the national park. The abstract and naturalistic human and animal forms are difficult to date but are thought to be several hundred to possibly over a thousand years old. The sites are not accessible to the public.

The Guadalupe Mountains were the last stronghold for the Mescalero Apaches. A marker at Manzanita Springs describes the last battle where the Indians were routed in 1869. The Indian settlement at that location was attacked, the village and winter stores destroyed, and the survivors driven into the mountains. With no hope of living through the winter, the Apaches surrendered and were placed on a reservation near Fort Stanton, New Mexico.

Poor conditions on the reservation led to a final revolt in 1880. That revolt resulted in a slaughter of the Mescaleros on a plateau near El Capitan. By the late 1880s, all the Mescaleros in the United States were on reservations.

The Butterfield Overland Stage was routed through Guadalupe Pass in 1858. A more southerly route with a dependable water supply and army protection was chosen after 11 months of operation. The ruins of the stage station, the Pinery, are located at the entrance to Pine Springs Campground.

The remnants of several ranching operations are evident in the park. Pipes that carried water from Smith Spring up the mountain slope to a stock tank in the Bowl are still visible. The remains of the Williams Ranch can be seen in the desert grassland west of the mountains. Much of the parkland was a working ranch until 1972, when the national park was established.

65. GUADALUPE RIVER STATE PARK

LOCATION
Comal and Kendall counties. 29 miles north of San Antonio on U.S. 281, 8 miles west on TX 46, 3 miles north on PR 31.
Mailing address: 3350 Park Road 31, Spring Branch, Texas 78070.
Phone: 210-438-2656. For all state park reservations, call 512-389-8900.

FACILITIES
Camping: 20 walk-in campsites with water nearby and composting toilets, 37 campsites with water only, 48 campsites with water and electricity, modern restrooms with showers, trailer dump station. Fees charged.

Recreation: picnic areas and playgrounds, 2-mile hiking trail, swimming in river, fishing, canoeing.

MAIN ATTRACTIONS
The Guadalupe is one of the most beautiful rivers in the state. Large bald cypress trees shade its winding, picturesque banks and make it ideal for swimming, canoeing, and fishing. The river, which makes three U-shaped curves through the park, separates the northern portion of the park from the developed southern section. The Guadalupe, with both tranquil portions and white-water rapids, is a favorite of canoeists. There are four sections of rapids in the park. Canoes may be carried through the picnic grounds and launched in the day-use area, but most people prefer to launch their canoes at the low-water crossings outside the park.

Honey Creek State Natural Area is adjacent to the state park and accessible only by guided tours. It contains a hardwood-lined creek with giant bald cypress trees, juniper-covered hills, and naturalized pastures. Ask the park rangers about touring this beautiful area.

In the mid 1800s, many German immigrants settled in Central Texas. Today, many of the towns in this area still reflect a distinctively German heritage. New Braunfels, 30 miles east on TX 46, is known for its German food. Landa Park, on the crystal springs that form the Comal River, is the site of Wurstfest in early November. The festival celebrates sausage, or wurst, and beer with traditional German singing, dancing, and music. Several outfitters along the Guadalupe River rent canoes and inner tubes.

Natural Bridge Caverns, one of the most scenic caves in Texas, is 16 miles west of New Braunfels on FM 1863.

HIKING

A short, maintained trail connecting the two campgrounds parallels the river and passes through the picnic areas. Unmarked trails follow the south riverbank in both directions from the picnic grounds. The portion of the park north of the river, which includes three primitive campgrounds on a hiking trail, is closed to the public until a ranger residence can be located there. Presently, there is no way to cross the river and warn campers of flash flooding.

ECOLOGY

The park preserves 1,900 acres of Central Texas Hill Country and a scenic section of the Guadalupe River. Sycamore, pecan, bald cypress, and hackberry trees shade the bottomlands and terraces along the river. Many of the large trees in the day-use area have been destroyed by flooding. Others lean in a downstream direction, attesting to the fury of the flooding common to Central Texas.

The river winds its sinuous course through limestone hills and plateaus, which themselves were carved by millions of years of erosion. Ashe juniper and oak trees dominate the dry uplands and provide the necessary habitat for the rare and beautiful golden-cheeked warbler. After rearing its young in the live oak-juniper woodlands of Central Texas, this colorful bird returns to the forests of Central America. About 260 species of birds, including many migrants, have been seen in the park. Other wildlife in the park are white-tailed deer, coyotes, gray foxes, bobcats, and raccoons. Armadillos are numerous, especially near the river, where they can easily burrow into the sandy banks.

The park is on the drainage zone for the Edwards Aquifer. Water seeps into the porous limestone hills and flows underground along an impervious layer of rock, emerging as springs wherever the rock is exposed to the surface. The springs form the San Antonio River in San Antonio, the Comal River in New Braunfels, the San Marcos River in San Marcos, and Barton Springs in Austin.

66. HASKELL CITY PARK

Haskell County. From U.S. 277, east on South 7th for 2 blocks; from U.S. 380, south on Ave. C for 6 blocks. Mailing address: 301 South 1st, Haskell, Texas 79521. Phone: 817-846-2333.

Facilities: 1-acre park with pull-through sites, 5 with water and electricity, 5 with water, electricity, sewage hookups; swimming pool, restrooms, picnic area, playgrounds. First night free, then fee. No reservations, open all year.

67. HILL COUNTRY STATE NATURAL AREA

LOCATION
Bandera County. 1 mile south of Bandera on TX 173, 10 miles west on FM 1077.
Mailing address: Route 1, Box 601, FM 1077, Bandera, Texas 78003. Phone: 210-796-4413.

FACILITIES
Camping: ten walk-in tent sites and 2 group sites 50–75 yards from parking lot, 3 designated backpacking areas 1.5 to 3.5 miles from trailhead, 6-acre shaded equestrian camping area, large barn with concrete floor and electricity (reservations required), hiking trail. Pit toilets, water faucet at parking lot with springwater which must be treated before drinking.

Recreation: hiking, horseback riding, mountain biking, 3 designated swimming areas in creek.

MAIN ATTRACTIONS
The rugged beauty of the 5,370 acres of this natural area attracts those who like the outdoors. This is not a park for party picnickers or RV campers. Thirty-four trails lead through the park, allowing adventurers to explore and make their own discoveries. But take care not to get lost. Campers must backpack 1.5 to 3.5 miles to three primitive camping areas with no water or other facilities. This is really getting away from city life. Since ground fires are prohibited, backpackers must use portable stoves and pack out all their garbage.

A majority of the park's visitors come to ride their horses. Riding clubs from all over Texas and surrounding states converge on the natural area for outings. Nine multi-use hiking, biking, and horse trails allow visitors to explore the canyons, springs, oak groves, and grassy savannas that make the Hill Country famous.

ECOLOGY

Visitors to this park will discover what the Texas Hill Country is really like. The rocky hills covered with scrubby junipers and oaks may look unimpressive, but closer investigation reveals a captivating beauty. Steep canyons harbor large trees, lush vegetation, and fern-lined springs. Sunfish dart under rocks in the spring-fed West Verde Creek. The picturesque, shallow creek provides a permanent oasis for wildlife. It winds through the hills providing water even when other, intermittent streams dry up.

A diversity of plants and animals live in the rugged terrain of the park. Visitors are likely to see white-tailed deer, armadillos, raccoons, skunks, and opossums, as well as a few snakes, lizards, and abundant birdlife. Turkeys, roadrunners, and quail scurry through the brush, and numerous sparrows, vireos, warblers, and other songbirds occur in the park, including the golden-cheeked warbler, which nests nowhere else but the juniper-covered hills of Central Texas.

The previous owner, Louise Lindsey Merrick, donated the ranch with the provision that it be "kept untouched by modern civilization, with everything preserved intact." We are fortunate to have access to such a large tract of unspoiled land in a part of Texas generally privately owned and inaccessible to the public.

68. HUECO TANKS STATE HISTORICAL PARK

LOCATION

El Paso County. 32 miles east of El Paso on U.S. 180, 6 miles north on FM 2775.
Mailing address: 6900 Hueco Tanks Rd. #1, El Paso, Texas 79938-8793. Phone: 915-857-1135. For all state park reservations, call 512-389-8900.

FACILITIES

Camping: 17 campsites with water and electricity, 3 without electricity, modern restrooms with showers, trailer dump station. Fees charged.

Recreation: picnic areas, hiking trails through the rocks, rock climbing, guided tours on weekends, amphitheater with summer programs.

MAIN ATTRACTIONS

The park preserves more than 3,500 Indian pictographs painted in an outcropping of intrusive igneous rock in the Chihuahuan Desert. The paintings vary from crude figures to intricate masks and detailed drawings of animals, people, and mythological figures. The colors of the drawings were made with combinations of mineral-based pigments. For example, masks are painted in red, black, gray, white, or a combination of colors. A.T. Jackson's *Picture Writing of Texas Indians* and Forrest Kirkland and W. W. Newcomb's *Rock Art of Texas Indians* discuss the drawings. Archaeological research completed since the latter book was published has assisted in dating the paintings.

HIKING

A series of unmarked trails leading through the large boulders enables the visitor to view many of the beautiful pictographs. Guided tours through the area are available on weekends. Some of the shorter trails are easily accessible, and longer, more rigorous hikes traverse the ridgetops.

ECOLOGY

About 34 million years ago, molten rock welled up within the earth and cooled before reaching the surface. Erosion over the intervening millennia stripped away the overlying limestone, revealing the hardened igneous rock to the elements. Today, the rocks stand as an island in the midst of the Chihuahuan Desert.

The igneous hills, composed of syenite porphyry, rise 300 to 450 feet above the desert floor and provide dramatic relief to the flat terrain. Weathering and other, undetermined factors have created large potlike depressions in the hills that collect rainwater. These basins, or huecos, have attracted humans for possibly 10,000 years. Animals tend to congregate at the water holes, especially migrating birds and large wandering mammals such as bobcats, coyotes, foxes, and mountain lions. A checklist of the birds in the park is available at the headquarters.

The temporary ponds support an interesting community of fairy shrimp, tadpole shrimp, and clam shrimp. The shrimp eggs survive the dry periods and hatch with the next rain. Many animals feed on the crustaceans, especially when the water level is low.

The mountains to the east channel water into the area of the tanks, and the soil, rich in material weathered from the igneous rocks, holds the moisture better than the surrounding desert soils. As a result, the vegetation in the area is distinctively different from the creosote bush, mesquite, yucca, agave, and thorny shrubs of the surrounding desert, which receives only eight inches of rain annually. Grasslands predominate, with galleries of Arizona oak and one-seed juniper growing in the sheltered canyons.

HISTORY

Artifacts of stone tools and projectile points indicate that the water reservoirs in the hills have attracted humans for possibly 10,000 years. The oldest paintings in the park date to the Desert Archaic period, several thousand years before the time of Christ. The first painters hunted small game and harvested edible plants.

By around A.D. 1000, a more sedentary farming culture had developed, with small villages of semisubterranean pit houses. Pictographs similar to those found in the southwestern pueblos suggest concurrent dates for some of the drawings. By 1400, the villages were abandoned. Early Spanish expeditions in 1581 and 1582 make no mention of any people living in the area.

The area of the tanks was probably not inhabited again until the Mescalero Apaches arrived in the late 1700s. They left their particular style of art, with pictures of horsemen, giant snakes, and dancing figures.

69. HUNTSVILLE STATE PARK

LOCATION

Walker County. 8 miles south of Huntsville off IH-45, Exit 109, west on PR 40, next to Sam Houston National Forest.
Mailing address: Box 508, Huntsville, Texas 77342-0508. Phone: 409-295-5644. For all state park reservations, call 512-389-8900.

FACILITIES

Camping: 127 campsites with water only, 64 campsites with water and electricity, 30 screened shelters, modern restrooms with showers, trailer dump station. Fees charged.

Recreation: picnic areas and playgrounds, 8 miles of hiking and nature trails with trail guide pamphlet, bicycle path, swimming in Lake Raven, fishing with 2 lighted piers, boating (no-wake speed limit), canoe and paddleboat rentals, miniature-golf course, guided horse-back rides, group picnic shelter for 75 people, store (summer only).

MAIN ATTRACTIONS

Huntsville State Park is located on the picturesque 210-acre Lake Raven. Shore and pier fishing is popular, with catches of crappie, bass, and catfish being typical. The shaded picnic grounds under tall pines and the wide variety of recreational opportunities available make this park a favorite, but also a crowded, retreat for nearby Houston and Huntsville city dwellers. Because use is heavy all during the summer and year-round on weekends, reservations are recommended for camping.

Nearby Huntsville was the home of Sam Houston, the commander in chief of the Texas revolutionary army and the republic's first president. Houston was also the state's first governor, but he relinquished the office when he refused to take the oath of allegiance to the Confederacy. His home and the Sam Houston Memorial Museum are in Huntsville.

HIKING

A 1-mile nature trail begins near the park entrance; ask for a trail guide leaflet and a hiking map. An 8-mile hiking trail circles the lake, passing through aromatic pine forests, hardwood bottoms, and creek drainages. There are no water and no camping on the trail. The Lone Star Hiking Trail, a hiking and backpacking trail through the Sam Houston National Forest, passes north of Huntsville State Park.

ECOLOGY

The 2,083-acre park lies in the Piney Woods of East Texas and is surrounded by Sam Houston National Forest. The dominant trees in the park are the towering pines, which shade the campgrounds and picnic areas. The snowy flowers of the dogwood decorate the woods in late March, and the leaves of sweetgum and red maple lend a colorful touch each fall.

Lake Raven was created in the thirties when the Civilian Conservation Corps impounded three creeks that run through the park. Hardwoods, including black willow, river birch, green ash, oak, and elm species, grow along the creek bottomlands.

A checklist to the birds of the park lists 223 species. Many species of wood warblers are attracted to the rich forestland during spring and fall migrations. In spite of its name, ravens are not found on the lake, merely the common crow. The red-cockaded woodpecker is a rare find in the park. Deer can be seen feeding in the early morning, and raccoons often raid garbage cans and unprotected food at night.

101

70. INKS LAKE STATE PARK

LOCATION
Burnet County. 9 miles west of Burnet on TX 29, south on PR 4. Mailing address: Route 2, Box 31, Burnet, Texas 78611. Phone: 512-793-2223. For all state park reservations, call 512-389-8900.

FACILITIES
Camping: primitive camping area on hiking trail, 151 campsites with water only, 56 campsites with water and electricity, 22 screened shelters, modern restrooms with showers, trailer dump station. Fees charged.

Recreation: picnic areas and playgrounds, 7.5 miles of hiking trails, swimming in lake, scuba diving, fishing with fishing piers, boating, boat rentals, 9-hole golf course, amphitheater, store.

MAIN ATTRACTIONS
Inks Lake, with 803 surface acres, is one of the most beautiful lakes in Central Texas; it is popular for fishing, boating, water sports, and scuba diving. Picturesque creeks and some of the most beautiful wildflower settings in the state add to the charm of the park.

Each April, the Highland Lakes Bluebonnet Trail, which passes through the park, attracts thousands of wildflower lovers. Festivals in many of the area communities coincide with the colorful display of roadside flowers. Longhorn Cavern State Park, which offers tours of the caverns, is a short distance south on PR 4.

HIKING
The 1,200-acre park includes open slopes bordering the lake and scenic woodlands. The upland wooded area has 7 miles of hiking trails with a primitive camping area a mile from the trailhead. There is no water on the trail.

ECOLOGY
Inks Lake is in the Central Texas mineral region, one of the most geologically interesting parts of the state. The area is characterized by colorful outcroppings of granite, schist, and gneiss, rocks formed underground and exposed millions of years later by erosion. The sandy pink soil and massive dome mountains provide quite a contrast to the chalky limestone hills of most of Central Texas.

The most common rock seen in the park is Valley Spring gneiss, formed from sedimentary rocks that were recrystallized deep in the earth by heat and pressure. The pink gneiss, a metamorphic rock more than 600 million years old, is one of the oldest rock formations in the state. Near the park, outcroppings of Packsaddle schist, a gray metamorphic rock, can be seen adjacent to the gneiss. Granite, formed by molten rock that intruded into the older rocks, forms pink fingers that spread across the pink and gray metamorphic rocks.

Wildlife is abundant in the park, and white-tailed deer are commonly seen in the campgrounds toward evening. Many species of waterfowl are attracted to the lake, and numerous songbirds frequent the shoreline woods, especially during migration.

71. IRAAN: ALLEY OOP PARK

LOCATION
Pecos County. Located in Iraan at intersection of TX 349 and U.S. 190.
Mailing address: P.O. Box 457, Iraan, Texas 79744. Phone: 915-639-2301.

FACILITIES
Four sites with water only, 6 with water, electricity, sewage hookups; flush toilets, dump station. This 15-acre park commemorates the author of the comic strip Alley Oop and the Yates Oil Field with the most productive wells in North America. One 1,283-foot-deep well produced 3,036 barrels per hour. Playground has dinosaur figures, picnic area, little shade. Fees charged, reservations accepted, open all year.

72. JOE POOL LAKE, LOYD PARK

Tarrant County. Grand Prairie, IH-20, exit south on Great Southwest Parkway, west on Harwood, south on Arlington Webb Rd., west on Ragland Rd. to park entrance. Mailing address: Trinity River Authority, 3401 Ragland Rd., Mansfield, Texas 76063. Phone: 817-467-2104. Camping: 221 campsites with water and electricity, restrooms, showers, group camping, walk-in primitive camping with chemical toilets, trailer dump station. Recreation: picnic areas, playgrounds, group pavilion, boat launch, fishing, designated swimming area, 5.5 miles of hiking and mountain bike trails, ball field. Reservations accepted. Fees charged. Open year-round.

The nearby Lynn Creek Park, with swimming, picnicking, playgrounds, and boat launches, is day-use only.

73. KERRVILLE-SCHREINER STATE PARK

LOCATION
Kerr County. 1 mile southwest of Kerrville on TX 16, 2 miles southeast on TX 173.
Mailing address: 2385 Bandera Hwy., Kerrville, Texas 78028. Phone: 210-257-5392. For all state park reservations, call 512-389-8900.

FACILITIES
Camping: 65 campsites with water nearby, 35 campsites with water and electricity, 20 campsites with water, electricity, and sewage hookups; 23 screened shelters, modern restrooms with showers, trailer dump station. Fees charged.

Recreation: picnic areas and playgrounds, 7 miles of hiking trails, mountain bike trails, swimming in the Guadalupe River, fishing with fishing pier, boating (15-mph speed limit), amphitheater, recreation hall, group screened shelter with kitchen.

MAIN ATTRACTIONS
The 517-acre park is divided into two units by TX 173. Picnicking, camping, and playgrounds are available in both units. Picnicking and fishing are the primary activities in the Flatrock Lake Unit, which borders the Guadalupe River. There is a fishing pier, and crappie, bass, and catfish are the main catches. A beach area has a designated swimming area; swimming is at your own risk.

Area attractions include Lyndon B. Johnson State Historical Park near Stonewall, which offers bus tours of the LBJ Ranch, a working pioneer farm, a herd of longhorns and bison, and a swimming pool.

Lyndon B. Johnson National Historic Park, an hour's drive away in Johnson City, has a reconstructed 1880-period ranch and exhibits.

The city of Kerrville is known for its music festivals on Memorial Day, Fourth of July, and Labor Day weekends and for the Texas State Arts and Crafts Fair on Memorial Day weekend. The park hosts the annual Easter Hill Country Bicycle Tour.

HIKING
A series of loop hiking trails totaling 7 miles leads from the larger Hill Country Unit. The trails traverse rolling terrain broken by scenic creeks and covered with mesquite trees, oaks, and grassy savannas. Trails lead from the picnic and day-use areas, circle around wooded hills, and parallel the park boundary.

ECOLOGY

The Flatrock Lake Unit offers picnicking and camping along the shaded banks of the Guadalupe River. Bald cypress, hackberry, sycamore, and pecan trees grow along the river; mesquite trees, live oaks, and grassy savannas dominate the uplands.

The vegetation of the Hill Country Unit is typical of the limestone hills of Central Texas. Plateau live oaks, Texas oaks, and Ashe junipers cover the ridges and the drainages that flow into the Guadalupe River.

Each spring, bluebonnets cover the grassy savannas in both units of the park. Indian blankets, Mexican hats, and a wide variety of other wildflowers add color to the rolling hills and riverbanks throughout the summer.

The park's many oaks and its shrubby vegetation provide abundant acorns and forage for a large population of deer and turkeys. At dusk, deer frequently graze along the roadsides in the Hill Country Unit. Other animals likely to be seen are armadillos, squirrels, rabbits, and many species of birds. Ask at the park entrance for a checklist of the birds.

74. KICKAPOO CAVERN STATE PARK

LOCATION

Kinney County. 22.5 miles north of Bracketville on RR 674. Mailing address: P.O. Box 705, Bracketville, Texas 78832. Phone: 210-563-2342.

FACILITIES

Camping: As of 1995, the park was undeveloped and open by reservation only. Camping is in an open area with undesignated sites and no potable water or restrooms. A group lodge with showers and flush toilets sleeps 14. Fees charged. Open January through September.

Recreation: Visitors can hike cross-country on old jeep trails, explore an undeveloped cave, and observe the plants, birds, and wildlife of the Edwards Plateau. You'll need to come prepared, though, with sturdy shoes for hiking the rocky hills, water, and powerful flashlights for cave exploration.

ECOLOGY

The 6,400-acre park preserves an unusual section of the Texas Hill Country. Besides the flora and fauna associated with a deep cave system, the park preserves one of the rare populations of pinyon pine trees growing in the rocky soils of the Edwards Plateau. These pines, normally growing in mountains and high deserts of the western United States, thrive in small, isolated pockets in several central Texas counties. True to form, a porcupine was in the top of one of the trees when I visited the park. Plateau live oaks, Ashe juniper, and mesquite trees with open grassy savannas cover the rocky hills of the park. Birdlife is abundant, and Brazilian (Mexican) freetail bats inhabit the cave during the summer.

75. KINGSVILLE: KAUFER-HUBERT MEMORIAL PARK AND SEAWIND RV RESORT

Kleberg County. 13 miles south of Kingsville on U.S. 77, 9 miles east on FM 628 to Baffin Bay; turn off U.S. 77 at the sign for the King's Inn. 20 acres on Baffin Bay. Mailing address: Route 1, Box 67D, Riviera, Texas 78379. Phone: 512-297-5738. Camping: 134 campsites with water, electricity, and sewage hookups; flush toilets, showers, trailer dump station. Reservations accepted by mail only with deposit. Fees charged. Recreation: picnic areas, fishing, boat ramp, recreation hall, 500-foot pier, 2-story observation tower, 1-mile exercise trail, playground, ball fields, sandy beach. Open all year. The nearby King's Inn is famous for its excellent seafood.

76. LAKE ARROWHEAD STATE PARK

LOCATION
Clay County. 9 miles south of Wichita Falls on U.S. 281, 7 miles east on FM 1954.
Mailing address: Route 2, Box 260, Wichita Falls, Texas 76301.
Phone: 817-528-2211. For all state park reservations, call 512-389-8900.

FACILITIES
Camping: 48 campsites with water and electricity, 19 sites with water, 4 equestrian camp sites, modern restrooms with showers, trailer dump station. Fees charged.

Recreation: picnic areas and playgrounds, equestrian area, swimming in lake, fishing, boating, water-skiing, pavilion, store.

MAIN ATTRACTIONS
Lake Arrowhead, with 13,500 acres, offers fishing and other water-related activities. Relief from the blazing summer sun is found only under the shade shelters in the picnic and camping

106

areas. Lake Arrowhead was formed in 1965 to provide water for Wichita Falls. The city deeded the park to the state in 1970.

Overgrazing of what used to be prairie has resulted in the invasion of thorny mesquite trees. The lakeshore around the picnic, camping, and playground areas is bulwarked with concrete and rocks to discourage erosion. The lake itself is a flooded oil field with many large offshore derricks.

77. LAKE B. A. STEINHAGEN

LOCATION

U.S. Army Corps of Engineers. Jasper and Tyler counties. Project office: 47 miles east of Livingston on U.S. 190, south on FM 92 on west side of reservoir.
Mailing address: 890 FM 92, Woodville, Texas 75979-9631. Phone: 409-429-3491.

Campground	water	fee area	flush toilets	season	dump station	electricity
Campers Cove	•			all		
East End	•			all		
Magnolia Ridge	•	•		all	•	•
Sandy Creek	•	•		all	•	•

FACILITIES

Camping: 4 parks on the reservoir have campgrounds. Fees vary. Individual sites may be reserved by calling 1-800-284-2267.

Recreation: swimming and fishing in lake, boat ramps, hunting.

MAIN ATTRACTIONS

Town Bluff Dam impounds approximately 10,950 acres; the lake has 160 miles of shoreline but averages only 7 feet in depth. Fishing is popular on the lake, with white bass, spotted bass, largemouth bass, and catfish being the common catches. The Neches River, which forms the lake, flows through the East Texas pine forests and

LAKE B. A. STEINHAGEN

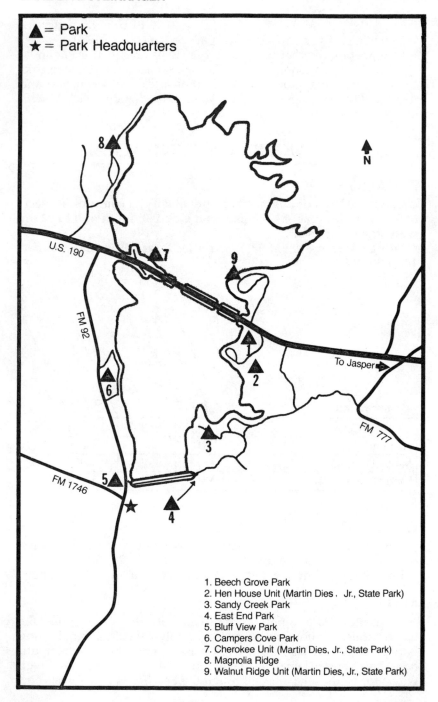

▲ = Park
★ = Park Headquarters

N

U.S. 190

FM 92

To Jasper

FM 777

FM 1746

8

7

9

1

2

6

3

5

4

1. Beech Grove Park
2. Hen House Unit (Martin Dies , Jr., State Park)
3. Sandy Creek Park
4. East End Park
5. Bluff View Park
6. Campers Cove Park
7. Cherokee Unit (Martin Dies, Jr., State Park)
8. Magnolia Ridge
9. Walnut Ridge Unit (Martin Dies, Jr., State Park)

108

swamps. Martin Dies, Jr., State Park is also located on the lake, and the Big Thicket National Preserve headquarters is south of Woodville off U.S. 69 on FM 420.

ECOLOGY

Shortleaf and loblolly pines and southern magnolias grow on the white-and-red sands around the lake, while dwarf palmettos and bald cypress and tupelo trees line the swampy inlets. The open water of the lake, its shallow inlets, and the rich woodlands provide food and shelter for numerous species of waterfowl, wading birds, and forest birds. Deer, squirrels, and other wildlife are also abundant.

A section of the property is operated by the Parks and Wildlife Department for wildlife management. Wild orchids and insectivorous plants have been found in a 4,000-acre section set aside for research.

78. LAKE BARDWELL

LOCATION

U.S. Army Corps of Engineers. Ellis County. Project office: 30 miles southeast of Dallas on IH-45 to Ennis, 3 miles southwest on TX 34.
Mailing address: Route 4, Box 60, Ennis, Texas 75119. Phone: 214-875-5711.

Campground	water	fee area	flush toilets	season	dump station	showers	electricity
High View	•	•		all	•		•
Love	•			Mar.-Oct.			
Mott	•	•		Mar.-Oct.	•		•
Waxahachie Creek	•	•		all	•	•	•

LAKE BARDWELL

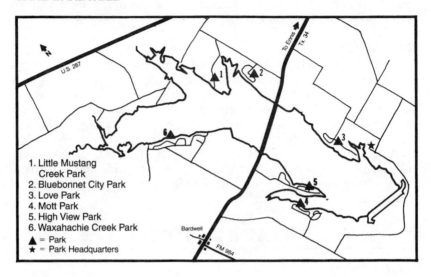

1. Little Mustang Creek Park
2. Bluebonnet City Park
3. Love Park
4. Mott Park
5. High View Park
6. Waxahachie Creek Park
▲ = Park
★ = Park Headquarters

FACILITIES

Camping: 4 of the parks have campgrounds. Fees vary. Campsites may be reserved by calling 1-800-284-2267.

Recreation: picnicking, nature trail at Waxahachie Creek Park, swimming in lake, fishing, boat ramps, water sports, hunting, concessions at High View Park.

MAIN ATTRACTIONS

Built for flood control of Waxahachie Creek and for local water supply, the reservoir covers 3,570 acres at a normal level with 25 miles of shoreline. Numerous species of waterfowl, ducks, herons, egrets, and cormorants frequent the lake, which is surrounded by rich blackland prairie farmland. Bluebonnets, Indian paintbrushes, and other wildflowers carpet the rolling shoreline each spring. Hunting is permitted in the ten wildlife management areas around the lake.

79. LAKE BASTROP NORTH SHORE RECREATION AREA

Lower Colorado River Authority. Bastrop County. 3.5 miles north of Bastrop on TX 95, 2.5 miles east on FM 1441. Mailing address: Box

546, Bastrop, Texas 78602. Phone: 512-321-3307. Camping: 22 camp-sites with water only, 44 campsites with water and electricity, 8 screened shelters with bunks, flush toilets, showers, trailer dump station. Fees charged. Recreation: swimming in lake, fishing, water-skiing, boat ramp, boat storage. Open all year. Facilities vary in quality. The south shore of the lake is being developed as part of Bastrop State Park. When completed, the north shore park will be closed until it can be redeveloped and also incorporated into the state park.

80. LAKE BELTON

LOCATION
U.S. Army Corps of Engineers. Bell and Coryell counties. Project office: 4 miles north of Belton on TX 317 to Belton Dam. Mailing address: 99 FM 2271, Belton, Texas 76513-9717. Phone: 817-939-1829.

Campground	water	fee area	flush toilets	season	dump station	cold-water showers	electricity
Cedar Ridge	●	●		all	●	●	●
Live Oak Ridge	●	●	●	all	●	●	●
Temple Lake	●	●	●	Apr.–Sept.	●	●	
Westcliff I	●	●	●	all	●	●	●

FACILITIES
Camping: Lake Belton's parks all have camping. Areas not listed on the matrix have minimal facilities (water, tables, pit toilets) and may be closed November–March. Fees at the parks vary. Campsites may be reserved by calling 1-800-284-2267.

Recreation: picnicking, swimming, fishing, water sports, boat ramps, marinas at Belton Lakeview and Cedar Ridge parks, hunting.

MAIN ATTRACTIONS
Built on the Leon River, Lake Belton covers 12,300 surface acres and has 136 miles of shoreline. White bass, largemouth bass, walleye

111

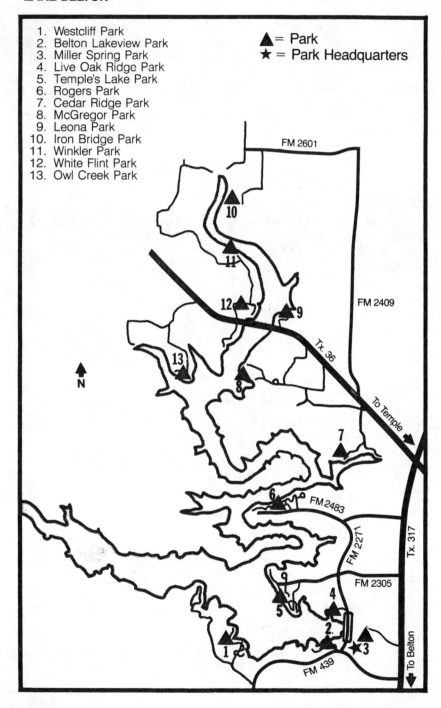

1. Westcliff Park
2. Belton Lakeview Park
3. Miller Spring Park
4. Live Oak Ridge Park
5. Temple's Lake Park
6. Rogers Park
7. Cedar Ridge Park
8. McGregor Park
9. Leona Park
10. Iron Bridge Park
11. Winkler Park
12. White Flint Park
13. Owl Creek Park

▲ = Park
★ = Park Headquarters

pike, and channel catfish are common catches in the lake. In the fall, the leaves of Texas oak and sumac color the shoreline with brilliant shades of red. Scenic cliffs rise above the lake, offering excellent panoramic views of the area.

Numerous species of ducks and other water birds overwinter on the reservoir. There are 3,900 acres of wildlife management areas for hunting. This is a metropolitan lake with more than 2.5 million visitors yearly.

81. LAKE BENBROOK

LOCATION
U.S. Army Corps of Engineers. Tarrant County. Project office: 12 miles southwest of Fort Worth on U.S. 377 to Benbrook. Lake access points on U.S. 377 at 1.2, 2.4, and 5.7 miles south of IH 20/820. Mailing address: Box 26619, Fort Worth, Texas 76126-0619. Phone: 817-292-2400.

Campground	water	fee area	flush toilets	season	dump station	cold-water showers	electricity
Holiday	•	•	•	all	•	•	•
Mustang	•	•	•	Apr.–Sept.	•	•	•
Rocky Creek	•				•		

FACILITIES
Camping: 3 parks have campgrounds, including two group pavilions. Campsites may be reserved 16 to 90 days in advance by calling 1-800-284-2267. Fees charged.

Recreation: picnicking, 7.3 miles of hiking and equestrian trails at Holiday Park, swimming, fishing, water sports, boat ramps, marinas at Dutch Branch (817-249-2696) and Rocky Creek (817-346-2199) offer boat rentals, golf course at Pecan Valley Park, hunting.

MAIN ATTRACTIONS
Lake Benbrook, on the Clear Fork of the Trinity River, covers 3,770 surface acres with 40 miles of shoreline. Cottonwood and willow

trees shade the shores, and oaks and other hardwoods forest the creek drainages. The trees provide good habitats for migrating song-birds, making the park attractive to bird-watchers. Fourteen hundred acres are managed for hunting.

Because of its proximity to Fort Worth, the lake is heavily used by city dwellers, especially on weekends. Fishing and water sports are the most popular activities.

HIKING

The 7.3 miles of trails make Benbrook one of the few Corps of Engineers lakes with extensive hiking and horseback-riding trails.

LAKE BENBROOK

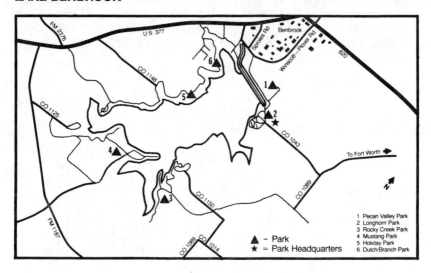

1 Pecan Valley Park
2 Longhorn Park
3 Rocky Creek Park
4 Mustang Park
5 Holiday Park
6 Dutch/Branch Park

▲ - Park
★ = Park Headquarters

82. LAKE BOB SANDLIN STATE PARK

LOCATION

Titus County. 10 miles southwest of Mount Pleasant on FM 127, south on FM 21.
Mailing address: Route 5, Box 224, Pittsburg, Texas 75686. Phone: 903-572-5531. For all state park reservations, call 512-389-8900.

FACILITIES

Camping: 75 campsites with water and electricity, 20 screened shelters, modern restrooms, showers, trailer dump station, 2 primitive camping areas on hiking trail. Fees charged.

Recreation: picnicking areas, group picnic shelter, playground, fishing pier, fish-cleaning shelter, bathhouse, 1.5-mile hiking trail.

MAIN ATTRACTIONS

The 9,460-acre Lake Bob Sandlin and adjoining Lake Monticello and Lake Cypress Springs offer numerous recreational opportunities for fishermen, water-sports enthusiasts, and those who just want a few days away from the city. Largemouth bass are the main attraction for fishermen, who also report good catches of crappie, channel catfish, white bass, and sunfish. Hikers enjoy the 1.5-mile loop hiking trail through deep woods and naturalized pastures within the park.

ECOLOGY

This park is within the Post Oak Savanna vegetation region of Texas, characterized by oaks, hickories, and other deciduous trees and grasslands. Because of its proximity to the Piney Woods, loblolly pine and sweetgum trees also grow abundantly within the park. Ferns, mosses, and other shade and moisture-loving plants thrive in the dense forests bordering the lake. Old home sites and pastures in the park have become naturalized with a combination of invading native plants and escaped ornamentals, such as Japanese honeysuckle and chinaberry trees.

The moist woods, streams, and shoreline provide excellent habitat for small mammals, frogs, turtles, and snakes. Visitors often see white-tailed deer grazing at dusk, armadillos rooting through the leaf-covered forest floor, and nutrias, South American beaverlike rodents, swimming along the shoreline. Birdlife is abundant, with both resident species and migrants in the spring and fall. The lake attracts herons, egrets, and numerous species of waterfowl.

83. LAKE BROWNWOOD STATE PARK

LOCATION

Brown County. 16 miles northwest of Brownwood on TX 279, 6 miles east on PR 15.

Mailing address: Route 5, Box 160, Brownwood, Texas 76801.

Phone: 915-784-5223. For all state park reservations, call 512-389-8900.

FACILITIES

Camping: 12 campsites with water only, 55 campsites with water and electricity, 20 campsites with water, electricity, and sewage hookups; 10 screened shelters, 17 cabins (with fireplaces, heat and air conditioning, and kitchenettes), 2 group lodges for 10 to 26 people, group facilities with dining hall and 4 bunkhouses that hold 8 people each, modern restrooms with showers, trailer dump station. Fees charged.

Recreation: picnic areas, hiking and nature trails with trail-guide booklet, swimming in lake, fishing, lighted pier, boating, paddleboat rentals, store (seasonal).

MAIN ATTRACTIONS

The park is on Lake Brownwood, which covers 7,300 acres and has 95 miles of shoreline. The sandy, shaded shores are ideal for picnicking, camping, and swimming. Water sports and fishing are major activities on the lake. Catches include black and white bass, largemouth bass, catfish, crappie, and bream.

The town of Brownwood received its name from Captain Henry S. Brown, a revolutionary soldier and the first white man to travel through the region. The first home in the area was built in 1854, but frequent Indian raids discouraged settlement by whites. After Chief Bigfoot and Chief Jape were defeated in 1874, the Anglo population increased rapidly.

HIKING

The park has two short trails: a hiking trail approximately one mile long and a three-quarter-mile nature trail. Ask for a trail-guide pamphlet at the entrance.

ECOLOGY

The 538-acre park is in the Cross Timbers and prairies region of Texas in an area of rolling hills separated by narrow valleys. The ridgetops are composed of erosion-resistant limestone, the slopes and valleys of softer shale and sandstone. The dam forming Lake Brownwood was constructed across a deep, narrow gap cut through one of the limestone ridges by Pecan Bayou.

Live oak trees cover the limestone ridges, while grasslands with invasions of mesquite and prickly pear cover the valleys, where the bedrock is shale. Cedar elms, post oaks, and hackberries are also numerous in the park.

The limestone beds exposed in and around the park are rich in fossils more than 310 million years old. More than 500 types have been found in the alternating layers of limestone and shale. Fossils are particularly abundant in the strata at the spillway. Ross Maxwell's *Geologic and Historic Guide to the State Parks of Texas* describes the geology of the area in detail.

84. LAKE BUCHANAN: BLACK ROCK PARK

Lower Colorado River Authority. Llano County. 12 miles west of Burnet on TX 29, 4 miles north on TX 261. 10 acres on Lake Buchanan. Mailing address: Box 220, Austin, Texas 78767-0220. Phone: 512-473-4083 or 1-800-776-7252, ext. 4083. Fax: 512-473-3298. Camping: the 10-acre park has 30 campsites with tables, water nearby, flush toilets, cold water wash-off showers, trailer dump station. Recreation: picnic sites and playground, swimming, fishing, boat ramp. Open all year. Fee charged. No reservations. Lake Buchanan is a picturesque lake for boating and bird-watching. Bald eagles winter on the lake.

85. LAKE CASA BLANCA STATE PARK

LOCATION
Webb County. 6 miles east of Laredo on U.S. 59, 1 mile north on Lake Casa Blanca Road.
Mailing address: P.O. Box 1844, Laredo, Texas 78044. Phone: 210-725-3826. For all state park reservations, call 512-389-8900.

FACILITIES
Camping: 5 sites with water, 6 sites with water, electricity; restrooms with showers, dump station, group campsites. Fees charged, group camp reservations. Open all year. Some facilities were still under development in late 1994.

Recreation: picnicking, 3 group pavilions available, playgrounds, boating, paddleboats and jet ski rental (weekends), fishing, swimming in lake, park store with fast food, golf course adjacent.

MAIN ATTRACTIONS
Recreation in this 370-acre park centers around water activities on Lake Casa Blanca. The watery habitat provides a home for wintering gulls, terns, herons, egrets, and other waterfowl and shorebirds. The brushy chaparral surrounding the lake includes blackbrush, huisache, mesquite, prickly pear, and other thorny shrubs typical of south Texas. The only hiking trails are paths along the lakeshore.

86. LAKE COLORADO CITY STATE PARK

LOCATION
Mitchell County. 30 miles east of Big Spring on IH-20, 5 miles south on FM 2836.
Mailing address: 4582 FM 2836, Colorado City, Texas 79512.
Phone: 915-728-3931. For all state park reservations, call 512-389-8900.

FACILITIES
Camping: 53 campsites with water only, 79 campsites with water and electricity, modern restrooms with showers, trailer dump station. Fees charged.

Recreation: picnic areas and playgrounds, hiking trail, swimming in lake, fishing, 2 fishing piers, boating, a covered fishing barge, and a meeting room.

MAIN ATTRACTIONS
The park is on the shore of a 1,618-acre lake, a reservoir that provides cooling water for a power plant adjacent to the park. The lakeshore has little shade for picnicking or camping, but there are nice sandy beaches for swimming and 2 fishing piers. In the summer, the lake is heavily used by motorboaters and does not offer a quiet retreat from the city.

ECOLOGY
The rolling terrain of the area is covered with scrubby mesquite trees, prickly pear cacti, agarita bushes, and a few junipers. In the spring and summer, wildflowers are sprinkled through the grasses, and bluebells can occasionally be found blooming along the shore.

One of the features of the park is a prairie dog town. In the morning or in the cool of the evening, the animals can be seen feeding and scurrying between their burrows. Other wildlife seen are grassland birds as well as migrating waterfowl during the winter.

87. LAKE CORPUS CHRISTI STATE PARK

LOCATION
San Patricio County. 35 miles northwest of Corpus Christi on IH-37, 4 miles south on TX 359, north on FM 1068.
Mailing address: Box 1167, Mathis, Texas 78368. Phone: 512-547-2635. For all state park reservations, call 512-389-8900.

FACILITIES

Camping: 60 campsites with water only, 23 campsites with water and electricity, 25 campsites with water, electricity, and sewage hookups; 25 screened shelters, modern restrooms with showers, trailer dump station. Fees charged.

Recreation: picnic areas and playgrounds, bird-watching, swimming in lake, fishing, 2 lighted piers, boating, pavilion. Paddleboats, canoes, pontoon boats, and ski boats can be rented.

MAIN ATTRACTIONS

Lake Corpus Christi, with 21,000 acres and 200 miles of shoreline, is the outstanding feature of the park. The lake was formed when the Nueces River was impounded in the thirties by the Civilian Conservation Corps to provide water for Corpus Christi, 35 miles southeast. The lake is noted for its abundance of big blue, yellow, and channel catfish, perch, bass, and crappie. Swimming, boating, and waterskiing are popular.

The rolling terrain of the 365-acre park is covered with thorny shrubs characteristic of the South Texas brush country and the lower Rio Grande Valley. Blackbrush acacia, lotebush, bluewood, mesquite, and lime prickly ash form a dense woodland around the shoreline.

The mild climate and diverse vegetation support more than 300 species of birds, making the area favored for bird-watching; a checklist is available at the entrance. Many species of shorebirds, wading birds, and waterfowl are attracted to the lake, and the woodlands provide habitat for a wide variety of migrating birds arriving from their trans-Gulf flight in the spring. Mammals common to the park include the spotted skunk, raccoons, and opossums.

The coastal region of Texas was once inhabited by Karankawa and Lipan Apache Indians, who resisted conversion to Christianity by the Spanish. The Nueces River, which forms the reservoir, was the disputed boundary between Texas and Mexico until the Mexican War established the Rio Grande as the official boundary.

88. LAKE CYPRESS SPRINGS

Franklin County. 4 parks administered by the water district. Mailing address: Franklin County Water District, Box 559, Mount Vernon, Texas 75457. Phone: 903-588-2352. Reservations accepted. Fees charged. Open all year.

W. D. Jack Guthrie Park, east of Mount Pleasant on IH-30 to Mount Vernon, south on FM 115, southeast on FM 21, south on FM

3007. Camping: 32 campsites with water and electricity, flush toilets, showers, trailer dump station, primitive camping. Recreation: playgound, boat ramp, designated swimming area, tennis, basketball, softfall.

Mary King Park, east of Mount Pleasant on IH-30 to Mount Vernon, south on FM 115, southeast on FM 21, south on FM 3007, south side of lake. Camping: 8 campsites with water and electricity, flush toilets, primitive camping. Recreation: boat ramp.

Walleye Park, south from Mount Vernon on FM 115, southeast on FM 21, south on FM 3122. Camping: 42 campsites with water and electricity, 4 screened shelters, flush toilets, showers, trailer dump station, primitive camping. Recreation: playground, group pavilion, boat ramp.

Overlook Park, south from Mount Vernon on FM 115, southeast on FM 21, south on FM 2723. Camping: primitive camping with tables, water, flush toilets, trailer dump station. Recreation: boat ramp.

89. LAKE GEORGETOWN

LOCATION

U.S. Army Corps of Engineers. Williamson County. Project office: 30 miles north of Austin on IH-35 to Georgetown, 4 miles west on FM 2338.
Mailing address: Route 5, Box 500, Georgetown, Texas 78626.
Phone: 512-863-3016. For reservations, call 1-800-284-2267.

FACILITIES

Jim Hogg Park has 148 sites with water and electricity, restrooms, showers, dump station, fishing dock. Open year round 6 A.M. to 10 P.M. with 24-hour exit. Cedar Breaks Park has 64 sites with water and electricity, restrooms, showers, dump station, 2 fishing docks. Open all year 6 A.M. to 10 P.M., closed at night except for emergencies. Russell Park is day-use only with swimming beach, boat launch, restrooms, and group picnic shelters. Open April 1 to Sept. 30. Fees charged for all parks. Tejas Camp has 12 tent sites with tables and water. Open all year, no fee. The 16-mile Good Water Trail connects Russell and Cedar Breaks parks via Tejas Camp.

MAIN ATTRACTIONS

Lake Georgetown, formerly called North Fork Lake, covers 1,310 acres at its normal level. The dam, completed in 1980, impounds the North Fork of the San Gabriel River.

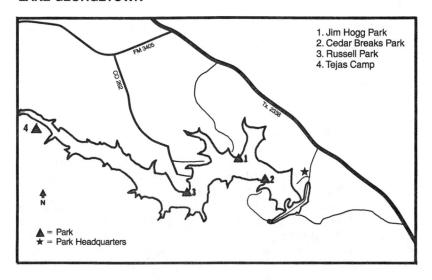

1. Jim Hogg Park
2. Cedar Breaks Park
3. Russell Park
4. Tejas Camp

▲ = Park
★ = Park Headquarters

90. LAKE GRANGER

LOCATION
U.S. Army Corps of Engineers. Williamson County. Project office: 32 miles north of Austin on IH-35 past Georgetown, 23 miles east on FM 971 through Granger.
Mailing address: Route 1, Box 172, Granger, Texas 76530. Phone: 512-859-2668.

Campground	water	fee area	flush toilets	season	dump station	showers	electricity
Friendship				Apr.–Sept.			
Wilson H. Fox	•	•	•	all	•	•	•
Taylor	•	•	•	Mar–Sept.	•	•	•
Willis Creek	•	•	•	all	•	•	•

121

FACILITIES

Camping: 3 parks with campgrounds, restrooms, showers. Campsites may be reserved 16 to 90 days in advance by calling 1-800-284-2267. Fees charged.

Recreation: picnicking, hiking trail at Taylor Park, swimming, fishing, boat ramps, hunting, pavilion.

MAIN ATTRACTIONS

Lake Granger, an impoundment of the San Gabriel River, covers 4,400 acres at its normal level. The Texas Parks and Wildlife Department manages 10,600 acres on the lake for wildlife and hunting.

The lake, in the Blackland Prairies region of Texas, is characterized by rolling hills and wooded creek drainages. In the fall, kettles of broad-winged hawks can be seen circling slowly overhead; in the winter, waterfowl frequent the lake, and ospreys often fly overhead. Chestnut-collared longspurs and a variety of sparrow species live in the fields. In the spring, migrating birds forage among the treetops, and wildflowers bloom abundantly, covering the hillsides overlooking the lake with bluebonnets, Indian paintbrushes, winecups, and other colorful species.

LAKE GRANGER

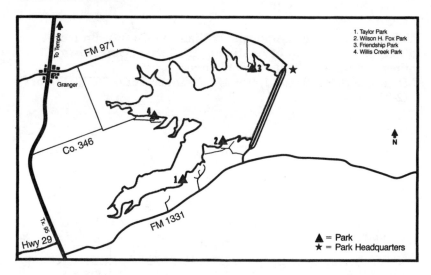

1. Taylor Park
2. Wilson H. Fox Park
3. Friendship Park
4. Willis Creek Park

▲ = Park
★ = Park Headquarters

91. LAKE GRAPEVINE

LOCATION

U.S. Army Corps of Engineers. Denton and Tarrant counties.
Project office: 23 miles northeast of Fort Worth on TX 121, past
Grapevine to dam.
Mailing address: 110 Fairway Dr., Grapevine, Texas 76051. Phone:
817-481-4541. For reservations, call 1-800-284-2267.

Campground	water	fee area	flush toilets	season	dump station	cold-water showers	electricity
Murrell	•	•		Apr.–Sept.			
Oak Grove	•	•		all			
Silver Lake	•	•	•	all	•	•	•
Twin Coves	•	•	•	Apr.–Sept.	•	•	•

FACILITIES

Camping: Silver Lake and Twin Coves have individual and group
sites, tent and RV camping, and accept reservations. Both parks have
gate attendants and close to day users at 10 P.M. Camping and day-
use fees are charged at all parks. Parks not listed are undeveloped.

Recreation: picnicking, two equestrian trails, nature trail in Twin
Coves Park, swimming area in Meadowmere Park, water sports,
fishing, boat ramps, marinas at Silver Lake, Oak Grove, and Murrell
parks, golf course below dam, hunting with permit. The nine-mile
Northshore hike and bike trail connects Rockledge Park and Twin
Coves Park. Another six-mile portion is on the west end of the lake.

MAIN ATTRACTIONS

Lake Grapevine, just north of the Dallas–Fort Worth airport, covers 7,380 acres and has 60 miles of shoreline. The lake is popular with
powerboat operators. Fishing for white bass is a favorite activity,
especially in the spring. Hunting is permitted in the 800-acre wildlife
management area. The recreational facilities of the lake are heavily
used by residents of the Dallas–Fort Worth metroplex, especially on
weekends. More than 5 million people visit the lake each year.

LAKE GRAPEVINE

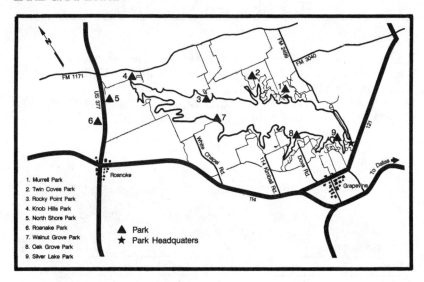

1. Murrell Park
2. Twin Coves Park
3. Rocky Point Park
4. Knob Hills Park
5. North Shore Park
6. Roanoke Park
7. Walnut Grove Park
8. Oak Grove Park
9. Silver Lake Park

▲ Park
★ Park Headquaters

92. LAKE HORDS CREEK

LOCATION

U.S. Army Corps of Engineers. Coleman County. 30 miles west of Brownwood on U.S. 84 to Coleman, 8 miles west on FM 53. Mailing address: HCR 75, Box 33, Coleman, Texas 76834-9320. Phone: 915-625-2322. For reservations, call 1-800-284-2267.

Campground	water	fee area	flush toilets	season	dump station	cold-water showers	electricity
Flat Rock	•	•	•	Apr.–Sept.	•	•	•
Friendship	•	•	•	all	•	•	•
Lakeside	•	•	•	all	•	•	•

FACILITIES

Camping: 3 parks, all with campgrounds. For the safety of campers, the gates to the parks are closed from 10 P.M. to 6 A.M. There are group camping areas with water and electric hookups and a covered pavilion. Some picnic areas are free; fees for campsites vary. Single campsites may be reserved by calling 1-800-284-2267. Call 915-625-2322 to reserve screened shelters and group pavilions.

Recreation: picnic areas, nature trail at Lakeside Park, swimming beach at Friendship Park, fishing, boat ramps, hunting, pavilion.

MAIN ATTRACTIONS

Lake Hords Creek is one of the smallest Corps of Engineers lakes, with only 500 surface acres at a normal level and an average depth of 17 feet. The reservoir provides water for the town of Coleman. Before the completion of the dam in 1948, the West Texas town had to supplement its water supply by importing water in railroad cars.

Largemouth bass and red-ear sunfish are caught in the lake. Hunting is allowed by permit on 800 acres of the property.

LAKE HORDS CREEK

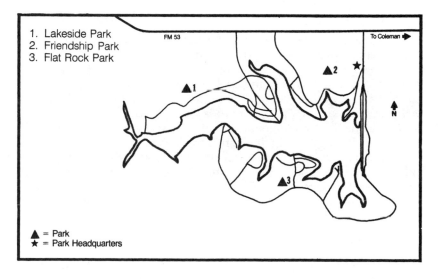

1. Lakeside Park
2. Friendship Park
3. Flat Rock Park

FM 53

To Coleman ➤

N

▲ = Park
★ = Park Headquarters

93. LAKE HOUSTON STATE PARK

LOCATION
Montgomery County. Forty-seven miles north of Houston on U.S.
59 to New Caney, 2 miles east FM 1485 to Encampment Road,
then south to park headquarters.
Mailing address: Route 7, Box 900, New Caney, Texas 77357-0900.
Phone: 713-354-6881. Fax: 713-354-7824. For all state park
reservations, call: 512-389-8900.

FACILITIES
Camping: 24 walk-in tent sites with water, 3 group lodges housing 20 people, kitchen/dining hall, restrooms, showers. The park
incorporates the facilities of an old Girl Scout Camp, which are
being renovated for use. Plans beyond 1995 include RV camping,
cabins, swimming pool, and equestrian trails.

Recreation: picnic areas, playgrounds, fishing and swimming in
Peach Creek and the East Fork of the San Jacinto River, canoeing,
hiking and biking on 10 miles of wooded trails.

MAIN ATTRACTIONS
First of all, Lake Houston State Park is not on or near Lake Houston, so don't plan a weekend of water skiing in the park. But the
park does offer ten miles of hiking trails and ten miles of waterfront
along the meandering Peach Creek and San Jacinto River. Opening
in 1994 as a day-use, weekend only park, the facilities will be gradually expanded as its master plan is developed. An extensive trail
system leads through pine-hardwood forests offering excellent bird-
watching, hiking and biking, and creek wading and swimming.
Anglers fish the San Jacinto River for catfish and bass. During periods of low water, the creeks run shin deep, perfect for wading, but
impossible to canoe. Located just thirty minutes from the chaos of
Houston freeways, the 4,913-acre park offers a calm respite for those
seeking the solitude of nature.

ECOLOGY
Situated at the confluence of scenic Peach Creek and the East Fork
of the San Jacinto River, the park includes loblolly-oak woodlands,
cypress bogs, open grasslands, a small lake, and shallow, tree-lined
creeks. The variety of habitats, from pine needle carpeted woodlands to swampy wetlands, sustains white-tailed deer, gray squirrels, raccoons, and a large number of birds. In an area fragmented by
freeways and subdivisions, the unbroken woodlands provide an

important refuge for the dwindling number of neotropical songbirds that require extensive tracts of contiguous forests to reproduce. The ten miles of trails allow visitors to discover delicate mushrooms in the spring and fall, the aroma of sunbaked pine needles, a cooling splash in a shaded creek in the summer, and the crimson leaves of sweetgum trees in the autumn.

94. LAKE JACKSONVILLE PARK

Cherokee County. 3 miles southwest of Jacksonville off U.S. 79 (College Ave.). Mailing address: Box 1390, Jacksonville, Texas 75766. Phone: 903-586-4160; City Parks Department, 903-586-6274. Camping: 10 campsites with water and electricity, 10 screened shelters, flush toilets, showers, trailer dump station. Reservations accepted. Fees charged. Recreation: picnic area, playground, park store open April to October, boat ramp, designated swimming area, fishing, hiking. Open all year.

95. LAKE LAVON

LOCATION
U.S. Army Corps of Engineers. Collin County. Project office: northeast of Dallas on TX 78, 5 miles past Wylie, 2 miles north on FM 386.
Mailing address: Box 1660, Wylie, Texas 75098-1660. Phone: 214-442-5711. For reservations, call 1-800-284-2267.

Campground	water	fee area	flush toilets	season	dump station	cold-water showers	electricity
Collin	•	•	•	all	•	•	•
East Fork	•	•	•	all	•	•	•
Lavonia	•	•	•	all	•	•	•
Clearlake	•	•	•	all	•	•	•

LAKE LAVON

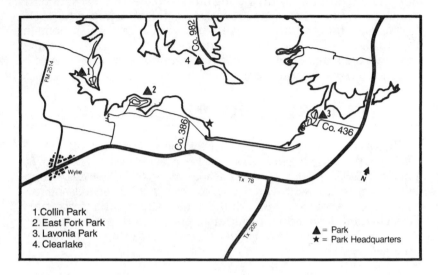

1. Collin Park
2. East Fork Park
3. Lavonia Park
4. Clearlake

▲ = Park
★ = Park Headquarters

FACILITIES

Camping: 6 parks with campgrounds. Campsites at East Fork and Lavonia parks, Lakeland and Ticky Creek can be reserved by calling 1-800-284-2267. Fees charged; Lakeland and Ticky Creek are free. Directions to the parks follow.

Collin Park (concessionaire): 5 miles north of Wylie on FM 2514.

East Fork Park: 3 miles northeast of Wylie on TX 78, 2 miles west on Skyview Dr.

Lavonia Park: 5 miles northeast of Wylie on TX 78, 2 miles west on County Road 486.

Clearlake: 7 miles north of Wylie on FM 2514, 6 miles east on FM 3286, 5 miles south on FM 982.

Ticky Creek (not shown on map): 7 miles north of Wylie on FM 2514, 6 miles east on FM 3286, 3 miles north on FM 982, 4 miles south on FM 3364.

Lakeland (not shown on map): 13 miles northeast of Wylie on TX 78, 2 miles west on County Road 550.

Recreation: picnic areas, horse trail, hiking (no trails), motorcycle trails near Lavonia Park, swimming at Collin Park, fishing, water sports, boat ramps, boat rentals at Collin Park, hunting.

MAIN ATTRACTIONS

Lake Lavon, averaging 14 feet deep, has 121 miles of shoreline and covers 21,400 surface acres at a normal level. The lake is surrounded

128

by rolling prairie with scattered trees. Fishing is good for large-mouth and hybrid striped bass, white crappie, and channel catfish. Wildlife management areas totaling 6,500 acres provide room for hunting and hiking. This is a metropolitan lake receiving heavy day use from the Dallas–Fort Worth area. Each year about 3 million people visit the park.

96. LAKE LEWISVILLE

LOCATION
Denton County. Refer to the map for directions and the matrix for itemized facilities.

Hidden Cove Park, operated by the City of The Colony. 721 acres. Mailing address: Route 2, Box 353H, Frisco, Texas 75034. Phone: information recording, 214-294-1115; office, 214-294-1445. Camping: 50 back-in sites with water and electricity, 38 screened shelters with electricity and water, and primitive backpacking areas. Group camping area with screened shelters and dining hall. Fees charged. Reservations accepted.

Lake Lewisville RV Resort. 680 acres. Mailing address: City of Lewisville Parks Department, Box 299002, Lewisville, Texas 75029-9002. Phone: 214-219-3550 or 436-7445. Camping: 119 campsites. Recreation: 18-hole golf course, marina, ball fields, swim beach, boat ramps.

Oakland Park and Pilot Knoll Park. Mailing address: U.S. Army Corps of Engineers, 1801 N. Mill St., Lewisville, Texas 75057. Phone: 214-434-1666. Camping: Oakland, 84 sites; Pilot Knob, 54 sites; Hickory Creek, 104 sites and group camp area. For reservations call 1-800-284-2267.

MAIN ATTRACTIONS
Lake Lewisville, on the Elm Fork of the Trinity River, covers 25,596 acres and has 200 miles of shoreline. The former Lake Dallas became part of the reservoir when a new dam impounded the river in 1955. Receiving more than 5 million visitors annually, the various parks on the lake are heavily used by residents of the Dallas–Fort Worth area. Hunting and hiking are allowed on the 9,000 acres set aside for wildlife management.

Campground	water	fee area	flush toilets	season	dump station	showers	electricity
Lake Lewisville St. Pk.	•	•	•	all	•	•	•
Lake Lewisville RV	•	•	•	all	•	•	•
Oakland (C. of E.)	•	•	•	all	•	•	•
Pilot Knoll (C. of E.)	•	•		Mar.–Oct.			
Hickory Creek (C. of E.)	•	•	•	all	•	•	•

An archaeological survey conducted in the area uncovered evidence including a *Clovis* point, of human occupation 10,000 to 11,000 years ago. Laws requiring surveys of areas targeted for federal and state construction have enabled archaeologists to piece together more information on the ways of life and migrations of the earliest Americans.

LAKE LEWISVILLE

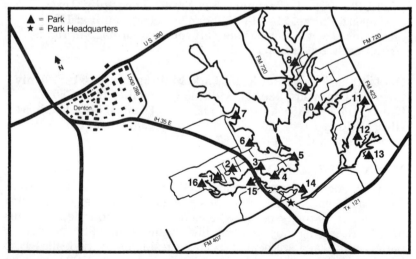

1. Sycamore Bend Park
2. Hickory Creek Park
3. Arrowhead Park
4. Oakland Park
5. Westlake Park
6. Willow Grove Park
7. Big Sandy Park
8. Little Elm Park
9. Cottonwood Park
10. Lake Lewisville State Park
11. Eastvale Park
12. Stewart Creek Park
13. East Hill Park
14. Lewisville Lake Park
15. Copperas Branch Park
16. Pilot Knoll Park

97. LAKE LIVINGSTON STATE PARK

LOCATION
Polk County. 2 miles south of Livingston on U.S. 59, 4 miles west on FM 1988, northwest on FM 3126, on the east shore of Lake Livingston.
Mailing address: Route 9, Box 1300, Livingston, Texas 77351.
Phone: 409-365-2201. For all state park reservations, call 512-389-8900.

FACILITIES
Camping: 16 campsites with water only, 97 campsites with water and electricity, group trailer area with water and electricity, 10 screened shelters with sleeping lofts (wheelchair access), modern restrooms with showers (wheelchair access), trailer dump stations. Fees charged.

Recreation: picnic areas and playgrounds, approximately 4 miles of hiking and nature trails, observation tower, swimming pool (summer only), fishing, marina (summer only), amphitheater, meeting room, store (summer only).

MAIN ATTRACTIONS
Water-oriented activities centered around Lake Livingston are the major attraction of the park. The lake has 84,800 surface acres and 452 miles of shoreline; it is 52 miles long. An interpretive trail and several miles of hiking trails wind through the park.

ECOLOGY
The 635-acre park is located in the pine-oak woodlands of East Texas. In the past, this area was managed exclusively for pine production, and most of the hardwoods were eliminated. Since the establishment of the park, the natural diversity of tree species is being allowed to develop. That diversity will support a greater variety of wildlife.

Both loblolly and shortleaf pines grow in the dense woods of the park, and the bottomlands are forested with willow, oak, elm, and hickory trees. Remnants of a tallgrass blackland prairie also occur, which provide habitat for grassland birds.

Waterfowl and open-water species such as gulls, terns, and loons are commonly seen on the lake. The endangered bald eagle and the osprey are occasionally sighted hunting for fish over the water. Warblers, seven species of woodpeckers, and many other woodland birds inhabit the forests. Ask for a checklist of the birds.

LAKE LIVINGSTON: WOLF CREEK PARK

San Jacinto County. Located on west shore of Lake Livingston. From Livingston west on U.S. 190 across lake, south on TX 156, east 3 miles on FM 224. Mailing address: Box 309, Coldspring, Texas 77331. Phone: 409-653-4312. 110 acres on Lake Livingston. Camping: 19 sites with water only, 54 sites with water and electricity; 30 sites with water, electricity, and sewage hookups; flush toilets, showers, laundry. Fees charged. Recreation: picnic areas, playgrounds, swimming in lake, fishing, water-skiing, boat ramp, flat-boat rentals, miniature golf course, pavilion, store, 9-hole golf course nearby. Open March 1 to November 31. Excellent facilities.

98. LAKE MEREDITH NATIONAL RECREATION AREA

LOCATION
Hutchinson, Moore, Potter counties. Headquarters: 38 miles northeast of Amarillo on TX 136, in Fritch. Mailing address: Box 1460, Fritch, Texas 79036. Phone: 806-857-3151.

FACILITIES
Camping: primitive campsites at Spring Canyon, Sanford-Yake, Fritch Fortress, and Blue West; covered picnic tables, restrooms. No hook-ups for RVs. Other undeveloped campgrounds have picnic tables, chemical toilets.

Recreation: picnicking, swimming at Spring Canyon below the dam, fishing, boating, marinas, docks, hunting.

MAIN ATTRACTIONS
Fishing, boating, and water sports bring visitors to this 21,600-acre reservoir. Fishing is good for walleye, catfish, bass, and crappie, and sailors enjoy the brisk breezes that sweep across the lake. Because the lake level fluctuates, the fishing and boat-launching areas on the western end of the lake are often mud flats. Boats are advised to listen for the wind warning siren, since violent thunderstorms can develop unexpectedly.

The campgrounds, equipped with tables and shade shelters, are on barren, rocky, windswept hilltops overlooking the lake. The lake has no swimming beaches, and swimming is not recommended. The dangerously steep shores are littered with loose rocks and covered, both below and above the fluctuating water level, with thorny mesquite bushes. Motorcycles and dune buggies often gather for events in the areas designated for off-road vehicles at Rosita Flats and Big Blue Creek parks.

NEARBY ATTRACTIONS

Alibates Flint Quarries National Monument is on the west end of Lake Meredith at Bates Canyon off TX 136. Prehistoric peoples throughout the Southwest used the rainbow-colored agatized dolomite for tools and weapons. Mining of the flint dates back 10,000 to 12,000 years. Guided tours are offered at 10 A.M. and 2 P.M. between Memorial and Labor days and by request at other times. Wear good walking shoes and take a canteen for the one-mile, steep loop trail to the quarries. Call the National Park Service office for reservations.

99. LAKE MINERAL WELLS STATE PARK

LOCATION

Parker County. 45 miles west of Fort Worth on U.S. 180, 2 miles east of Mineral Wells.
Mailing address: Route 4, Box 39C, Mineral Wells, Texas 76067.
Phone: 817-328-1171. For all state park reservations, call 512-389-8900.

FACILITIES

Camping: 20 backpack sites accessed by 2.5-mile trail (no water available), 31 campsites with water only, 77 campsites with water and electricity, wheelchair access to a few campsites, equestrian camping area at trailhead, 15 screened shelters, group facility—with screened shelters, kitchen, and dining hall for 80 people, modern restrooms with showers, trailer dump station. Fees charged.

Recreation: picnic areas and playgrounds, 12 miles of multi-use trails (hiking, biking, horses), 5 miles of hiking and nature trails, rock climbing and rappelling, swimming in lake, fishing with 6 piers (one lighted), boating (15-mph speed limit), boat ramp, boat rentals. Jet skis, water skiing, and tubing are not allowed.

MAIN ATTRACTIONS

The 646-acre Lake Mineral Wells offers fishing, swimming, and boating. Separate hiking and horseback-riding trails traverse the deep canyons and wooded hills of the park.

In the early 1900s, Mineral Wells was a nationally famous health spa. The mineral water was first discovered in 1885 in the Crazy Well, at what is now the intersection of U.S. 281 and 180. The waters, containing sodium sulfate, chlorides, magnesium, and calcium, were believed to cure a long list of illnesses. In 1934, there were 150 commercial wells in operation in Mineral Wells. The large Baker Resort Hotel, now abandoned, is an example of the affluence that once graced the town.

HIKING, MOUNTAIN BIKING, AND HORSEBACK RIDING

The hiking, biking, and equestrian trails begin at the end of the paved road. An equestrian campground is located at the trailhead for the 8.5-mile horseback-riding loop. For hikers and backpackers, there is a primitive camping area without water at the end of the hiking trail. Obtain permits and information at the park entrance.

ECOLOGY

The 2,853-acre park features steep hills overlooking the scenic lake, deep ravines, and open savannas. Post oaks and blackjack oaks are scattered through the savannas, and the ravines are heavily wooded with pecans, cedar elms, cottonwoods, and red oaks. Ashe juniper, Texas oak, plateau live oak, mesquite, and hackberry trees are also abundant in the park.

Sand, clay, and gravel deposited more than 300 million years ago form the red, brown, and yellow sandstones, the conglomerate rocks, and the sandy soil of the park. An aquifer, or water-bearing stratum of rock, with mineral-rich water underlies the area.

100. LAKE O. C. FISHER

LOCATION

U.S. Army Corps of Engineers. Tom Green County. Project office: west of San Angelo on FM 2288.
Mailing address: 3900 Mercedes Road, San Angelo, Texas 76901-2630. Phone: 915-949-4757.

FACILITIES

Camping: 4 parks with campgrounds. Fees vary. Individual and group campsites at Dry Creek and Red Arroyo. Campsites may be reserved by calling 1-800-284-2267. Rangers patrol Dry Creek and Red Arroyo and lock the gates between 10 P.M. and 6 A.M.

Recreation: nature trail and bicycle and jogging trails at Red Arroyo Park, off-road-vehicle area, swimming, fishing, boat ramps, hunting.

LAKE O. C. FISHER

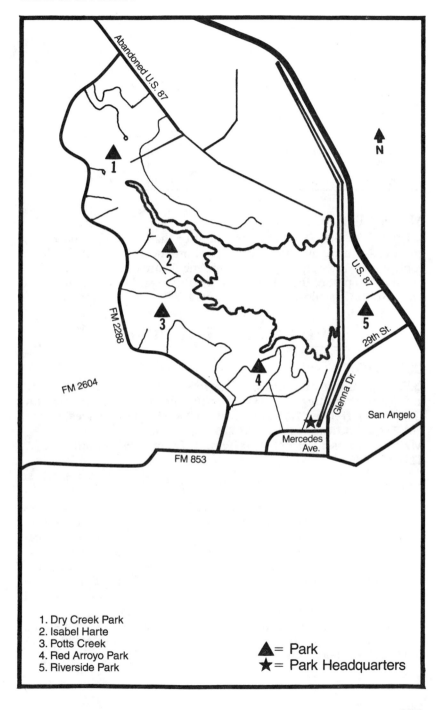

1. Dry Creek Park
2. Isabel Harte
3. Potts Creek
4. Red Arroyo Park
5. Riverside Park

▲ = Park
★ = Park Headquarters

Campground	water	fee area	flush toilets	season	dump station	showers	electricity
Dry Creek	•	•	•	all	•	•	•
Isabel Harte	•			all			
Potts Creek	•			all			
Red Arroyo	•	•	•	all	•	•	•

MAIN ATTRACTIONS

Lake O. C. Fisher, an impoundment of the North Concho River, covers 5,440 acres and has 27 miles of shoreline. It was built for flood control and water storage in the San Angelo area. Angelo State University uses part of the property for a wildlife and ranching research area. Hunting is allowed by permit on 4,000 acres of federal land.

101. LAKE O' THE PINES

LOCATION
U.S. Army Corps of Engineers. Marion, Upshur, Harrison, Camp, and Morris counties. Project office: 16 miles north of Marshall on U.S. 59 to Jefferson, 2.5 miles west on TX 49, 4.4 miles west on FM 729, 2.5 miles south on FM 726.
Mailing address: Drawer W, Jefferson, Texas 75657. Phone: 214-665-2336.

FACILITIES
Camping: Lake O' the Pines has 7 parks with campgrounds. Parks not listed on the matrix either do not have camping or have been closed. Some campsites are free; fees at others vary. Individual campsites may be reserved by calling 1-800-284-2267. Alley Creek and Johnson Creek have group campgrounds that can be reserved. A gate attendant is on duty at Brushy Creek, Johnson Creek, Alley Creek, and Buckhorn Creek parks. Rangers patrol those parks, and the gates are closed from 11 P.M. to 6 A.M.

Recreation: exhibits at project office, swimming in lake, fishing, boat ramps, water sports, marinas, hunting, amphitheater at Johnson Creek Recreation Area for summer films.

Campground	water	fee area	flush toilets	season	dump station	showers	electricity
Alley Creek	•	•	•	Mar.–Sept.	•	•	•
Brushy Creek	•	•	•	all	•	•	•
Buckhorn Creek	•	•	•	Mar.–Sept.	•	•	•
Cedar Springs	•			all	•		
Hurricane Creek	•		•	all			
Johnson Creek	•	•	•	all	•	•	•
Oak Valley	•			all			

MAIN ATTRACTIONS

Built on Cypress Creek for flood control and water storage, the lake covers 18,700 surface acres at a normal level; it has 144 miles of shoreline. White crappie, largemouth bass, spotted bass, and bluegill sunfish are common catches. Hunting is allowed on part of the property.

Lake O' the Pines is in the Piney Woods of East Texas. The shore is heavily forested with loblolly pines and a variety of oaks and other hardwoods. The diverse vegetation, varying from the well-draining uplands to creek bottoms and the open lake, supports an abundant population of wildlife, especially birds. Located on the Central Flyway, the area attracts many migrating songbirds in the spring and fall as well as waterfowl in the winter. A checklist of the birds is available at the project office.

HISTORY

Archaeological surveys conducted in the reservoir area have uncovered numerous artifacts from the various tribes collectively known as the Caddo Indians. In 1541, the first Europeans explored what is now East Texas and found the Caddos, a culturally advanced confederation of tribes. They were originally very cordial to Europeans but later rebelled against the depredations inflicted upon them by the Spanish.

In 1835, the Caddos were forced to sign a treaty in which they ceded all their lands, which had been included in the Louisiana Purchase in 1803, to the U.S. government. They were forced to move at their own expense beyond the borders of the United States to Texas.

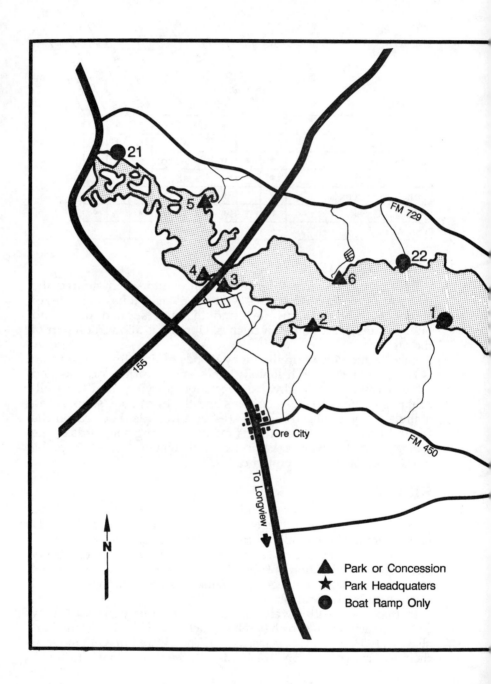

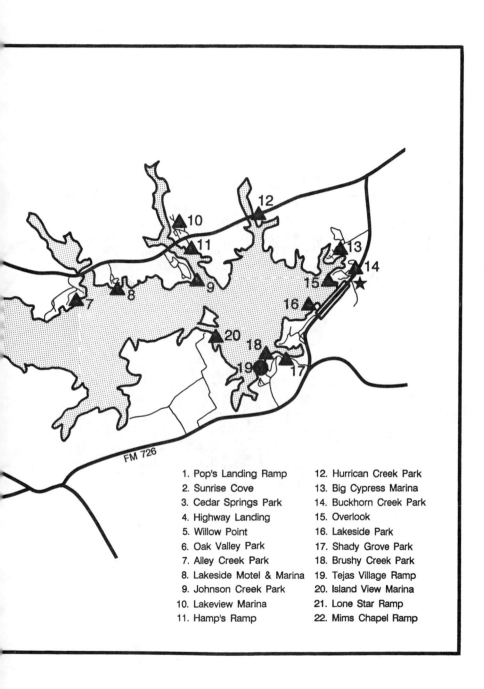

1. Pop's Landing Ramp
2. Sunrise Cove
3. Cedar Springs Park
4. Highway Landing
5. Willow Point
6. Oak Valley Park
7. Alley Creek Park
8. Lakeside Motel & Marina
9. Johnson Creek Park
10. Lakeview Marina
11. Hamp's Ramp
12. Hurrican Creek Park
13. Big Cypress Marina
14. Buckhorn Creek Park
15. Overlook
16. Lakeside Park
17. Shady Grove Park
18. Brushy Creek Park
19. Tejas Village Ramp
20. Island View Marina
21. Lone Star Ramp
22. Mims Chapel Ramp

The Caddos found no peace in Texas, and after Texas gained its independence from Mexico they were driven into Oklahoma. East Texas is rich in the archaeological heritage of those inhabitants of the Piney Woods.

Jefferson, ten miles east of the lake, has many beautifully reconstructed buildings from the mid 1800s. Before railroads crossed the state, the town was the main port of entry for East Texas. Steamboats carried goods down Big Cypress Bayou to the Red River, which connected with the Mississippi and New Orleans. Restored buildings and museums in Jefferson depict the rich history of the area.

102. LAKE PAT MAYSE

LOCATION
U.S. Army Corps of Engineers. Lamar County. Project office: 12 miles north of Paris on U.S. 271 past Powderly, west on FM 906. Mailing address: P.O. Box 129, Powderly, Texas 75473-0129. Phone: 214-732-3020.

Campground	water	fee area	flush toilets	season	dump station	hot-water showers
Lamar Point	•	•		all	•	
Pat Mayse East	•	•		all	•	
Pat Mayse West	•	•	•	all	•	•
Sanders Cove	•	•	•	all	•	•

FACILITIES
Camping: Lake Pat Mayse has campgrounds at 4 parks. Fees are charged.

Recreation: picnicking, nature trails, swimming, water sports, fishing, boat ramps, hunting.

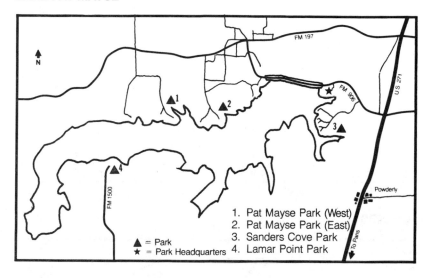

1. Pat Mayse Park (West)
2. Pat Mayse Park (East)
3. Sanders Cove Park
4. Lamar Point Park

▲ = Park
★ = Park Headquarters

MAIN ATTRACTIONS

Lake Pat Mayse covers 5,990 acres and has 67 miles of shoreline. The park includes gently rolling grasslands and forests of oak, pine, elm, and hickory. The lake was formed by impounding Sanders Creek, a tributary of the Red River. Fishing is excellent in the lake, especially for largemouth and sand bass, white crappie, and channel and flathead catfish. Public hunting and hiking are permitted on the 14,925-acre wildlife management area. Game species include white-tailed deer, squirrels, quail, and doves.

Visitors to this area should look for historic homes in Paris. Also, Gambill Wildlife Refuge, northwest of Paris on FM 79, then west on FM 2820, is a good bird-watching area.

103. LAKE PROCTOR

LOCATION

U.S. Army Corps of Engineers. Comanche County. Project office: 5.5 miles northeast of Comanche on U.S. 377, 2 miles north on FM 2861.
Mailing address: Route 1, Box 71A, Comanche, Texas 76442.
Phone: 817-879-2498. For reservations, call 1-800-284-2267.

Campground	water	fee area	flush toilets	season	dump station	showers	electricity
Copperas Creek	•	•	•	all	•	•	•
High Point	•			all	•		
Promontory	•	•	•	all	•	•	•
Sowell Creek	•	•	•	all	•	•	•

LAKE PROCTOR

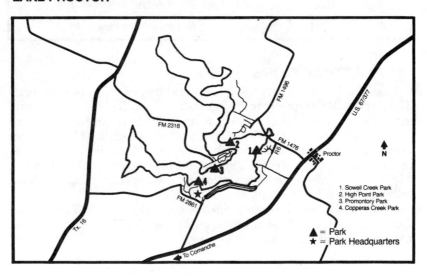

1. Sowell Creek Park
2. High Point Park
3. Promontory Park
4. Copperas Creek Park

▲ = Park
★ = Park Headquarters

FACILITIES

Camping: Lake Proctor has camping at 4 parks. Campsites in High Point Park are free; fees at others vary. Inquire about group camping areas at Copperas Creek, Sowell Creek, and Promontory parks.

Recreation: picnicking, swimming, fishing, water sports, boat ramps, hunting, amphitheater at Copperas Creek Park.

MAIN ATTRACTIONS

Built for flood control and water storage on the Leon River, the reservoir covers 4,610 acres and has 38 miles of shoreline. The lake is a prime spot for largemouth bass, as well as crappie and catfish. Early spring through June is the best time for fishing. Located on the Central Flyway, the lake is popular for waterfowl hunting. As many as 100,000 ducks may be seen on the lake during migration. Ask at the entrance facility or the project office for a brochure on fishing and hunting in the area.

The open meadows bordering the campgrounds are blanketed with colorful wildflowers in the spring. Ground squirrels and quail scurry through the bluebonnets and Indian paintbrushes, and meadowlarks crouch beside their dome nests of grass.

104. LAKE SAM RAYBURN

LOCATION

U.S. Army Corps of Engineers. Jasper, San Augustine, Nacogdoches, Sabine, and Angelina counties. East of Lufkin. Project office: southeast of Lufkin on TX 63, east on FM 255 to dam. Mailing address: Route 3, Box 486, Jasper, Texas 75951. Phone: 409-384-5716. For reservations, call 1-800-284-2267.

Cassells-Boykin County Park: 22 miles south of Lufkin on U.S. 69 to Zavalla, 4 miles east on TX 147 to FM 3123, turn north into park before reaching the bridge. Mailing address: P.O. Box 908, Lufkin, Texas 75902-0908. Phone: 409-632-5531. Camping: 10 multi-use paved sites, 17 primitive tent sites, restrooms, dump station; no water available.

FACILITIES

Camping: 14 parks on Sam Rayburn Reservoir with campgrounds. Marinas run by private concessions at Shirley Creek, Jackson Hill, Powell, and Twin Dikes offer camping areas with electric hookups. Shirley Creek and Powell parks have cabins and mobile home rentals. Parks not listed on the matrix do not have camping. Some campgrounds are free; others have fees. Individual campsites may not be reserved. Write the project headquarters for further information. Refer to Angelina National Forest for further information on parks operated by the U.S. Forest Service.

(Text continues on page 146)

LAKE SAM RAYBURN

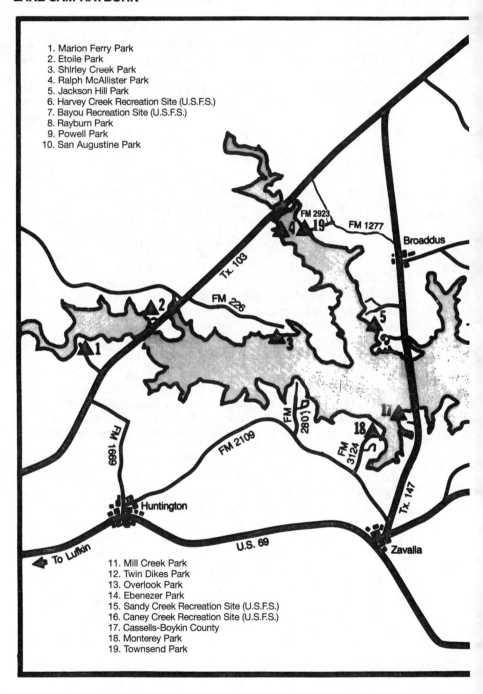

1. Marion Ferry Park
2. Etoile Park
3. Shirley Creek Park
4. Ralph McAllister Park
5. Jackson Hill Park
6. Harvey Creek Recreation Site (U.S.F.S.)
7. Bayou Recreation Site (U.S.F.S.)
8. Rayburn Park
9. Powell Park
10. San Augustine Park

11. Mill Creek Park
12. Twin Dikes Park
13. Overlook Park
14. Ebenezer Park
15. Sandy Creek Recreation Site (U.S.F.S.)
16. Caney Creek Recreation Site (U.S.F.S.)
17. Cassells-Boykin County
18. Monterey Park
19. Townsend Park

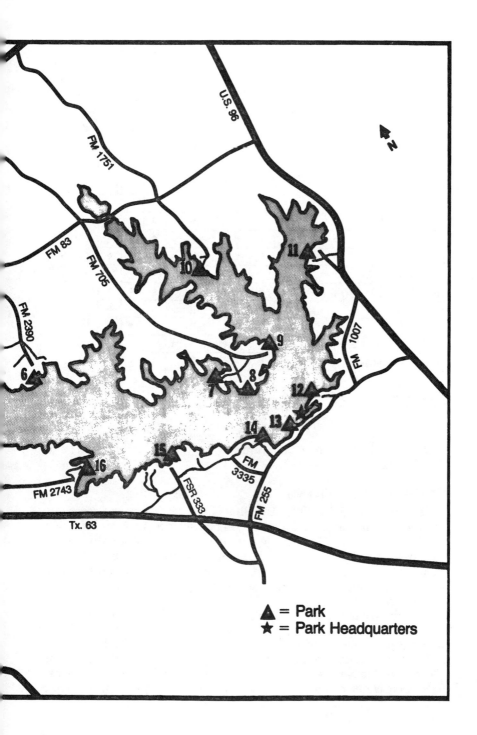

▲ = Park
★ = Park Headquarters

(*Text continued from page 143*)

Campground	water	fee area	flush toilets	season	dump station	cold-water showers	electricity
Cassells-Boykin	•	•	•	all	•		
Ebenezer	•			all			
Etoile	•			all			
Jackson Hill	•	•		all	•	•	•
Mill Creek	•	•	•	all	•	•	•
Powell	•	•	•	all	•	•	•
Rayburn	•			all	•		
San Augustine	•	•	•	all	•	•	•
Shirley Creek	•	•	•	all	•	•	•
Twin Dikes	•	•	•	all	•	•	•
Sandy Creek (USFS)	•	•	•	Mar.–Sept.		•	
Caney Creek (USFS)	•	•	•	all	•	•	
Harvey Creek (USFS)		•		all			
Townsend Park (USFS)	•	•		all		•	

Recreation: picnic area, boat ramp, water related activities on Lake Sam Rayburn. Fees charged. Open all year.

MAIN ATTRACTIONS

The lake, formed on the Angelina River, is the largest reservoir entirely within the state. It covers 114,500 surface acres and has 560 miles of shoreline; its average depth is 25 feet. Originally called McGee Bend, the reservoir was renamed in 1963 to honor the late House Speaker, Sam Rayburn, from Bonham. In addition to flood control and water storage, the dam serves as a source of hydroelectric power.

Fishermen can expect excellent catches, including largemouth bass, both black and white bass, walleye pike, striped bass, Florida bass, and bream. Squirrel and waterfowl hunting is popular in the area.

The lake, located in the midst of Angelina National Forest, has a red-and-white-sand shoreline heavily wooded with pines and oaks. The open water of the lake attracts many waterfowl in the winter, and the numerous wooded inlets provide ideal habitats for wading birds and shorebirds. Gulls, terns, and occasionally a bald eagle or an osprey can be seen flying over the lake. During the spring and fall, the forest is a stopover for many species of migrating songbirds.

Archaeological surveys of the area have uncovered dozens of ancient campsites and at least one large village site. It is believed that the region was occupied over the past thousand years by at least five distinct cultural groups, including some Caddoan groups. There is evidence that numerous tribes lived in the area around 1650, and the Cherokees occupied the land from about 1828 to 1839.

105. LAKE SOMERVILLE (CORPS OF ENGINEERS PARKS)

LOCATION
U.S. Army Corps of Engineers. Burleson, Lee, and Washington counties. Project office: 14 miles northwest of Brenham on TX 36, half mile west of Somerville.

Campground	water	fee area	flush toilets	season	dump station	showers	electricity
Yegua Creek	•	•	•	all	•	•	•
Big Creek	•	•	•	all	•	•	•
Overlook	•	•	•	all	•	•	•
Rocky Cove	•	•	•	all	•	•	•
Welch Park	•	•	•	all		•	

Mailing address: Box 549, Somerville, Texas 77879.
Phone: 409-596-1622. For reservations, call 1-800-284-2267.

FACILITIES
Camping: 4 parks with Corps-operated campgrounds on Lake Somerville. Write the project office for information on the group camping area at Rocky Creek Park. Welch Park is a primitive camping area run by the city of Somerville. Lake Somerville State Recre-

ation Area has 2 units, on opposite shores, with camping (see separate listing). Fees vary.

Recreation: nature trail, equestrian trail, swimming and fishing in lake, boat ramps, water sports, hunting, marinas at Overlook and Big Creek parks with stores, piers, boat rentals, cabins, and campsites.

LAKE SOMERVILLE

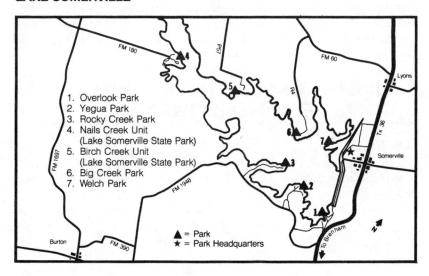

1. Overlook Park
2. Yegua Park
3. Rocky Creek Park
4. Nails Creek Unit
   (Lake Somerville State Park)
5. Birch Creek Unit
   (Lake Somerville State Park)
6. Big Creek Park
7. Welch Park

▲ = Park
★ = Park Headquarters

MAIN ATTRACTIONS

The lake, built on Yegua Creek, a tributary of the Brazos River, provides flood control and water storage for the area. At nonflood levels, the lake covers 11,460 acres and has 85 miles of sandy shoreline. Fishing is good for largemouth bass, white bass, channel catfish, and white crappie. Hunting is allowed on 3,500 acres leased by the Texas Parks and Wildlife Department.

Yegua Creek and Big Creek parks have short nature trails leading through post oak, live oak, mesquite, and eastern red cedar. In the summer, the fields are carpeted with colorful wildflowers, such as coreopsis, Indian blankets, and winecups. Quail, meadowlarks, and ground squirrels going to and from their nests dart through the fragrant flowers.

LAKE SOMERVILLE STATE PARK

LOCATION

Refer to map with Lake Somerville, Corps of Engineers parks.

Birch Creek Unit: 25 miles southwest of Bryan on FM 60, 8 miles southwest of Lyons on FM 60, south on PR 57. Mailing address: Route 1, Box 499, Somerville, Texas 77879. Phone: 409-535-7763.

Nails Creek Unit: 29 miles west of Brenham on U.S. 290, 13 miles north on FM 180. Mailing address: Route 1, Box 61C, Ledbetter, Texas 78946. Phone: 409-289-2392. For all state park reservations, call 512-389-8900.

FACILITIES

Camping: Birch Creek, primitive camping (50 sites) on a 13-mile hiking trail (no water), 103 campsites with water and electricity. Nails Creek, 40 campsites with water and electricity, 20 equestrian campsites with water at Nails Creek, group trailer area with dining hall at Birch Creek, modern restrooms with showers, trailer dump station. Fees charged.

Recreation: picnic areas and playgrounds, 29 miles of hiking and nature trails, interpretive exhibits, swimming in lake, fishing, boating, wheelchair access to facilities.

MAIN ATTRACTIONS

Lake Somerville, with 11,460 acres, is popular for boating, water sports, swimming, and fishing. Catches of largemouth bass, white bass, channel catfish, and crappie are common. The tall oaks and gently sloping lakeshore provide a scenic setting for picnicking and camping, and the sandy beaches are good for swimming. The lake was formed in 1967 by impounding Yegua Creek 20 miles upstream from its confluence with the Brazos River. The 5,200-acre park was acquired in 1969 from the Army Corps of Engineers.

Nearby attractions include the University of Texas Winedale Museum, at Round Top on TX 237, which features early Texas architecture and furnishings. Washington-on-the-Brazos State Historical Park, a day-use area, is 21 miles northeast of Brenham on TX 105.

HIKING

In addition to the 640-acre Birch Creek Unit in Burleson County and the 300-acre Nails Creek Unit in Lee County, the park includes 4,260 acres of property connecting the two units. The backpacker or day hiker can enjoy 29 miles of hiking and nature trails in this area, including a 13-mile trail between the units. The Texas Parks and

Wildlife Department allows hunting in the wildlife management area adjacent to the 13-mile trail—do not camp in that area during hunting season.

ECOLOGY

The soil of the park was formed from weathered Yegua sandstone and clays from the Caddell formation deposited more than 42 million years ago. Petrified wood that is 40 million years old may be found in the park. The sandy soil supports a luxuriant growth of post and blackjack oak trees and dense stands of yaupon holly bushes.

Wildflowers are abundant throughout the spring and summer. The yellow heads of coreopsis, with their reddish centers, and white daisy-like fleabane decorate the roadsides. Bright yellow-and-red gaillardias, the delicate pink flowers of sensitive briers, and purple winecups add to the spring display of color.

The reservoir has created a variety of wildlife habitats in addition to the naturally occurring post oak and hickory woods, scattered grasslands, and bottomland forests. Waterfowl frequent the open waters, wading shorebirds the mud flats and marshes, and prairie species the cleared pasturelands.

Wildlife in the park is abundant. White-tailed deer, armadillos, and rabbits are commonly seen, especially at dusk, while foxes, coyotes, and raccoons are more secretive. Many species of water birds are attracted to the lake. In the winter, olivaceous cormorants are common, and bald eagles and ospreys are occasionally sighted. The habitats around the lake attract more than 260 species of birds. A checklist is available at the park entrance.

106. LAKE STILLHOUSE HOLLOW

LOCATION

U.S. Army Corps of Engineers. Bell County. 9 miles southwest of Temple on IH-35 to Belton, 4 miles west on U.S. 190. Project office: 3 miles west of Belton on U.S. 190, 2 miles south on FM 1670.
Mailing address: 99 FM 2271, Belton, Texas 76513. Phone: 817-939-1829. For reservations, call 1-800-284-2267.

FACILITIES

Camping: 3 Corps-operated parks on the lake with campgrounds. Some campsites are free; fees at others vary. Individual sites may be reserved. Parks not listed on the matrix do not have camping.

Recreation: picnicking, nature trail at Chalk Ridge Falls Park below the dam, exercise trail at Overlook Park, swimming at Stillhouse and Dana Peak parks, fishing, water sports, boat ramps, marina at Stillhouse Park, hunting.

Campground	water	fee area	flush toilets	season	dump station	cold-water showers	electricity
Dana Peak	•	•	•	all	•	•	•
Stillhouse	•		•	Apr.–Sept.		•	
Union Grove	•	•	•	all	•		•

MAIN ATTRACTIONS

Lake Stillhouse Hollow, on the Lampasas River, covers 6,430 acres at its normal level and has 58 miles of shoreline. The lake has more than one million visitors a year, primarily boaters and swimmers. Bird-watching is also popular. A large number of waterfowl can be seen in the winter, as well as an occasional osprey. Hunting is allowed on 4,381 acres of the wildlife management area.

LAKE STILLHOUSE HOLLOW

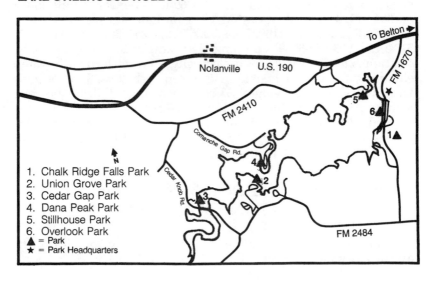

To Belton
Nolanville   U.S. 190   FM 1670
FM 2410
Comanche Gap Rd.
Cedar Knob Rd.
N
1. Chalk Ridge Falls Park
2. Union Grove Park
3. Cedar Gap Park
4. Dana Peak Park
5. Stillhouse Park
6. Overlook Park
▲ = Park
★ = Park Headquarters
FM 2484

107. LAKE TAWAKONI STATE PARK

LOCATION
Hunt County. 50 miles east of Dallas on U.S. 80 to Wills Point, north on FM 47, north on FM 2475 to White Deer Landing Rd. Mailing address: c/o Public Lands Region 8, 1638 Park Rd. 16, Tyler, Texas 75706-9132. Phone: 903-595-2938.

FACILITIES
As of early 1995, this park is undeveloped and open only by guided tour from Purtis Creek State Park. Proposed facilities include 68 campsites with water and electricity, 15 screened shelters, restrooms, showers, trailer dump station.

MAIN ATTRACTIONS
Situated with 5 miles of shoreline on the south side of the 36,700-acre Lake Tawakoni, this park offers visitors a variety of water-oriented activities. The 400-acre park also has a half-mile nature trail and ample day-use picnicking and playground areas. The Sabine River Authority operates day-use parks on the lake.

LAKE TAWAKONI: WIND POINT PARK

Sabine River Authority. Hunt County. 51 miles northeast of Dallas on U.S. 67, 15 miles southeast on U.S. 69 to Lone Oak, 1 mile south on FM 513, 4 miles west on FM 1571, on Lake Tawakoni. Mailing address: Route 1, Box 1100, Lone Oak, Texas 75453. Phone: 903-662-5134; fax: 903-662-5749. Camping: 140 campsites with water only, 103 campsites with water and electricity, 70 campsites with water, electricity, and sewage hookups; 15 screened shelters, 8 cabins with kitchenettes, 2 group lodges with kitchen, flush toilets, showers, laundromat, trailer dump station. Reservations accepted. Fees charged. Recreation: picnic areas and playgrounds, baseball diamonds, nature trail, swimming, 300-foot lighted fishing pier, boat ramps, marina, store. Open all year.

108. LAKE TEXANA: BRACKENRIDGE PLANTATION CAMPGROUND

Lavaca-Navidad River Authority. Jackson County. 25 miles northeast of Victoria on U.S. 59 to Edna, 6 miles east on TX 111. 250 acres on Lake Texana. Mailing address: Box 429, Edna, Texas 77957. Phone: 512-782-5229. Camping: 18 campsites with water and electricity, 82 campsites with water, electricity, and sewage hookups; group campsite with all hookups; flush toilets, showers, trailer dump station. Reservations accepted. Fees charged. Recreation: picnic areas, hiking trails, swimming in reservoir, fishing, water-skiing, boat ramp, marina, playground, golf course nearby, pavilion, store. Open all year. Good facilities. The park is located on the site of the old town of Texana.

LAKE TEXANA: MUSTANG WILDERNESS PARK

Lavaca-Navidad River Authority. Jackson County. 30 miles northeast of Victoria on U.S. 59. From U.S. 59, exit Loop 522 at Ganado, west 1 mile to FM 2982, south 2.1 miles, left on County Road 249 to park entrance. 250 acres on Lake Texana. Mailing address; Box 429, Edna, Texas 77957. Phone: 512-782-5229. Camping: 29 primitive campsites, which you must hike to; no water, tables, or restrooms. Fees charged. Recreation: 5 miles of hiking trails, fishing, boating, boat ramp. Open all year.

LAKE TEXANA STATE PARK

LOCATION
Jackson County. 25 miles northeast of Victoria on U.S. 59 to Edna, 6 miles east on TX 111.
Mailing address: Box 760, Edna, Texas 77957-0760. Phone: 512-782-5718. For all state park reservations, call 512-389-8900.

FACILITIES
Camping: 55 campsites with water only, 86 campsites with water and electricity, modern restrooms with showers, trailer dump station. Fees charged.
Recreation: picnic areas and playgrounds, swimming in lake, fishing, with 2 lighted piers, boating, pavilion.

MAIN ATTRACTIONS
The park is located on the shores of Lake Texana, an impoundment of the Navidad River. The lake, with 11,000 surface acres and 125 miles of shoreline, is suitable for all water sports, including boat-

ing, canoeing, fishing, and swimming. There are three fishing piers, and catches of crappie, sunfish, bass, and catfish are common.

The 575-acre park is on the Gulf Coast prairie in the wooded Navidad River bottom. Large live oaks, hackberries, elms, and pecans shade the camping and picnicking areas. Numerous hawks spend the winter along the shores of the lake. Many waterfowl and shorebirds can be seen on the lake, and deer, armadillos, rabbits, and squirrels are common.

Lake Texana is named after the extinct town of Texana, which was located below the dam. This county seat was an important shipping and trading center until 1880, when its citizens refused to vote financial support to a railroad between Rosenberg and Victoria. The railroad company established Edna 8 miles west of Texana, and within three years the county seat was transferred and Texana ceased to exist.

109. LAKE TEXOMA

LOCATION
U.S. Army Corps of Engineers. Grayson and Cooke counties.
Project office: 3.5 miles north of Denison on TX 75A.
Mailing address: Route 4, Box 493, Denison, Texas 75020. Phone: 903-465-4990.

FACILITIES
Camping: See the matrix for parks with camping. Preston Bend and Juniper Point have gate attendants, with gates open from 6 A.M. to 10 P.M. There is free primitive camping on the Cross Timbers Hiking Trail.

Recreation: picnicking, hiking on the Cross Timbers Hiking Trail, swimming, water sports, fishing, boat ramps, hunting.

MAIN ATTRACTIONS
Built on the Red River, bordering Texas and Oklahoma, Lake Texoma is the tenth-largest reservoir in the United States. It serves as a flood control and water conservation facility and provides hydroelectric power to the surrounding area. Up to 70 megawatts of electricity can be generated by the power plant. Tours of the plant are offered in the afternoons.

At a normal level, the lake covers 89,000 acres and has 580 miles of shoreline. Denison Dam, a rolled earthfill dam 15,200 feet long, is the twelfth largest in volume in the United States. Eisenhower State

Campground	water	fee area	flush toilets	vault toilets	season	dump station	showers	electricity	swimming beach	cabins
Big Mineral	•	•		•	summer	•			•	•
Dam Site	•	•	•	•	summer	•	•	•		
Flowing Wells	•	•		•	summer					
Juniper Point	•	•	•		summer	•	•	•		
Mill Creek	•	•	•	•	summer					
Preston Bend	•	•	•		summer	•	•	•		
Preston Fishing Camp	•	•	•		summer	•	•	•		•
Cedar Mills	•	•		•		•				•
Paradise Cove	•	•	•	•		•	•	•		
Paw Paw Creek	•	•	•	•	all		•	•		•
Rock Creek	•	•	•	•		•		•		•
Walnut Creek	•	•	•		all	•	•	•		•

Park, Hagerman National Wildlife Refuge, and Tishomingo National Wildlife Refuge in Oklahoma are also on the reservoir.

Lake Texoma is one of the most popular Corps of Engineers lakes in the country. Several privately operated facilities for boat storage and overnight accommodations are available. Large striped bass may be caught in the lake, along with crappie, white bass, black bass, catfish, and sunfish. Wildlife management projects provide hunting areas. Separate hunting and fishing licenses are required for Texas and Oklahoma, but a special fishing license is available for those fishing only in the lake.

HIKING

The 14-mile-long Cross Timbers Hiking Trail meanders through Juniper Point, Cedar Bayou, Paw Paw Creek, and Rock Creek parks. In addition to those sites, hikers may camp at the primitive sites along the trail. Wilderness camping permits and maps are available at the dam headquarters. The trail brochure covers some of the history and plant and animal life of the Cross Timbers vegetation zone of Texas.

LAKE TEXOMA

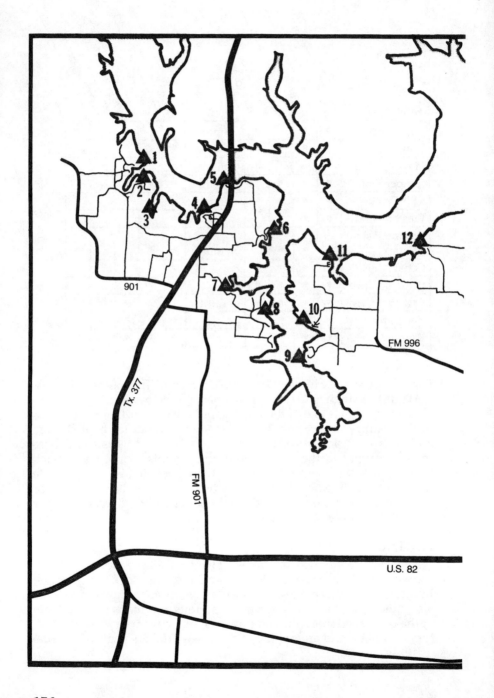

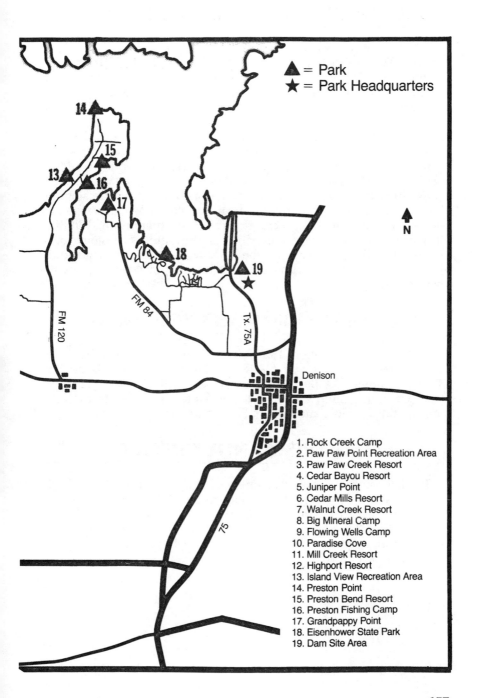

▲ = Park
★ = Park Headquarters

14 ▲
15 ▲
13 ▲ ▲ 16
▲ 17
▲ 18
▲ 19
★

N

FM 120
FM 84
Tx. 75A

Denison

75

1. Rock Creek Camp
2. Paw Paw Point Recreation Area
3. Paw Paw Creek Resort
4. Cedar Bayou Resort
5. Juniper Point
6. Cedar Mills Resort
7. Walnut Creek Resort
8. Big Mineral Camp
9. Flowing Wells Camp
10. Paradise Cove
11. Mill Creek Resort
12. Highport Resort
13. Island View Recreation Area
14. Preston Point
15. Preston Bend Resort
16. Preston Fishing Camp
17. Grandpappy Point
18. Eisenhower State Park
19. Dam Site Area

157

110. LAKE TRAVIS: PACE BEND PARK

Travis County. Location: 30 miles west of Austin on U.S. 71, right on FM 2322, 4 miles to park entrance. Address: 2701 FM 2322, Spicewood, Texas 78669. Phone: 512-264-1482. Administered by Travis County Parks, Box 1748, Austin, Texas 78767. Phone: 512-473-9437.

Camping: 20 sites with water, electricity, restrooms, showers, dump station, reservations accepted; 419 primitive sites with no facilities. Fees charged. Open all year. Primitive camping (tables, toilets) is also available at Arkansas Bend and Cypress Creek parks.

Recreation: the park encompasses 1,520 acres on a four-mile-long peninsula on Lake Travis. The rugged park features scenic limestone cliffs dropping straight into the water, as well as gentle sloping beaches ideal for swimming and boating. No roads cut across the mile-wide, two-mile-long central area of the peninsula. Wildlife thrives in the oak-juniper woodlands and mesquite-bluestem grass savannas of the central area of the park, while the bordering shorelines receive heavy recreational use. Archaeological sites are presently in review.

LAKE TRAVIS: MANSFIELD DAM

Travis County. Location: 13.5 miles west of Austin on U.S. 183, or 9 miles west on U.S. 71, then take Loop 620 to dam. Administered by Travis County Parks, Box 1748, Austin, Texas 78767. Phone: 512-473-9437. Camping: camp sites with tables, water, flush toilets; picnicking, boating, fishing, and hiking. Fees charged, open all year.

LAKE TRAVIS: SANDY CREEK PARK

Travis County. Location: 13 miles west of Austin on U.S. 183, 2 miles west on FM 1431, 7 miles south to Lime Creek Road. Administered by Travis County Parks, Box 1748, Austin, Texas 78767. Phone: 512-473-9437. Camping: camp sites with tables, water, flush toilets, dump station; picnicking, boating, fishing, and hiking. Fees charged. Open all year.

112. LAKE WACO

LOCATION

U.S. Army Corps of Engineers. McLennan County. Project office: west of Waco on FM 1637.

Mailing address: Route 10, Box 173G, Waco, Texas 76708. Phone: 817-756-5359. For reservations, call 1-800-284-2267.

Campground	water	fee area	flush toilets	season	dump station	cold-water showers	electricity
Airport	•	•		all	•	•	•
Speegleville I	•	•		all	•	•	•
Speegleville III	•	•		all	•	•	•
Midway	•			all			

LAKE WACO

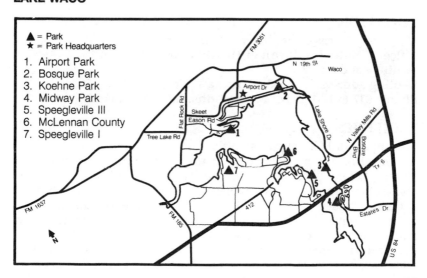

▲ = Park
★ = Park Headquarters

1. Airport Park
2. Bosque Park
3. Koehne Park
4. Midway Park
5. Speegleville III
6. McLennan County
7. Speegleville I

FACILITIES

Camping: Lake Waco has Corps of Engineers campgrounds at 4 parks. Fees vary. Three group sites may be reserved.

At Airport Park, obtain the key for the campgrounds and showers from the gatekeeper.

Speegleville I Park has camping only; it is not a day-use area. Inquire about group camping.

Recreation: picnic and swimming areas at Airport Park, fishing, water sports, boat ramps, marinas at Airport and Speegleville III parks, hunting, amphitheater at Speegleville I Park with summer programs on Saturday nights.

MAIN ATTRACTIONS

Built for flood protection and water storage for the city of Waco and nearby areas, Lake Waco covers 7,240 acres at its normal level and has 60 miles of shoreline. The lake is heavily used by residents of Waco and the surrounding area for fishing, boating, and swimming—each year, more than 3 million people visit the park. Hunting is permitted on 3,000 acres by permit only.

112. LAKE WHITNEY (CORPS OF ENGINEERS PARKS)

LOCATION

U.S. Army Corps of Engineers. Bosque and Hill counties. Project office: 18 miles southwest of Hillsboro on TX 22, south of Whitney at dam.
Mailing address: Box 5038, Laguna Park, Texas 76634-5038.
Phone: 817-694-3189. For reservations, call 1-800-284-2267.

FACILITIES

Camping: 10 Corps parks on the lake with campgrounds. Parks not listed on the matrix either do not have camping areas or are closed. Lofers Bend, McCown Valley, and Cedron Creek have attendants on duty, and entrance is limited to campers. The park gates are closed from 10 P.M. to 6 A.M. Soldiers Bluff also has restricted entry. Cedron Creek, Lofers Bend, and McCown Valley have wheelchair access to some facilities. Water to the parks may be cut off during freezes. Some campsites are free; fees at others vary. Sites may be reserved. Juniper Cove Marina, 817-694-3129, is operated by a concessionaire.

Recreation: picnicking, nature trail with trail-guide pamphlet at Lofers Bend Park, swimming, fishing, boat ramps at all but Soldiers Bluff, marina at Lofers Bend park, hunting.

Campground	water	fee area	flush toilets	season	dump station	cold-water showers	electricity
Cedar Creek	•			all			
Cedron Creek	•	•	•	Mar.–Oct.	•	•	•
Kimball Bend	•			all			
Lofers Bend	•	•	•	Mar.–Oct.	•	•	•
Plowman Creek	•	•	•	all	•	•	•
Riverside	•			all			
Soldiers Bluff	•			all			
Steeles Creek	•			all			
Walling Bend	•			all			
McCown Valley	•	•	•	all	•	•	•
Juniper Cove Marina	•	•	•	all	•	•	•

MAIN ATTRACTIONS

Lake Whitney was built to control flooding on the Brazos River, to generate hydroelectric power, and to act as a reservoir for the local water supply. The lake covers 23,550 acres at a normal level and has 190 miles of shoreline; hunting is permitted on 14,000 acres. Check with project office for permits and details. More than 2 million people visit the lake each year.

ECOLOGY

The rolling hills around the lake consist of grasslands and scattered patches of elm, oak, and hickory woodlands. Though the area had more woodlands before the trees were cut for farms and pastureland, the overall vegetation has not changed much in the past few hundred years. Overgrazing has resulted in the encroachment of prickly pear, broomweed, and mesquite in the pastures. On the edges of the lake, live oaks, junipers, post oaks, and cedar elms dominate, with occasional osage oranges, cottonwoods, and pecans.

Deer, raccoons, armadillos, and squirrels are common to the lake woodlands, and a wide variety of birds frequent the area. Bison, antelope, bear, javelina, and beaver were once abundant but have been eliminated since the coming of the pioneers to Texas.

LAKE WHITNEY

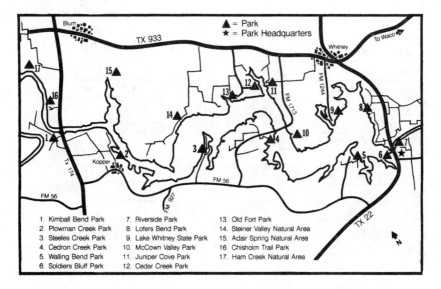

1. Kimball Bend Park
2. Plowman Creek Park
3. Steeles Creek Park
4. Cedron Creek Park
5. Walling Bend Park
6. Soldiers Bluff Park
7. Riverside Park
8. Lofers Bend Park
9. Lake Whitney State Park
10. McCown Valley Park
11. Juniper Cove Park
12. Cedar Creek Park
13. Old Fort Park
14. Steiner Valley Natural Area
15. Adair Spring Natural Area
16. Chisholm Trail Park
17. Ham Creek Natural Area

HISTORY

Before the land was flooded by Lake Whitney, an archaeological survey was conducted by the Smithsonian Institution in cooperation with the University of Texas. In studies conducted between 1947 and 1950, more than 70 sites of ancient human occupation were documented. The 9 sites that were thoroughly excavated supplied evidence that this area had been occupied by various native American groups from approximately 1000 B.C. to the nineteenth century A.D.

Pictographs in one of the rock shelters show abstract human forms in red pigment. They may have been drawn by groups living in the shelter more than a thousand years ago. In the 1770s, the Tawakonis resided on the land now covered by the lake. In the mid 1800s, at least three different tribes lived in the area; they were removed to reservations in 1869. One tribe, a Choctaw group, camped in what is now Lofers Bend Park.

LAKE WHITNEY STATE PARK

LOCATION
Hill County. 18 miles southwest of Hillsboro on TX 22 to Whitney, 4 miles west on FM 1244, on the east side of Lake Whitney. See map with Lake Whitney, Corps of Engineers Parks. Mailing address: Box 1175, Whitney, Texas 76692. Phone: 817-694-3793. For all state park reservations, call 512-389-8900.

FACILITIES
Camping: 71 campsites with water only, 31 campsites with water and electricity, 35 campsites with water, electricity, and sewage hookups; 21 screened shelters; group facility with 8 screened shelters, kitchen, and dining hall; modern restrooms with showers, trailer dump station. Fees charged.

Recreation: picnic areas and playgrounds, short trails along edge of lake, minibike trail, swimming in lake, fishing, boating, 2,000-foot unlighted airstrip, recreation hall.

MAIN ATTRACTIONS
The 15,760-acre Lake Whitney has more than 250 miles of scenic shoreline, ranging from steep cliffs to sandy beaches. The gradually sloping shores of the lake are pleasant for swimming. Fishing, boating, and water sports are the primary activities of park visitors.

ECOLOGY
The 955-acre park is on a peninsula predominantly composed of grasslands and old field vegetation. Elm-hackberry woodlands occur along the lakeshore and drainages of Whitney and Frazier creeks. The common trees are cedar elm, hackberry, pecan, live oak, post oak, cottonwood, and mesquite. The prairies in the park and around the lake come to life each spring with thousands of wildflowers—bluebonnets and Indian paintbrushes cover the rolling hills with a blanket of color that seems to merge with the sky-blue water of the lake.

Almost 200 species of birds have been sighted in the park, including many waterfowl, shorebirds, quail, hawks, swallows, warblers, orioles, and sparrows. A bird checklist is available. Deer, skunks, raccoons, cottontail rabbits, and armadillos are commonly seen, especially at dusk and dawn.

113. LAKE WRIGHT PATMAN

LOCATION

U.S. Army Corps of Engineers. Bowie and Cass counties. 8 miles southwest of Texarkana off U.S. 59. Project office: 10 miles north of Queen City off U.S. 59.
Mailing address: Box 1817, Texarkana, Texas 75501-1817. Phone: 903-838-8781. For reservations, call 1-800-284-2267.

Campground	water	fee area	flush toilets	vault toilets	season	dump station	showers	electricity
Clear Springs	•	•	•	•	all	•	•	•
Herron Creek	•			•	all			
Intake Hill	•			•	all	•		
Jackson Creek	•			•	all			
Malden Lake				•	all			
Rocky Point	•	•	•		all	•	•	•
Piney Point	•	•	•		Apr.–Oct.		•	•
Kelly Creek	•	•	•		all	•	•	•
Big Creek Landing	•	•		•	all			•

FACILITIES

Camping: Corps of Engineers-operated campgrounds at 7 of the parks on Wright Patman Lake. Fees at campgrounds vary. Individual sites may not be reserved. Big Creek, Paradise Cove, and Kelly Creek camping areas are operated by concessionaires. There is a group camping area at Clear Springs Park. Campsites at Atlanta State Park are on the south side of the reservoir.

Recreation: swimming and fishing in lake, boat ramps, water sports, hunting. Amphitheater, playground, and nature trail at Rocky Point Park.

MAIN ATTRACTIONS

The lake, originally named Lake Texarkana, was renamed in honor of Congressman Wright Patman in 1973. Formed by impounding the Sulphur River, it covers 33,750 surface acres and has 203 miles of shoreline and an average depth of 12 feet. Visitor use has increased yearly to more than 4 million in the last decade.

WRIGHT PATMAN LAKE

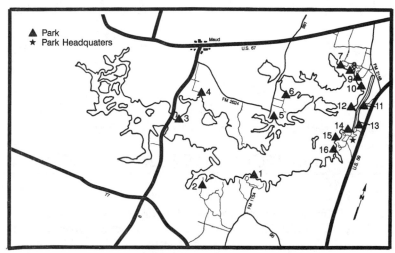

1. Atlanta State Park
2. Jackson Creek Park
3. Malden Lake Park
4. Herron Creek Park
5. Kelly Creek Park
6. Big Creek Park
7. Clear Springs Park
8. North Shore Park
9. Intake Hill Park
10. Paradise Cove
11. Oak Park
12. Elliot Blutt Park
13. Sulphur Point Park
14. Spillway Park
15. Piney Point Park
16. Rocky Point

ECOLOGY

The lake is near the Texas-Arkansas border in the East Texas Piney Woods. Pines and various oaks and other hardwoods are the dominant trees of the forested shoreline. Dogwood trees, scattered throughout the woodlands, bloom profusely in the spring.

Many wading birds and waterfowl, including loons, grebes, and ducks, overwinter on the large lake. Occasionally, a bald eagle or an osprey will be seen flying over the water hunting fish. During spring and fall migrations, warblers, swallows, and other birds find a welcome refuge in the rich woodlands.

114. LITTLEFIELD CITY OVERNIGHT PARK

Lamb County. In Littlefield, half mile north of U.S. 84 on U.S. 385 (Hall Ave.). Mailing address: P.O. Box 1267, Littlefield, Texas 79339. Phone: 806-385-5161. Camping: 36 RV sites with electricity and water, 8 include covered tables and sewage hookups. Free facility offered by the city for travelers needing an overnight stay. No reservations. Open all year.

115. LLANO CITY AND COUNTY PARKS

Llano County. 2 adjacent parks, 3 miles west of Llano on FM 152. Mailing address: Chamber of Commerce, 700 Bessemer, Llano, Texas 78643. Phone: 915-247-5354. Camping: 100 campsites with water, electricity, and sewage hookups; no tables, flush toilets nearby, primitive camping with tables and water nearby. No reservations. Fees charged for RV sites. Recreation: picnicking, playground, swimming pool, golf course, exercise trail, community center.

116. LOCKHART STATE PARK

LOCATION
Caldwell County. 2 miles southwest of Lockhart on FM 20. Mailing address: Route 3, Box 69, Lockhart, Texas 78644. Phone: 512-398-3479. For all state park reservations, call 512-389-8900.

FACILITIES
Camping: 10 campsites with water and electricity, 10 campsites with water, electricity, and sewage hookups; modern restrooms with showers. Fees charged.

Recreation: picnic areas and playgrounds, short trails, swimming pool (summer only), fishing in Clear Fork Creek, 9-hole golf course, court for basketball and volleyball, recreation hall.

MAIN ATTRACTIONS
This park has the distinction of having the only state-operated golf course—those in other parks are operated by concessionaires. The 9-hole, 3,000-yard, par-35 course was constructed in the thirties by the Civilian Conservation Corps. The course crosses Clear Fork Creek several times and borders rich bottomland forests near the creek and post oak woodlands along the hillsides.

The Battle of Plum Creek was fought near the park on August 11, 1840. A group of Texas rangers and volunteers attacked a band of Comanche warriors and their families. The Indians, who had repeatedly raided settlements during the summer months, were driven westward by their defeat.

ECOLOGY

The 263-acre park encompasses riparian woods, paralleling the Clear Fork of Plum Creek, and post oak woodlands, covering the rocky hillsides. The deeper soil deposited along the banks of the creek supports pecans, hackberries, and sycamores. Cardinals and white-throated sparrows dart through the brush bordering the creek, and the drill of woodpeckers resounds through the early-morning air.

In the fall, hundreds of cedar waxwings are attracted to the sweet berries of the hackberry trees. Robins flock to the yaupon hollies growing under the oaks and elms on the hills and devour the shiny red berries. In the spring, wildflowers blanket the streamside, and sunfish build their nests in the clear pools below several picturesque rock dams along the creek.

117. LOST MAPLES STATE NATURAL AREA

LOCATION

Bandera County. 48 miles west of Kerrville on TX 39, south on FM 187. 5 miles north of Vanderpool.
Mailing address: HC 01, Box 156, Vanderpool, Texas 78885. Phone: 210-966-3413. For all state park reservations, call 512-389-8900.

FACILITIES

Camping: 8 primitive camping areas with composting toilets on hiking trails, 30 campsites with water and electricity; modern restrooms with showers, trailer dump station. Fees charged.

Recreation: picnic areas and playgrounds, 10 miles of hiking trails, half-mile developed nature trail along the Sabinal River, interpretive exhibits, wading and limited swimming in river, fishing.

MAIN ATTRACTIONS

Lost Maples State Natural Area is famous for the bigtooth maple trees that grow in the protected Sabinal River Canyon and along tributary creeks. During late October and early November when climatic conditions have been favorable, the maples turn spectacular colors of scarlet, burgundy, and orange; up to 6,000 people may visit the park each weekend. If possible in the fall, plan weekday visits to avoid the crowds. The entrance facility houses excellent graphic exhibits on the maples and other aspects of the park's ecology. This beautiful and unique park is well worth a visit.

Prehistoric humans inhabited the Sabinal River Canyon more than 10,000 years ago, hunting the now extinct giant bison and mammoths. Later groups occupying the canyon left middens of heat-fractured stones, charcoal, and animal bones. Lipan and Mescalero Apaches, who displaced the earlier Tonkawas, raided Anglo settlers from bases within the canyon until the mid 1800s.

HIKING

Ten miles of hiking trails, marked for easy orientation, lead through the scenic Sabinal River Canyon and down fern-lined, spring-fed streams. There is no water on the trails; obtain information and trail maps from the ranger station. The designated primitive camping areas are located along the trails, some on high ridges, others on the shaded banks of winding streams. Some of the primitive camping areas are within 1 mile of the trailhead, and some are several miles farther. Lost Maples offers one of the most interesting hiking and backpacking opportunities in the state park system.

ECOLOGY

Nestled deep in the Central Texas Hill Country, Lost Maples consists of 2,174 acres of plateau grasslands, steep limestone canyons, and wooded slopes and bottomlands. The Sabinal River and other shallow, spring-fed streams cut canyons up to 300 feet deep through the rugged terrain. Numerous springs and seeps along the drainages support a rich diversity of plant and animal life.

The bigtooth maple trees, *Acer grandidentatum*, that grow in the park occur in isolated populations widely distributed throughout the western United States and northern Mexico. They require a fairly protected habitat of moderate temperature, humidity, and moisture. The Sabinal River Canyon in the park is the southeastern limit of the trees.

There is a noticeable diversity of plant life in the park, from the evergreen woodlands of the upper canyon slopes to the deciduous woods in the canyon bottoms. Grassy openings dominate the upland plateaus, with Ashe junipers and plateau live oaks occurring on the dry limestone slopes. Bigtooth maples, Texas and Lacey oaks, walnuts, and other deciduous trees and shrubs grow in the damper lower canyons.

The diverse conditions support more than 350 species of plants, many of which are unusual. Rare plants in the park include the spice-bush, sycamore-leaf snowbell, Texas barberry, canyon mockorange, crossvine, witch hazel, and Texas madrone.

A rich avian and mammal community adds to the natural splendor of the park. More than 200 species of birds have been recorded, including the golden-cheeked warbler, which nests only in Central Texas, black-capped vireo, green kingfisher, zone-tailed hawk, and golden and bald eagles; ask for a checklist at the park headquarters. The most often seen mammals are white-tailed deer, rock squirrels, and armadillos. Gray foxes, ringtails, bobcats and javelinas are common but seldom encountered. Occasionally, a porcupine or mountain lion is seen in the park.

The unusual variety of plant and animal life at Lost Maples is of such significance that the park was the first to be designated a state natural area. To merit that designation, an area must contain "prime examples of ecological systems, biological features, or geological formations of exceptional educational and scientific value." The designation allows for low-density use to protect the park's scenic beauty and natural features. Because of the shallow root system of the maples, compaction of the soil by hikers could damage these beautiful trees. That is one of the ecological factors that led to the decision to develop only about 4 percent of the total acreage of the park.

118. LUBBOCK: BUFFALO SPRINGS LAKE PARK

Lubbock County Water Control and Improvement District. Lubbock County. 5 miles southeast of Lubbock on FM 835. Mailing address: Route 10, Box 400, Lubbock, Texas 79404. Phone: 806-747-3353. Camping: campsites with no hookups, 36 campsites with water and electricity, 44 campsites with water, electricity, and sewage hookups; flush toilets, showers, trailer dump station. Fees charged. Recreation: picnic areas and playgrounds, hiking trails, horseback riding, fishing, boat ramps, marina, boat rentals, store, restaurant. Open all year. Good facilities.

119. LYNDON B. JOHNSON NATIONAL GRASSLAND

LOCATION
Wise County. 34 miles northwest of Fort Worth on U.S. 287 to Decatur, 4 miles north on FM 730, then 3 miles west on Red Deer Rd. to Clayborn Road, then a fourth mile to Portwood Road, north half mile to Forest Service Road 902, west to Black Creek Lake. Mailing address: Box 507, Decatur, Texas 76234. Phone: 817-627-5475.

FACILITIES
Camping: Black Creek Lake, 7 primitive campsites with water and pit toilets, unimproved camping available throughout grasslands. No fees charged.

Recreation: boating and fishing on Black Creek and Cottonwood lakes, hunting, horseback riding. A 4-mile hiking trail connects the two lakes.

MAIN ATTRACTIONS

The LBJ National Grassland covers 20,315 acres of oak savanna and grassland in Wise and Montague counties in numerous unconnected parcels. Tenant farmers and poor farming practices had turned this prairie land into exhausted farmland by the thirties. During the Dust Bowl era, the federal government bought up the wasted farms to demonstrate soil conservation principles and to show how the land could be used for grazing and recreational purposes. The grasslands are managed for cattle grazing, oil and gas production, watershed improvement, fishing, hunting, and other recreational pursuits. Game species include white-tailed deer, turkey, quail, squirrel, and rabbit. The lakes are stocked with bass, catfish, and bream. Horseback riding and hunting are the most popular activities in the grasslands.

LYNDON B. JOHNSON NATIONAL GRASSLAND

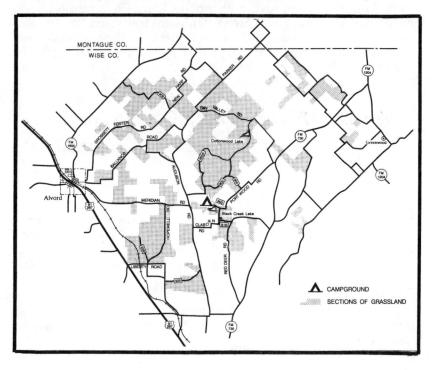

120. MARLIN: FALLS ON THE BRAZOS

Falls County. 28 miles southeast of Waco on TX 6 to Marlin, 4 miles southeast to FM 712, southwest to the Brazos River. Mailing address: Box 628, Marlin, Texas 76661. Phone: 817-883-3203. Camping: 6 campsites with water and electricity, 7 tent sites, flush toilets, trailer dump station. Reservations accepted. Fees charged. Recreation: picnic areas and playgrounds, fishing, boat ramp, pavilion, store. Open all year.

121. MARTIN CREEK LAKE STATE PARK

LOCATION
Rusk County. 25 miles south of Marshall on TX 43, south on FM 1716.
Mailing address: Route 2, Box 20, Tatum, Texas 75691. Phone: 903-836-4336. For all state park reservations, call 512-389-8900.

FACILITIES
Camping: 60 campsites with water and electricity, 21 screened shelters, group shelter, modern restrooms with showers, trailer dump station, primitive camping on island. Fees charged. The entrance gate is locked from 10 P.M. to 6 A.M.

Recreation: picnic areas, fishing pier, swimming, boating, hiking, playground, park store, bait, canoe rental.

MAIN ATTRACTIONS
This park preserves 286 acres of pine-hardwood forest along the shores of a lake impounded to cool a lignite-fired electric power plant. The beautiful woodlands are forested with a variety of oaks, sweetgum, elms, river birch, eastern red cedar, yaupon, and farkleberry. Nature trails lead through the dense woods, along a historic roadway, through creek bottoms, and around an island reached by a footbridge. Those who want to get away from the crowds can use the primitive camping and picnic area on the island. Visitors who come about the end of October have a special treat: the woods come alive with brilliant hues of red, yellow, and burgundy.

Birds and small animals abound in the park. Look for herons, egrets, and waterfowl along the shores and deer, rabbits, and squirrels in the woods. Fishermen catch largemouth bass, crappie, catfish, and sunfish in the 6,000-acre lake. Since the lake is artificially warmed by the power plant, fishing is good year-round.

HISTORY

The Caddo Indians historically occupied this part of the state. Later, displaced Choctaws, Cherokees, Kickapoos, and remnants of other tribes moved into the area, eventually to be exterminated or driven to Oklahoma. Part of an old Indian trail, later widened for wagons and named Trammel's Trace, runs through the park. The wagon road was a major route to Arkansas. Evidence of the roadbed still remains near the fishing pier.

122. MARTIN DIES, JR., STATE PARK

LOCATION

Jasper and Tyler counties. 50 miles east of Livingston on U.S. 190, on the east side of Lake B. A. Steinhagen.
Mailing address: Route 4, Box 274, Jasper, Texas 75951. Phone: 409-384-5231. For all state park reservations, call 512-389-8900.

FACILITIES

Camping: 68 campsites with water only, 115 campsites with water and electricity, 46 screened shelters, modern restrooms with showers, trailer dump station. Fees charged.

Recreation: picnic areas and playgrounds, short nature trails in Walnut Ridge and Hen House Ridge units, swimming in Lake B. A. Steinhagen at Hen House Ridge, 2 lighted fishing piers and cleaning stations, boat ramp, boat rentals, dining hall, convenience store nearby.

MAIN ATTRACTIONS

The 705-acre park, which preserves a prime example of deep East Texas beech woodlands, is located on the 13,000-acre Lake B. A. Steinhagen. Nature trails wind through the mixed pine-hardwood forests, around sloughs bordered by bald cypress, and along the lake. In the spring, the snowy blossoms of dogwood trees and magnolias decorate the woods; in the fall the leaves of beeches and maples thrill the visitor with their brilliant hues of gold, red, and burgundy.

The park is separated into three units: Cherokee, Walnut Ridge, and Hen House Ridge. The Cherokee Unit is on an island and is for day-use only. The campgrounds and other facilities are located in the other two units.

Fishing and boating are popular activities on the scenic lake. Catches include catfish, crappie, sunfish, and white, spotted, and largemouth bass.

Area attractions include the Big Thicket National Preserve Visitor Station, with interpretive programs and nature trails along scenic Village Creek, 25 miles south of Woodville off U.S. 69 on FM 420. Woodville is the home of the Dogwood Festival, held on the last Saturday in March.

ECOLOGY

Martin Dies, Jr., State Park, named after the senator who helped obtain funds for its formation, is situated in the Big Thicket area of the East Texas Piney Woods. The park is on an old river terrace in the alluvial floodplain of the Neches River. The rich bottomland soil supports a well-developed upper- and middle-story forest. Shallow sloughs leading into the lake reach through the woodlands like long fingers.

The floodplain forest hosts a wide variety of trees from towering pines, hickories, magnolias, and American hollies to the beautiful but smaller flowering dogwoods, silver bells, fringe trees, and redbuds. Bald cypress, tupelo, and moss-covered oak trees line the sloughs and shore. Approximately 60 species of trees grow in the rich environs of the park. Ask at the entrance for lists of the trees and birds found in the area.

Lake B. A. Steinhagen was formed when the Neches River was dammed just below its confluence with the Angelina River. The Neches River Corridor Unit of the Big Thicket National Preserve begins below the dam and extends all the way to Beaumont. The state park, the units of the national preserve, and private sanctuaries protect remnants representative of the complex woodlands that once formed the Big Thicket of East Texas, the biological crossroads of seven major ecological systems.

More than 350 species of birds occur in the area, and many are seen in the state park. The large pileated woodpecker, with its flaming red crest, darts noisily from tree to tree, while stately herons and egrets pace back and forth through the sloughs like ballet dancers in slow motion.

123. MASON: FORT MASON CITY PARK

Mason County. One-half mile south of Mason on U.S. 87. Mailing address: P.O. Box 68, Mason, Texas 76856. Phone: 915-347-6656. Camping: 11 sites with water, electricity, sewage hookups, 6 with water, electricity; dump station, hot showers. This 23-acre city park includes a community building, rodeo arena, playground, and pavilion. Fees charged, reservations accepted. Open all year.

124. MATAGORDA ISLAND STATE PARK

LOCATION
Calhoun County. 7 miles offshore from Port O'Connor, accessible only by boat.
Mainland mailing address: Box 117, Port O'Connor, Texas 77982.
Phone: 512-983-2215; no phone on the island.

FACILITIES
Camping: primitive camping on beach or bay side, pit toilets, rinse shower. NO drinking water, NO electricity, NO services.

Recreation: boat dock on bay side, swimming beach on gulf side of island, beachcombing, bird-watching, photography, fishing.

MAIN ATTRACTIONS
This state park provides the ultimate escape from civilization. If you want the "lost on a desert island" experience, charter a boat or take the weekend ferry to this 38-mile-long, 4-mile-wide barrier island. Before you leave, consider what is really necessary for survival in a hostile environment, because all you'll have is what you take. Besides your favorite novel, take plenty of water, sunscreen, insect repellent, and comfortable clothes. Pack light. If the ranger with the weekend park shuttle is not around, you'll have to walk the 1.5 miles from the bayside dock to the gulfside beach. And if you want shade, you'll have to take an umbrella.

The park has two designated campgrounds. Army Hole Campground is adjacent to the boat dock on the bayside. Beach Campground is 2.5 miles from the dock on the Gulf side of the island. Facilities at both are minimal but include covered picnic tables, and pit toilets. Army Hole has a cold-water shower.

Only the southern tip of the 24-mile island is not part of the combined state park and wildlife management area. The park contains 7,325 acres and 2 miles of beach, and the wildlife management area has 36,568 acres. The park is open all year, but access to the management area may be limited during hunting season. Dove, quail, and waterfowl hunting and regulated deer hunting from fixed stands are permitted in the management area. Between October and April, whooping cranes frequent the marshy areas of the island, which is across the bay from the Aransas National Wildlife Refuge.

125. McCLELLAN CREEK NATIONAL GRASSLAND/LAKE McCLELLAN

LOCATION

Gray County. 50 miles east of Amarillo on IH-40, 5 miles north on TX 70, 8 miles east on FM 2477.

Mailing address: Route 1, Box 55B, Cheyenne, Oklahoma 73628-9725. Phone: 405-497-2143.

FACILITIES

Camping: 8 campsites with water and electricity in North Shore Recreation Area. Fees charged. Open all year.

Recreation: picnicking, fishing, boating, store, hiking trail.

MAIN ATTRACTIONS

Fishing and boating on the 350-acre Lake McClellan are the main attractions of this park, managed by the U.S. Forest Service. Open grasslands and heavy woods provide a variety of habitats for quail, turkey, squirrels, deer, rabbits, and coyotes. Waterfowl frequent the lake, especially during spring and fall migrations, and bald eagles in the winter.

126. McKINNEY FALLS STATE PARK

LOCATION

Travis County. 7 miles southeast of Austin on U.S. 183, 2 miles west on Scenic Loop Rd. to McKinney Falls Parkway.

Mailing address: 5208 McKinney Falls Parkway, Austin, Texas 78744. Phone: 512-243-1643. For all state park reservations, call 512-389-8900.

FACILITIES

Camping: 14 campsites with water only, 70 campsites with water and electricity; group camp with dining hall, kitchen, and 6 screened shelters that hold 8 people each; modern restrooms with showers, trailer dump station. Fees charged.

Recreation: picnic areas and playgrounds, 3.5-mile hike and bike trail, three-quarter-mile nature trail with trail-guide booklet, interpretive exhibits, 18-hole golf course nearby, amphitheater.

MAIN ATTRACTIONS

The outstanding feature of the 949-acre park, only a 15-minute drive from Austin, is tree-lined Onion Creek and its two picturesque waterfalls. Shaded picnic areas and playgrounds are scattered along the 1.7 miles of winding shoreline. Ruins of nineteenth-century stone buildings, one of the first gristmills in Central Texas, and stone fences built with slave labor can be seen. Swimming is allowed in the creek seasonally when contaminants are in low concentration. However, McKinney Falls is one of the most attractive state parks in Texas.

HIKING

A 3.5-mile hike and bike trail runs along the creek, behind the campgrounds, and past the entrance facility. Artifacts of human occupation since A.D. 500 have been found in Smith Rockshelter, an undercut area on a bluff overlooking the creek. A three-quarter-mile nature trail begins at the visitor center and passes through Smith Rockshelter.

ECOLOGY

The park, at the confluence of Onion and Williamson creeks, encompasses two major ecological regions: the Blackland Prairies and the Edwards Plateau. Since humans have eliminated the wildfires that once cleared the prairies, most of the grasslands typical of that region in the park are now overgrown with shrubs and trees. Trees common to the Edwards Plateau, such as plateau live oak, Ashe juniper, Texas persimmon, and mesquite, dominate the dry rocky uplands.

Moisture-loving plants thrive along the creek corridors. Pecan, sycamore, ash, soapberry, and majestic bald cypress trees shade the quiet pools and meandering channels. A small stand of the rare Texas peach bush, *Prunus minutiflora,* is located in the park.

At one time, bison and pronghorn antelope roamed the prairies surrounding the park. Now, the most commonly seen animals are the earless lizards that scamper over the bare limestone rocks, pausing only to wave their striped tails as a diversionary maneuver. Early-morning risers may chance upon a raccoon, opossum, skunk, deer, or rabbit. Eastern fox squirrels live in the trees, and armadillos root in the soft soil bordering the creek. Many birds, including turkeys, quail, migratory shorebirds, and waterfowl, frequent the rich woodlands and waterways; a checklist of the birds is available.

One mile east of the park is an unimposing hill called Pilot Knob, the remains of a volcano that erupted under the sea approximately 80 million years ago. The ash sediments from the volcano were compressed under millions of years of sand and mud deposits. They form the layer of green clay visible under the limestone ledge of the lower falls. Uplifting of the earth's surface some 25 million years ago brought the area above sea level, allowing the elements to begin the slow process of erosion that formed the land as we see it today.

HISTORY

Humans have been attracted to the beauty and life-sustaining resources of Onion Creek for more than 1,500 years. Archaeologists have uncovered artifacts from a succession of prehistoric encampments in the Smith Rockshelter. Those early nomads subsisted on the abundant mammals, fish, berries, nuts, and roots of the area.

Thomas F. McKinney, one of Stephen F. Austin's original 300 colonists in Texas, settled on 2,500 acres of land around Onion Creek in the 1850s. The massive stone walls of McKinney's two-story house, which burned in the 1940s, can be seen on a hill above the lower falls.

McKinney, who made his fortune as a merchant-trader, was the principal financier of the Texas Revolution. By the end of the Civil War, however, he was near bankruptcy and was forced to sell his property. Most of the land was purchased by the grandfather of J. E. and Annie Smith, who donated 632 acres to the state in 1970.

127. MERIDIAN STATE PARK

LOCATION

Bosque County. 40 miles southwest of Hillsboro on TX 22, 4 miles southwest of Meridian.

Mailing address: Box 188, Meridian, Texas 76665. Phone: 817-435-2536. For all state park reservations, call 512-389-8900.

FACILITIES

Camping: 7 campsites with water and electricity, 8 campsites with water, electricity, and sewage hookups; 11 screened shelters; group facility with 7 screened shelters, kitchen, and dining hall; modern restrooms with showers, trailer dump station. Fees charged.

Recreation: picnic areas and playgrounds, hiking and nature trails, swimming in lake, fishing, boating (5-mph speed limit), pavilion.

MAIN ATTRACTIONS

The 70-acre lake, impounded in the thirties by the Civilian Conservation Corps, and the densely wooded hillsides provide a tranquil and scenic setting for the park. Fishing for largemouth bass, crappie, channel catfish, and sunfish, as well as bird-watching, nature hikes, swimming, and picnicking are popular activities here.

Area attractions include the Texas Safari Ranch, a drive-through game park with thousands of exotic grazing animals and a carnival-like headquarters. The ranch is 10 miles southeast of the park on TX 6, then west on FM 3220.

HIKING

A number of nature trails, some with interpretive signs, lead through the various habitats within the park. The Shinnery Ridge Trail, 1.6 miles round trip, passes through oak-juniper woods and grassy prairies. The 2.3-mile Bosque Trail circles the lake. For a shorter walk, try the Little Forest and Little Spring trails, .4 and .7 mile respectively. The plants, animals, ecology, and geology of the park are explained on signs along the Shinnery Ridge, Bosque, and Little Springs nature trails.

ECOLOGY

Meridian State Recreation Area is located in the Lampasas cut plains region on North Central Texas. The plants on the limestone hills and bluffs overlooking the lake are similar to those of the Edwards Plateau of Central Texas, but the vegetation of the floodplain around the park's lake resembles that of East Texas riparian lowlands.

The steep hillsides are covered with Ashe juniper, post oak, blackjack oak, and Texas mountain laurel. In the fall, the crimson leaves of Texas oaks add a splash of color to the woodlands, and in the spring the cascading violet flowers of Texas mountain laurels fill the air with an aroma reminiscent of grape Kool-Aid. Bluebonnets, gaillardias, Indian paintbrushes, and mountain pinks blanket the roadsides with color.

The endangered golden-cheeked warbler finds the northern limit of its range in the juniper-oak woodlands surrounding the park. This colorful warbler breeds only in the restricted range of the Ashe junipers in Central Texas. Bird-watchers come from across the nation to see this tiny bird, which winters in Central America.

Almost 200 species of birds have been seen along the dry stony hillsides and the moist luxuriant bottomlands of the park. Black-capped vireos (also endangered), black-chinned hummingbirds, painted buntings, and many migrating warblers, hawks, and flycatchers can be seen in the spring. Wintering birds include pied-billed grebes, ducks, flickers, purple finches, rufous-sided towhees, and various sparrows. Ask for a checklist at the park headquarters.

Late evening and early morning are the best times to see the mammals in the park. White-tailed deer feed in the open areas; raccoons, skunks, and opossums forage for food; and foxes may occasionally be seen bounding across the roads.

128. MISSION TEJAS STATE HISTORICAL PARK

LOCATION
Houston County. 20 miles northeast of Crockett on TX 21, in Weches.
Mailing address: Route 2, Box 108, Grapeland, Texas 75844.
Phone: 409-687-2394. For all state park reservations, call 512-389-8900.

FACILITIES
Camping: 3 campsites with water only, 7 campsites with water and electricity, 5 campsites with water, electricity, and sewage hookups; modern restrooms with showers. Fees charged.
Recreation: picnic areas and playgrounds, nature trails with trail-guide booklet, historical structures, pavilion.

MAIN ATTRACTIONS
In 1690, the Spanish built the mission San Francisco de los Tejas, the first mission in East Texas, to bring Christianity to the Tejas Indians. After three years of Christian influence, the Indians, whose name means "friend," rebelled and drove the Spaniards away. The location of the park is based on the discovery of a cannon believed to have been buried by the fleeing Spaniards. In the 1930s, the Civilian Conservation Corps built a hewn-log structure to commemorate the original mission. A pioneer dogtrot log cabin, built nearby in 1828, was moved to the park and reconstructed in 1974. Stop at the entrance to the park for historical brochures.

HIKING
The park has two trails through the scenic, aromatic Piney Woods. An interpretive booklet for the forest trail and a bird checklist are available. The forest trail loops around a small pond bordered with dogwood, American holly, winged elm, oak, and red maple trees. A 2-mile hiking trail leads through the deep woods, enabling visitors to experience some of the beauty and uniqueness of East Texas.

ECOLOGY

The 118-acre park, located on the edge of Davy Crockett National Forest, is heavily wooded with pines and several species of oaks. Willow, sassafras, and mulberry trees grow in moist areas, as do beautyberry and elderberry. Rattan vines twine around the trees as they reach for the sky.

The deep woods, especially at night, are an unforgettable experience. The tall pines and oaks filter the moonlight, giving the woods an almost ghostly appearance. Owls hooting in the shadows add to the mystique of the experience. The howl of coyotes and the startled response of a frightened cottontail remind the visitor that many of nature's creatures do not sleep at night.

HISTORY

The first Spanish explorers were impressed with the friendliness and cultural advancement of the Tejas Indians of East Texas. When the de León expedition reached the area in 1690, the Indians greeted them and invited them into the chief's lodge. In the house, a 50-foot-high structure with ten beds and reed mats, the men feasted on tamales, nuts, beans, and corn prepared in various ways.

The priests constructed a chapel in four days in the Indian village and dedicated it as San Francisco de los Tejas. The mission symbolized Spain's first formal possession of the country that became Texas. The Spanish constructed another mission in the area. By 1693, smallpox and drought had caused the Tejas to become hostile, causing the missionaries to flee, burning the mission behind them. The mission was reestablished in 1716 on the Neches River and eventually moved to San Antonio in 1731.

Mission Tejas was on the Old San Antonio Road, or El Camino Real, which was blazed in 1691 to connect the East Texas missions with Mexico City. Today TX 21 follows that route from near the Louisiana border to San Marcos, where it merges with IH-35 and continues south to Mexico.

The reconstructed log house near the park entrance is an excellent example of a pioneer home from the early 1800s. The house was built by Joseph Rice in 1828 on the Old San Antonio Road about 16 miles from the park. As his family grew, Rice enlarged the house—originally a one-room cabin—to three rooms with lofts for sleeping and storage as well as broad front and back porches. The breezeway, or dogtrot, separating the rooms was used during the hot summers for dining, sitting, and sleeping.

Caddoan Mounds State Historic Site is north of Weches on TX 21. The park interprets the history of the Caddo Indians through displays of their artifacts and mounds. There is no camping at the site.

129. MONAHANS SANDHILLS STATE PARK

LOCATION
Ward County. 30 miles southwest of Odessa on IH-20 to PR 41, 5 miles east of Monahans.
Mailing address: Box 1738, Monahans, Texas 79756. Phone: 915-943-2092. For all state park reservations, call 512-389-8900.

FACILITIES
Camping: 5 campsites with water only, 19 campsites with water and electricity; modern restrooms with showers, trailer dump station. Fees charged.

Recreation: picnicking, group dining hall, self-guided nature trail, hiking in dunes, interpretive exhibits, ranger-led programs, store, sandsurfing, guided nature trail, guided ATV tour of dunes by reservation.

MAIN ATTRACTIONS
Picnicking and frolicking down the giant dunes are the most popular activities in the park. The park store rents surfboards for sand surfing, a favorite sport. The Sandhills Museum, in the park headquarters, has exhibits explaining the significant botanical, geological, and archaeological features of the park. A self-guided nature trail leads through the dunes from the museum.

Nearby attractions include the Odessa Meteor Crater, a national historic site 25 miles east just off IH-20, and the Million Barrel Museum in Monahans.

ECOLOGY
The 3,840-acre park is located in the sandy plains near the western edge of the Edwards Plateau. The sand is part of a vast area of dunes known locally as the Sahara of the Southwest. The wind-blown sand was formed by years of wind erosion of Quaternary sandstone formations a million years old. The dunes are composed of well-sorted grains of quartz ranging from light gray to golden in color. The reddish brown sands in the area are quartz grains stained with iron oxide.

Most of the sand is covered with vegetation, which helps brace the dunes from the force of the wind. However, the park preserves a spectacular region of unstabilized dunes. The wind creates intricate wavelike patterns across the dunes, reminding one of ripple marks at the surf's edge. Sculptured by the restless wind, the dunes arc dramatically across the sky, with contours and shadows that merge to form an ever-changing scene of inspiring beauty. West Texas is far from the roaring surf and ocean spray, but the Monahans sandhills are as picturesque as any found along the Texas coast.

The plants and animals of the sandhills country comprise one of the most ecologically interesting communities in Texas. In order to survive, an organism must be especially adapted to the shifting sand, burning sun, nutrient-poor soil, and low annual rainfall. But the dunes are far from barren or lifeless. An amazing variety of life thrives in this rugged habitat.

The colorful dunes support desert plants such as yucca and sagebrush. Annual flowers bloom and quickly set their seeds before being inundated by the advancing sand. At different seasons, the dunes may be painted with the blooms of sunflowers, wild buckwheats, bindweeds, Indian paintbrushes, and evening primroses.

One of the most unusual plants adapted to these harsh growing conditions is the Havard shin oak, *Quercus havardii,* which is only three to four feet tall at maturity. The trees produce large acorns eaten by javelinas, prairie chickens, bobwhite quail, and rodents. The miniature trees cover thousands of acres and comprise one of the largest, but shortest, oak forests in North America.

The vegetation covering much of the sand stabilizes the dunes and provides habitat for gray foxes, coyotes, skunks, jackrabbits, armadillos, bobcats, pack rats, and kangaroo rats. Dominant grasses include sand bluestem, giant sandreed, and *Panicum* species. The many footprints in the sand attest to rampant nocturnal activity, but the animals themselves are seldom seen. The tiny footprints of a kangaroo rat spotted beside the slithering trail of a snake end in a confused jumble. The outcome is left to your imagination.

Groundwater is close to the surface in the sand country. Depressions between the dunes are sometimes filled with water, creating ideal spots to see wildlife in the early morning. In the past, Indians, settlers, and the railroad depended on the easily obtainable water during their passage across this desolate country.

130. MOTHER NEFF STATE PARK

LOCATION
Coryell County. 15 miles northwest of Temple on TX 36, 5 miles north on TX 236.
Mailing address: Route 1, Box 58, Moody, Texas 76557. Phone: 817-853-2389. For all state park reservations, call 512-389-8900.

FACILITIES

Camping: 24 campsites with water nearby, 6 campsites with water and electricity, flush toilets, showers, trailer dump station. Fees charged.

Recreation: picnic areas and playgrounds, hiking trail, fishing in the Leon River, tabernacle, pavilion.

MAIN ATTRACTIONS

The first state park in Texas, Mother Neff preserves a scenic section of the Leon River. Giant oaks, cottonwoods, pecans, and cedar elms shade the luxuriant bottomland around the steep banks of the river. Bird-watching is popular in the park, as are fishing and picnicking along the picturesque river. Mother Neff is one of the most pleasant small parks in Texas.

Surrounded by cultivated farmland, the 259-acre park encompasses three distinct vegetation types, including about a hundred acres of prairies, a hundred acres of rugged limestone hills, and 50 acres of rich bottomland forests with many giant trees growing along the winding Leon River. More than 130 species of birds have been sighted in the park; ask for a checklist at the headquarters. It is easy to see why the original owner, pioneer Isabella Neff, wanted to preserve this beautiful area.

In 1916, Isabella Eleanor Neff, who had come to Texas from Roanoke, Virginia, with her husband in 1854, donated 6 acres along the Leon River to the state. One of her sons, Pat Neff, who was governor from 1921 to 1925, donated another 250 acres to establish Mother Neff Park. As governor, Neff created the Texas State Parks Board in 1923, and Mother Neff Park became the hub of the still-expanding park system. During the thirties, the Civilian Conservation Corps constructed the stone headquarters, the pavilion, and the tabernacle. The tabernacle, which is often used for weddings and church services, must be reserved several months in advance.

HIKING

A short hiking trail leads along a creek in the juniper-oak uplands. The trail follows the creek to a historic water hole, called the Wash Pond, used by Indians and early settlers and to a rock shelter or shallow cave used by the Tonkawas as a campsite.

131. MULESHOE NATIONAL WILDLIFE REFUGE

LOCATION
Bailey County. 20 miles south of Muleshoe on TX 214. Mailing address: Box 549, Muleshoe, Texas 79347. Phone: 806-946-3341.

FACILITIES
Camping: 6 campsites with tables and water, group camp area. No reservations. No fees. Open all year.

Recreation: auto tour of refuge, picnic area, nature trail, prairie dog town, bird-watching, wildlife photography. The refuge roads are open during daylight hours.

MAIN ATTRACTIONS
Winter visitors to this refuge can witness one of the grandest wildlife spectacles in North America: between 10,000 and 20,000 sandhill cranes. The magnificent birds begin arriving about the end of September and stay until March. The birds roost at night in the three small lakes on the refuge when water is available. At dawn they rise en masse and, bugling their piercing call, circle and leave to feed in nearby grain fields. You will never forget the sight of thousands of these 3-foot-tall birds, with their 6.5-foot wingspans, clouding the sky.

The area's agricultural practices are a factor in the large number of sandhills. Pumping the aquifer for irrigation lowered the lakes, making them a protected nighttime roost for the cranes. The birds find ample grass, leftover grain, and insects in the fields surrounding the refuge. Two factors could adversely affect the cranes in the future. Government regulations allow farmers to profit by converting marginal cropland to grass, which could greatly reduce the food available. This and other complex factors have caused the cranes' population to drop from past highs of 200,000 to a winter peak of 20,000 in the refuge. Another threat lurks along the Platte River in Nebraska, where the cranes gather before migrating to the Arctic tundra to breed. A dam is proposed for the area, which would destroy much of the cranes' habitat.

In addition to the sandhills, thousands of ducks and other waterfowl winter in the refuge, depending on the amount of water in the lakes. The refuge bird list includes 283 species, with many migrants that stop over in the spring and fall. Burrowing owls perch on burrows in the prairie dog town, and golden eagles and other raptors soar in the sky. Coyotes, badgers, rabbits, and small mammals live in the shortgrass prairie that surrounds the playa lakes.

132. MUSTANG ISLAND STATE PARK

LOCATION
Nueces County. On PR 53, 14 miles south of Port Aransas or 14 miles east of Corpus Christi, on the Gulf of Mexico. Mailing address: Box 326, Port Aransas, Texas 78373. Phone: 512-749-5246. For all state park reservations, call 512-389-8900.

FACILITIES
Camping: primitive camping area on beach (occasionally closed due to flooding), 48 paved RV sites with water and electricity, modern restrooms with showers, trailer dump station; on-beach camping with chemical toilets, rinse showers. Fees charged.

Recreation: picnicking, swimming in the Gulf of Mexico, surfing, bathhouse with cold-water showers, fishing.

MAIN ATTRACTIONS
Swimming in the rolling surf, beachcombing, and playing in the sand are the primary activities at the park. Visitors will find some of the best surfing in Texas along the jetties of the fish pass, a cut through the island to the inland bay. Fishing is popular from the jetties.

ECOLOGY
The barrier islands that parallel the crescent-shaped Texas coast are of extreme ecological importance. The islands provide a variety of wildlife and plant habitats and protect the bays and the mainland shoreline. Seldom are hurricanes powerful enough to breach the islands with wind-driven waves.

Mustang Island has six distinct habitats, each of which supports a characteristic community of plants and animals: beaches, primary dunes, secondary dunes, marshes, tidal flats, and the bay. The shells of many marine organisms litter the open beaches. The primary and secondary dunes support an interesting variety of salt- and wind-adapted plants. Morning glories spread across the dunes, and sea oats and other grasses grasp for a sandy foothold.

Freshwater marshes are sustained by the rains, while salt marshes are more permanent; the marshes are the nursery grounds for many species of fish. Birds are abundant both in the marshes and along the mud flats on the inner shoreline. The mud flats support many organisms that attract shorebirds and wading birds. Ducks and waterfowl frequent the protected bay and lagoon between the island and the mainland.

The dunes are very fragile. The plants fight the wind-driven sand and, if undisturbed, will stabilize the dunes and protect them from erosion. Many dunes in the park have been reconstructed and are now at their natural height of about 15 to 20 feet. Except in the primary dunes immediately adjacent to the beach, hiking through the dunes should be avoided.

The main animals seen in the park are birds, rodents, and snakes. Rattlesnakes are common in the grassy secondary dunes, where they feed on ground squirrels, pocket gophers, and cotton rats. The tracks of raccoons, opossums, black-tailed jackrabbits, striped skunks, and coyotes can be seen leading across the dunes, an indication of the active nightlife of the wild community.

133. NAVARRO MILLS LAKE

LOCATION
U.S. Army Corps of Engineers. Navarro County. Project office: 16 miles southwest of Corsicana on TX 31 to Navarro Mills, 1.5 miles northwest on FM 667.
Mailing address: Route 1, Box 33-D, Purdon, Texas 76679-9707.
Phone: 817-578-1431.

Campground	water	fee area	flush toilets	season	dump station	cold-water showers	electricity
Liberty Hill	•	•	•	all	•	•	•
Oak	•	•	•	all	•	•	•
Wolf Creek	•	•	•	all	•	•	•

FACILITIES
Camping: 3 Corps-operated parks on the lake with campgrounds. Campsite fees vary. Camping areas at Oak, Wolf Creek, and Liberty Hill parks may be reserved by calling 1-800-284-2267.

Recreation: picnicking, hiking, swimming, fishing, boat ramps, marina at Liberty Hill Park, hunting.

MAIN ATTRACTIONS

Lake Navarro Mills, an impoundment of Richland Creek, covers 5,070 acres and has 38 miles of shoreline. Catfish and crappie are the primary game fish in the lake. Public hunting and hiking are permitted on 3,550 acres reserved for wildlife management.

NAVARRO MILLS LAKE

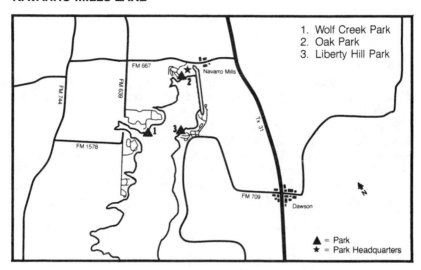

1. Wolf Creek Park
2. Oak Park
3. Liberty Hill Park

▲ = Park
★ = Park Headquarters

134. PADRE ISLAND NATIONAL SEASHORE

LOCATION

Kleberg County. 20 miles southeast of Corpus Christi on PR 22. Mailing address: 9405 S. Padre Island Dr., Corpus Christi, Texas 78418. Phone: Visitors Center, 512-949-8068; headquarters, 512-937-2621.

FACILITIES

Camping: free primitive camping on beach, 40 paved campsites with water only, modern restrooms with showers at Malaquite Beach, trailer dump station. Entrance and camping fees charged.

Recreation: picnicking, nature trail with trail-guide pamphlet, interpretive exhibits, swimming in the Gulf of Mexico, surfing, fishing, boating, pavilion, store.

MAIN ATTRACTIONS

Padre Island has more than 100 miles of expansive beaches with scenic dunes formed by the sea and shaped by the wind. Swimming, surfing, sunbathing, and fishing are the most popular activities. Shells and other interesting finds from the sea make beachcombing an adventure. More than 350 species of birds attract bird-watchers from across the nation, and the large, picturesque dunes thrill photographers. The variety of habitats on the island offers unparalleled opportunities for nature study. Most of the beach is accessible only by foot or with a four-wheel-drive vehicle.

HIKING

The three-quarter-mile Grasslands Nature Trail leads visitors through the rolling, grassy coastal sands that occupy a major portion of the island.

Sixty-five miles of beach and dunes stretch between Malaquite Beach and the Port Mansfield Channel. The south side of the channel to the southern tip of Padre Island covers another 35 miles. Though there are no facilities or drinking water on the beach, the entire stretch offers exciting beachcombing. Primitive camping is allowed on the beach but not in the ecologically delicate dunes.

Be sure to stop at the ranger station at Malaquite Beach for information about the ecology of the island, details about hiking and camping on the island, and pamphlets on the park's vegetation, birds, and other wildlife. If you are interested in undertaking a long hike, you will either have to hike back the way you came or have a friend with a four-wheel-drive vehicle pick you up. There is no ferry across the channel, so, if you are interested in hiking on the southern part of the island, you will have to drive to South Padre Island, east of Brownsville.

ECOLOGY

Padre Island is 113 miles long and, at most, 3 miles wide. The constant winds, salty ocean spray, sandy soil, lack of fresh water, and hot, shadeless summer days create an environment in which survival is not easy. Yet many plants and animals have successfully adapted and even thrive under the harsh conditions. Eight distinct habitats, each with its own characteristic plant and animal communities, exist within the park: beaches, foredunes, actively moving dune fields, grasslands, ponds and marshes, tidal flats, the Laguna Madre, and spoil banks, islands formed from dredging operations.

The flat beach slopes gently into the Gulf; it is generally devoid of vegetation but is the home of countless sea creatures. The shells of whelks, clams, scallops, and sand dollars litter the beach like confetti. Small fish can be seen skating across the surf and leaping above the waves. Porpoises are common offshore, and on rare occasions a whale has been stranded on the beach.

Paralleling the beach is a ridge of wind-sculptured sand dunes. These dunes are fairly well stabilized by a delicate mat of vegetation. Evening primroses with yellow flowers sparkle with early-morning dew, and the railroad vine, a morning glory, spreads its roots as far as 20 feet to help hold the shifting sand. Sea oats and other grasses silhouetted against the sky on the towering dunes help even the inexperienced photographer take professional-looking pictures. When human activity or violent weather destroys the fragile vegetation, the dunes quickly erode away.

Rolling sand hills covered by a variety of grasses and small herbaceous plants occupy most of the island behind the foredunes. Many small mammals inhabit this area, including kangaroo rats, pocket gophers, cotton rats, rice rats, ground squirrels, and jackrabbits. Coyotes prey on the small animals, as do rattlesnakes, which are numerous in the grasslands.

Low-lying marshy areas are interspersed with the grasslands. These slowly draining areas contain fresh water after rains and salt water after severe storms. Here grow cattails, marshhay cordgrass, and other plants tolerant of both fresh and salt water. Dunes constantly driven by the winds border the western side of the island. Also on the western shore are tidal flats, which attract a large number of wading birds and shorebirds.

The Laguna Madre provides a protected shelter for the many birds that nest on the spoil banks created by dredging the Intracoastal Canal. Millions of migrating waterfowl spend their winter in this long body of shallow water.

Despite the inhospitable environment, more than 350 species of birds and 400 plant species make Padre Island their home. Shorebirds and gulls soar overhead, and colorful wildflowers and dune grasses nod gracefully in the prevailing breezes. The ceaseless roar of the surf echoes across the island with a primordial cry unchanged since first recorded by human ears. Unfortunately, garbage from ships, offshore oil rigs, and thoughtless vacationers litters almost every yard of the beautiful shoreline.

HISTORY

Padre Island, first charted in 1519, was originally named Las Islas Blancas, the White Islands. In the intervening centuries, many storm-driven ships were wrecked on the silver beaches. In 1553, a 20-ship Spanish treasure fleet caught in a hurricane lost many of its galleons to the raging sea.

In 1800, the island was granted to Padre Nicolás Balli by the Spanish government. Balli started the first ranch on the island, and cattle grazed the sandy grasslands until 1970, when the national seashore was established.

135. PALMETTO STATE PARK

LOCATION
Gonzales County. 21 miles southeast of Lockhart off U.S. 183. Mailing address: Route 5, Box 201, Gonzales, Texas 78629. Phone: 210-672-3266. For all state park reservations, call 512-389-8900.

FACILITIES
Camping: 21 campsites with water nearby, 18 campsites with water and electricity, one site with water, electricity, sewage; modern restrooms with showers, trailer dump station. Fees charged.

Recreation: picnic areas and playgrounds, nature trails with trail-guide pamphlet, bird-watching and wildflower gazing; fishing, tubing, and canoeing on the San Marcos River; recreation hall.

MAIN ATTRACTIONS
The botanically unique 263-acre park is located on the spring-fed San Marcos River. The most unusual features of the scenic park are the unique plant and animal communities associated with naturally occurring artesian springs and swamps. The area had numerous warm springs, mud boils, and peat deposits until the mid 1900s. However, drilling for oil and water had lowered the water table, thus eliminating those interesting hydrologic features. The park derives its name from the dwarf palmettos that grow abundantly in the swamps. Palmettos, common to East Texas marshy areas, are not usually found in dry Central Texas. The river and warm artesian wells in the park provide the right environment for lush vegetation.

There are two nature trails in the park. One leads along the steep banks of the San Marcos River, the other through the palmetto swamp. A fountain of warm sulfur-rich water flows from a natural artesian well near the start of the Palmetto Nature Trail. The spring powers one of the few operational ram-jet pumps in existence today. The pump, installed in 1936, uses no electricity; it derives its power solely from the naturally occurring water pressure of the well.

ECOLOGY

The ecological diversity of Palmetto State Park is the result of the various habitats created by the river, artesian springs, and swamps. The naturally flowing artesian wells maintain the water level in the swamps, enabling the dwarf palmettos and other acid-loving plants to thrive in an area far west of their natural habitat. Rich hardwood bottomlands occur along the river, while the uplands are dominated by a post oak–little bluestem community.

The distribution of many eastern and western species of plants and animals merges in this area. Approximately 240 species of birds have been sighted in the park. Many are near the western limit of their ranges, making Palmetto one of the most interesting birding spots in Central Texas. The pileated woodpecker, yellow-crowned night heron, barred owl, and the Kentucky, prothonotary, and northern parula warblers all nest in the vicinity. Ask at the park headquarters for a bird checklist.

Eastern gray squirrels and canebrake rattlesnakes are other animals in the area not usually seen farther west. The fox squirrel, pygmy mouse, eastern cottontail, raccoon, armadillo, and white-tailed deer also make their homes in the park.

The abundance and diversity of plants, particularly wildflowers, in the park area have attracted amateur and professional botanists for many years. The annual phlox cultivated worldwide is derived from a native phlox discovered in this area by Scottish botanist Thomas Drummond.

The anaqua tree, a subtropical species that reaches its northern limits in Central Texas, occurs along riverbanks in the park. The evergreen leaves have the texture of sandpaper. In the spring, the open hillsides are ablaze with bluebonnets, Indian paintbrushes, red phlox, larkspurs, and gaillardias. The fall-blooming species—goldenrod, wild hibiscus, turk's caps, and sunflowers—are no less spectacular.

HISTORY

The area was settled in 1879 by Adolph Otto and his wife, Christine. A community, named Ottine by combining their names, developed around Otto's sawmill and cotton gin. The area quickly became a popular spot for botanists from around the country and the world. Also, people were attracted to the warm sulfur springs for their alleged healing qualities. Today, the Texas Warm Springs Foundation is near the park entrance.

In 1933, the Texas State Parks Board acquired Ottine Swamp and constructed the park recreation hall with Civilian Conservation Corps labor. The historic building stands in the picnic area near the playgrounds.

136. PALO DURO CANYON STATE PARK

LOCATION
Randall County. 26 miles south of Amarillo on IH-27 to Canyon, 12 miles east on TX 217.
Mailing address: Route 2, Box 285, Canyon, Texas 79015. Phone: 806-488-2227. For all state park reservations, call 512-389-8900.

FACILITIES
Camping: 43 campsites with water nearby, 102 campsites with water and electricity, modern restrooms with showers, trailer dump station.

Recreation: picnic areas and playgrounds, 50 miles of hiking trails, interpretive exhibits (summer only), swimming in creek, miniature railroad through canyon, horse rentals, state longhorn herd, amphitheater with a drama production each summer, store.

MAIN ATTRACTIONS
Palo Duro Canyon, formed by the erosive action of the Prairie Dog Town Fork of the Red River and its numerous tributaries, resembles a miniature Grand Canyon. The name "Palo Duro" is Spanish for "hard wood," referring to the rot-resistant junipers growing throughout the canyon. The state park, encompassing more than 17,000 acres, is one of the largest in Texas. Part of the official state longhorn herd, a reminder of past days, can be seen grazing along the entrance road.

The interpretive center, open in summer, explains the cultural and geologic history of the park. Each summer, in the amphitheater, the Texas Panhandle Heritage Foundation performs a drama about early pioneers in the region. Another popular attraction is the winding Sad Monkey Railroad, which provides impressive views of some of the unusual formations in the canyon.

Nearby attractions include the Panhandle-Plains Historical Museum in Canyon, one of the best museums in the state. Buffalo Lake National Wildlife Refuge is 12 miles southwest of Canyon.

HIKING AND HORSEBACK RIDING
The beauty of the canyon, evident from the scenic overlook and the loop drive, is better appreciated by hikers or horseback riders along the many trails. The park has 5 miles of marked trails and approximately 50 miles of unmarked trails. Camping is not allowed along the trails. In summer, always carry water with you.

ECOLOGY

Palo Duro Canyon is on the Caprock Escarpment, which divides the High Plains and the Rolling Plains of North Texas. Examples of plants and animals from each area occur in the park. The canyon, averaging 700 feet deep and a half mile to 2 miles wide in the park, provides a refuge for plants and wildlife. This protected canyon, plus the park's perennial springs, woodlands, and permanent waterways, supports a great diversity of vegetation and animal life.

Rocky Mountain, Pinchot, and one-seed junipers, mesquite trees, and other drought-resistant plants grow on the arid canyon slopes and along the canyon rim. In contrast, stately cottonwood and hackberry trees shade the streams winding through the canyon. Life-giving springs, which may flow at a rate of 15 gallons per minute, are produced where water-bearing strata are exposed; these springs form miniature oases for moisture-dependent plants.

Vast herds of bison used to roam the canyon, but they were extirpated by the buffalo hunters. Pronghorn antelope, unimpeded by the barbed wire fences, still occur in small numbers on the adjoining plains. Imported African aoudad sheep are established in the canyon.

More than 200 species of birds have been recorded in the park. In the spring and fall, kettles of circling Mississippi kites ride thermals rising from the canyon by day and roost in the tall cottonwoods bordering the streams by night. In a 1983 survey, 22 golden eagle nests were spotted in the canyon. Beavers, which make their homes in the creeks, and mule deer are best sighted in the early morning or at dusk.

To the west extends the flat unbroken prairie of the High Plains, or Llano Estacado, formed from millions of years of deposits originating in the Rocky Mountains and carried eastward by streams and rivers. The Prairie Dog Town Fork of the Red River, no more than a low-water creek most of the year, has carved through 800 feet of sediments and exposed strata hundreds of millions of years old.

The most prominent layers exposed in the park are the brick-red shale, sandy clay, and sandstone, formed by sediments from the Permian oceans of 225 million to 270 million years ago. The colorful layers are laced with veins of white crystal gypsum or satin spar. The force of erosion is evident along the creeks, as banks of red clay with alternating layers of gypsum crumble into the streambeds.

Covering the Permian sediments, which make up the canyon floor, are 300 feet of red, yellow, lavender, and gray shales and sandstones from the Triassic age, approximately 200 million years old. The harder layers of sandstone are resistant to erosion and form ridges, ledges, cliffs, and many outstanding features throughout the park. Sad Monkeys, Spanish Skirts, and Santana's Face are the imaginative names of some of the most prominent formations. The Lighthouse, the best-known landmark, is a 75-foot pillar of soft mudstone capped by a layer of erosion-resistant sandstone.

This layer cake of colorful sedimentary rock was covered during the Cretaceous by many more layers of sediments, which were eventually removed by erosion. During the Tertiary period, from 3 million to 11 million years ago, clay, sand, chalk, caliche, and gravel were deposited to create the Ogallala formation, an important aquifer, or water-bearing stratum. The Ogallala provides the irrigation water that has turned the arid Panhandle into one of the most productive farming regions in the country. A surface layer of sand, clay, and gravel, deposited during the Pleistocene epoch some 1 million years ago, underlies the grasslands so attractive to ranchers.

HISTORY

Palo Duro Canyon has been a center of human activity for more than 12,000 years. Paleo-Indian nomads hunted the mammoths and other Ice Age animals that grazed on the rich grasslands in the canyon. During the 1800s, the canyon was the domain of the Comanches, who in 1874 were defeated by the U.S. Army. A historical marker designates the site of that last major Indian battle in Texas. The Indians were led by the fierce war chief Quanah Parker.

Charles Goodnight established one of the largest ranches in Texas in Palo Duro Canyon in 1876. He began with 1,600 head of longhorn cattle and lived in a dugout house similar to the one exhibited along the park loop road. Later, Goodnight and his partner John Adair founded the J.A. Ranch; they were among the first to use controlled breeding to improve their herd, which eventually numbered 100,000.

137. PAMPA: HOBART STREET PARK

Gray County. In town on TX 70, one block north of U.S. 60. Mailing address: P.O. Box 2499, Pampa, Texas 79066-2499. Phone: 806-669-5770. Five acres with 12 sites with water, electricity, primitive camp sites; dump station, flush toilets, playground, picnicking. Open year round, no reservations.

PAMPA: RECREATION PARK

Gray County. On U.S. 60, 2 miles east of intersection with TX 70. Mailing address: P.O. Box 2499, Pampa, Texas 79066-2499. Phone: 806-669-5770. One hundred thirty-four acres on Old City Lake; 25 campsites with water, electricity; flush toilets, dump station, group campsites. Recreation: picnic area, playgrounds, boating, fishing, 2-mile hiking trail. Open year round, fees charged, no reservations.

138. PEDERNALES FALLS STATE PARK

LOCATION

Blanco County. 40 miles west of Austin on U.S. 290, 7 miles north on FM 3232.

Mailing address: Route 1, Box 450, Johnson City, Texas 78636. Phone: 210-868-7304. For all state park reservations, call 512-389-8900.

FACILITIES

Camping: primitive camping area on hiking trail, 70 campsites with water and electricity, modern restrooms with showers, trailer dump station. Fees charged.

Recreation: picnic areas and playgrounds, 7-mile hiking trail, nature trail with trail-guide booklet, swimming in river, tubing, fishing, canoeing, amphitheater.

MAIN ATTRACTIONS

The most outstanding feature of the park is the boulder-strewn, cascading Pedernales Falls. The river, which has cut deep channels through the limestone, spills down two waterfalls into deep pools. There are two scenic overlooks and a trail to the falls. Though the bedrock is limestone, the river bottom is sandy. The sand of the Pedernales and other Central Texas rivers is carried by streams from the weathered granite formations exposed in the Llano region.

Hours can be spent scampering over the exposed rocks leading upstream from the falls. Like giant stairsteps, the strata tilt gently upward, each successive layer younger than the one below it. The river, cascading over the tilted bedrock, forms the falls that give the park its name.

Fishing is popular all along the Pedernales River, but because of hazardous water conditions, swimming, wading, and tubing are prohibited near the falls. Below the falls, the shady shoreline and the cool river provide a welcome respite from the heat of summer afternoons. The normally calm river can rise rapidly and become a torrent after thunderstorms. Access to the river is prohibited when flooding is likely.

Nearby attractions include the Lyndon B. Johnson National Historical Park, 9 miles west in Johnson City. An interpretive center describes the development of the Texas cattle industry, and a reconstructed pioneer ranch with a house, barns, and longhorn cattle illustrates the early life-style.

Lyndon B. Johnson State Historical Park is near Stonewall, 14 miles west of Johnson City. Tours of the LBJ Ranch, a working cattle ranch, are offered. A swimming pool and picnic areas are available in the park.

HIKING

The 7-mile Wolf Mountain Trail leads across rugged uplands and crystalline streams and down steep riverbanks into the shady riparian woodlands. Off the trail, about 2 miles from the trailhead, are areas designated for primitive camping. The camping area has no water and no facilities.

The short loop of the Hill Country Nature Trail begins in the car-camping area. The trail booklet, available at the park headquarters, describes the plants, wildlife, and ecology of this special part of Texas known as the Hill Country.

ECOLOGY

Pedernales Falls State Park, formerly the 4,800-acre Circle Bar Ranch, stretches 9 miles along the Pedernales River. The park, situated on the eastern edge of the Edwards Plateau, encompasses dry rolling grasslands, rugged cedar brakes, oak-mesquite woodlands, botanically rich spring-fed canyons, and lush riverbanks lined with bald cypress.

The park provides an excellent example of the Edwards Plateau, which stretches west of Austin for more than 300 miles. The dominant plants are the Ashe juniper and the plateau live oak. Texas oak, mesquite, and small shrubs such as evergreen sumac, aromatic sumac, silktassel, and agarita are common on the dry rocky hillsides. Grama, bluestem, and muhly grasses grow in the upland clearings.

The area is dissected by many canyons rich with moisture-loving plants. Spicebush, a small shrub favored by early settlers for tea and seasoning, sycamore, Mexican plum, black cherry, and box elder trees grow in the protected environment. In contrast to the dry hillsides, lush vegetation lines the springs and seeps along the stream bottoms. Arrowhead Pool, on the Wolf Mountain Trail, is a large arrow-shaped pool at the bottom of a cascading, fern-lined waterfall.

Twin Falls Overlook, reached by the trail from the campgrounds, is at the confluence of two creeks, each with a picturesque waterfall. This ecologically sensitive area is so easily damaged by human use that hiking beyond the overlook is prohibited.

The area around the Pedernales Falls is scoured of most vegetation by periodic flooding. A few wildflowers find a temporary hold in silty patches among the rocks. Desert plants such as sotol, yucca, and prickly pear cacti grow in the fast-draining sandy soil above the flood line. Castor bean, poison hemlock, and snow-on-the-mountain are abundant on the sandy beaches below the falls. Those three plants are poisonous. The poison hemlock can easily be confused with the carrot plant, but it is extremely toxic, particularly the foliage.

Wildlife is abundant in the park. Turkey, deer, raccoons, skunks, opossums, armadillos, and more than 150 species of birds, including the bald eagle and golden-cheeked warbler, may be seen. A bird checklist is available from the entrance facility. Deer commonly graze along the roadsides and near the camping and picnicking areas. At dusk, armadillos plow noisily through the underbrush bordering the river, rooting for insects in the sandy soil.

139. PERRYTON: WOLF CREEK PARK

Ochiltree County. 12 miles south of Perryton on U.S. 83, 5 miles east, on Lake Fryer. Mailing address: Route 2, Box 20, Perryton, Texas 79070. Phone: 806-435-4559. Camping: 107 campsites with water and electricity, group camping area with electricity, chemical toilets, trailer dump station, bathhouse with hot showers, flush toilets. Fees charged. Recreation: picnic areas, hiking trails, fishing, boat ramp, store, restaurant. Open all year.

140. PORT ARANSAS PARK

Nueces County. On the beach at Port Aransas. Mailing address: Box 18608, Corpus Christi, Texas 78480. Phone: 512-749-6117. Camping: primitive camping on beach, 75 RV sites with water, electricity, and showers; flush toilets, trailer dump station. Fees charged. Recreation: swimming in the Gulf of Mexico, 1,240-foot lighted fishing pier, boating, concessions. Open all year. Good facilities for RVs; open beach camping.

141. PORT LAVACA LIGHTHOUSE BEACH AND BIRD SANCTUARY

Calhoun County. 25 miles southeast of Victoria on U.S. 87 to TX 35, eastern city limits of Port Lavaca on Lavaca Bay. Mailing address: Box 105, Port Lavaca, Texas 77979. Phone: 512-552-9796. Camping: 51 sites with water, 32 with water and electricity, 19 sites with water, electricity, sewage, 19 covered shelters with cable TV; flush toilets, showers, trailer dump station. Recreation: picnic areas and playgrounds, swimming pool, lighted fishing pier, boat ramp, store, one-half-mile trail with bird observation tower. Open all year, fees charged, reservations accepted. Facilities are poor here for tents but adequate for RVs.

142. POSSUM KINGDOM STATE PARK

LOCATION
Palo Pinto County. 85 miles west of Fort Worth on U.S. 180 to Caddo, 17 miles north on PR 33.
Mailing address: Box 36, Caddo, Texas 76429. Phone: 817-549-1803. For all state park reservations, call 512-389-8900.

FACILITIES
Camping: 55 campsites with water only or with water nearby, 61 campsites with water and electricity, 6 cabins, modern restrooms with showers, trailer dump station. Fees charged.

Recreation: picnic areas and playgrounds, swimming in Possum Kingdom Lake, fishing pier, boating, water-skiing, canoe and paddleboat rentals, state longhorn herd, store (summer only).

MAIN ATTRACTIONS
The 19,800-acre Possum Kingdom Lake, 34 miles long with 310 miles of shoreline, offers visitors swimming, fishing, water sports, and excellent scuba diving in its clear waters. Catches of black bass, striped bass, perch, and walleye pike are common. Rainbow trout are stocked in the cool waters discharged from the dam. Morris Sheppard Dam was built on the Brazos River in 1941 by the Brazos River Authority. The hydroelectric power plant at the dam can produce up to 22.5 megawatts of electricity.

ECOLOGY
The Brazos River, one of the major river systems in Texas, has cut through more than 200 feet of limestone and shale layers in the area of the park. The result is a meandering riverbed with steep cliffs and narrow canyons. New boating enthusiasts can explore the flooded canyons, with cliffs more than 100 feet high.

The exposed rock layers, part of the Canyon Group, were formed from sediments deposited in shallow seas around 280 million years ago. Geologists have studied the exposed strata because they are the same age as some of the limestones that hold oil reserves deep beneath the surface in West Texas.

Ashe juniper, mesquite, Texas oak, live oak, and redbud trees dominate the park, and pecans grow along the creek drainages.

There is a large population of white-tailed deer, many tame enough to eat from your hands. Mountain lions, bobcats, and coyotes also find a protected home in the area. Many waterfowl frequent the reservoir, and the endangered golden eagle and ospreys are occasionally sighted. Turkeys and quail inhabit the mixed grassland savannas scattered through the rocky hills. A portion of the Texas state longhorn herd grazes the uplands of the park.

143. PURTIS CREEK STATE PARK

LOCATION
Henderson and Van Zandt counties. 10 miles northwest of Athens on U.S. 175 to Eustace, 3 miles north on FM 316. Mailing address: 14225 FM 316, Eustace, Texas 75124. Phone: 903-425-2332. For all state park reservations, call 512-389-8900.

FACILITIES
Camping: 59 campsites with water and electricity, modern restrooms, showers, trailer dump station. Fees charged.

Recreation: fishing, 2 lighted piers, fish-cleaning station, boat dock, 1.3-mile hiking trail, playground, picnic area, swimming.

MAIN ATTRACTIONS
This park, with 1,533 acres of woodlands and pastures, was designed for the fisherman. It even has its own ponds for raising fish to stock the lake. Brush and trees were left in the 355-acre impounded lake to provide habitat for fish. Though fishermen report record catches of catfish, crappie, and bluegill, it is the largemouth bass that make this park popular. The park's catch-and-release policy allows many people to catch a trophy-size bass. All bass must be released back into the lake alive, but regular limits govern the other fish. Because the lake is so small, only 50 boats are allowed on the water at a time. Boats are not allowed to create a wake, so they must travel at idle speed. People without boats can fish along the bank or from the lighted piers.

If fishing is not your forte, you can enjoy the forest of tall oaks, elms, walnuts, pecans, and eastern red cedars. Woodpeckers, warblers, vireos, and other woodland birds flit through the trees, and cormorants, herons, kingfishers, and waterfowl are attracted to the lake. The hiking trail provides a pleasant walk through a good example of the Post Oak Savanna vegetation region of Texas. Tours of the undeveloped Lake Tawakoni State Park leave Purtis Creek on the last Saturday of the month. Reservations and a conservation passport are required.

144. QUEEN CITY: MOORE'S LANDING COUNTY PARK

Cass County. Wright Patman Lake. 9 miles north of Queen City on U.S. 59, west on County Rd. 3659 to County Rd. 3658 to park. Mailing address: P.O. Box 184, Queen City, Tx 75572. Phone: 903-796-4502 or 756-5181. Camping: 46 campsites with water and electricity, flush toilets, showers, trailer dump station, group camp area, primitive camping. Recreation: picnicking, playground, group pavilion, boat ramp, designated swimming area, hiking. No reservations. Fees charged. Open all year.

145. RAY ROBERTS LAKE STATE PARK

LOCATION
Denton County.
Isle DuBois Unit: IH-35 north of Denton, east on FM 455 at Sanger, across dam to park entrance.
Johnson Branch Unit: Closed.
Mailing address: 100 PW 4137, Pilot Point, Texas 76266-8944.
Phone: 817-686-2148. For all state park reservations, call 512-389-8900.

FACILITIES
Camping: 115 campsites with water and electricity, 69 walk-in tent sites, restrooms, showers, trailer dump station; 14 equestrian sites. Fees charged.

Recreation: picnicking, pavilions, park store, hike and bike trails, equestrian trail, lighted fishing pier, swimming beach, boat launch.

MAIN ATTRACTIONS
Twelve thousand acres of recreation land surround the 29,000-acre Ray Roberts Lake. The Isle DuBois Unit consists of 1,400 acres near the dam and has a 4-mile hike and bike trail and a 12-mile multi-use hike/bike/equestrian trail. The remainder of the public land around the lake is a wildlife management area with no camping. Several satellite parks on the lake have boat launches and restrooms.

Oaks and hickories of the Eastern Cross Timbers region forest the park and provide habitat for fox squirrels and other small mammals. Waterfowl and occasional bald eagles winter on the reservoir. Several archaeological sites have been recorded in the park.

146. RUSK-PALESTINE STATE PARK/TEXAS STATE RAILROAD

LOCATION
Palestine Unit: 46 miles south of Tyler on TX 155 to Palestine, 2 miles east on U.S. 84, Rusk Unit: 41 miles south of Tyler on U.S. 69 to Rusk, 3 miles west on U.S. 84.
Mailing address: Route 4, Box 431, Rusk, Texas 75785. Phone: 903-683-5126. Texas State Railroad reservations, 800-442-8951 (Texas only). For all state park reservations, call 512-389-8900.

FACILITIES
Camping: Palestine Unit, 12 campsites with water. Rusk Unit, 16 campsites with water and electricity, 32 campsites with water, electricity, and sewage hookups; 45 group trailer sites with electricity and water, screened dining hall, modern restrooms with showers (wheelchair access), trailer dump station. Fees charged.

Recreation: Palestine Unit, Texas State Railroad Depot, picnic areas. Rusk Unit, Texas State Railroad Depot, picnic areas and playgrounds, half-mile nature trail with pamphlet on vegetation and wildlife, period buildings, fishing on a 15-acre stocked lake, tennis courts, pavilion, store (summer only).

MAIN ATTRACTIONS
The Rusk and Palestine units of the state park are located at either end of the 25.5-mile-long Texas State Railroad in Cherokee and Anderson counties, respectively. Two large Victorian depots complete with antique furnishings set the mood for a ride into the past on the turn-of-the-century railroad, which features steam locomotives and period coaches.

The 4-hour round trip takes passengers over wooden trestles and winding tracks through the heart of the East Texas Piney Woods. The railway winds past rural farmland through scenic woods, parallels sandy creeks, and crosses the Neches River. In the spring, the snow-white blossoms of the dogwoods and the colorful redbud trees add an extra dimension of beauty to the ride.

The trains can be boarded from either the Rusk or the Palestine Unit; they leave the depots at 11 A.M. and 1:30 P.M. The trains operate on weekends only in the spring and fall, from Thursday through Monday in the summer; they do not run from November through mid March.

The Texas State Railroad was constructed in 1896 to haul wood and iron ore to a foundry near Rusk operated by the prison system.

In 1906, the 5-mile line was extended another 5 miles and eventually connected Rusk and Palestine. It became a common carrier but was never profitable. From 1921 to 1969, the railroad was leased to private companies; it was transferred to the Parks and Wildlife Department in 1972.

Camping, fishing, and a short trail by the lake are available at the 100-acre Rusk Unit. The campgrounds are adjacent to the highway, and road traffic is considerable. The lake is stocked with bass, catfish, and perch.

Jim Hogg State Historical Park, home of the first native-born Texas governor, is in Rusk. It is open for day use only.

147. SABINE NATIONAL FOREST

LOCATION

East of Lufkin on the Texas-Louisiana border, on Toledo Bend Reservoir.
Mailing address, Tenaha Ranger District: 101 S. Bolivar, San Augustine, Texas 75972. Phone: 409-275-2632 or 2635. Mailing address, Yellowpine Ranger District: Box F, Hemphill, Texas 75948. Phone: 409-787-3870.

Campground	water	fee area	flush toilets	chemical toilets	season	dump station	cold-water showers	boating	fishing	swimming	trails
Indian Mounds	•	•		•	Mar.–Oct.			•	•		
Lakeview	•	•		•	Mar.–Oct.			•	•		•
Ragtown	•	•	•		Mar.–Sept.	•	•	•	•		•
Red Hills Lake	•	•	•		Mar.–Oct.	•	•	•	•	•	•
Willow Oak	•	•		•	all			•	•		

FACILITIES

Sabine National Forest has 5 parks with campgrounds. Fees charged.

RV sites are located at Indian Mounds, Lakeview, and Ragtown on Toledo Bend Reservoir, and at Red Hills Lake. Willow Oak, with tent camping, is also on Toledo Bend Reservoir.

Individual campsites cannot be reserved. Primitive camping, at no charge, is allowed anywhere in the forest, except when hunting or logging is in progress. For maps and information on day-use areas, write the headquarters. Directions for reaching the parks are as follows.

Indian Mounds: 6.6 miles east of Hemphill on FM 83, 4 miles south on FM 3382, 1 mile east on FSR 130.

Lakeview: 9 miles south of Hemphill on TX 87, 5 miles east on FM 2928.

Ragtown: 13 miles southeast of Center on TX 87, 6.5 miles east on FM 139, 4 miles east on FM 3184, 1.5 miles east on FSR 132.

Red Hills Lake: 10.5 miles north of Hemphill on TX 87, north of Milam.

Willow Oak: 15 miles southeast of Hemphill on TX 87.

MAIN ATTRACTIONS

Sabine National Forest comprises 152,482 acres of pine-hardwood woodlands in Jasper, Sabine, San Augustine, Newton, and Shelby counties. Its eastern border is Toledo Bend Reservoir, with 186,500 surface acres and 650 miles of shoreline. The reservoir is a popular spot for fishing and boating.

All the parks in the forest, except Red Hills, are located on the reservoir. Red Hills is situated in the rolling hills, towering pines, and diverse hardwoods characteristic of the deep Piney Woods. There is a 17-acre lake with a sandy swimming beach, a bathhouse, and an interesting but poorly marked hiking trail. In the early spring, trilliums and other woodland flowers bloom on the rich forest floor. Only boats without motors are allowed on Red Hills Lake.

148. SABINE PASS BATTLEGROUND STATE HISTORICAL PARK

LOCATION

Jefferson County: 15 miles south of Port Arthur on TX 87 to Sabine Pass, then 1.5 miles south on FM 3322.
Mailing address: c/o Sea Rim State Park, P.O. Box 1066, Sabine Pass, Texas 77655. Phone: 409-971-2451.

FACILITIES

Camping: 10 RV sites with water and electricity, tent camping, restrooms, dump station. Fees charged.

Recreation: fishing and crabbing along one-fourth-mile shore, fish cleaning shelter, boat launch, covered picnic tables.

HISTORY

In 1863, Lt. Dick Dowling and 46 other Texans in an earthen fort were attacked by a 22-ship Union armada. Though armed with only 6 cannons, they were able to repel the Union forces and protect important shipping lanes from capture. The 56-acre park encompasses a point of land at the mouth of Sabine Lake.

149. SAM HOUSTON NATIONAL FOREST

LOCATION

40 miles north of Houston via IH-45 or U.S. 59.
Mailing address: Raven Ranger District: Box 1000, New Waverly, Texas 77358. Phone: 409-344-6205. Mailing address: Double Lake, 308 N. Belcher, Cleveland, Texas 77327. Phone: 713-592-6461. Stubblefield Lake and Kelley Pond, Drawer 1000, New Waverly, Texas 77358. Phone: 409-344-6205.

Campground	water	fee area	flush toilets	season	cold-water showers	concessions	boating	fishing	swimming	trails
Double Lake	•	•	•	all	•	•	•	•	•	•
Kelley Pond										•
Stubblefield Lake	•	•	•	all	•		•	•		•

FACILITIES

The whole forest is open for free primitive camping, except during hunting season and logging operations. Contact the headquarters for information on hunting camps.

Individual campsites cannot be reserved; group campgrounds, available at Double Lake, may be reserved. Swimming fee at Double Lake. Write the headquarters for maps and for information on day-use areas. The following parks have camping facilities. Fees charged.

Double Lake: 2 miles west of Coldspring on TX 150, south on FM 2025, east on FSR 210.

Kelley Pond: 11 miles west of New Waverly on FM 1375, south on FSR 204.

Stubblefield Lake: 11 miles west of New Waverly on FM 1375, 3 miles north on FSR 215.

MAIN ATTRACTIONS

Sam Houston National Forest consists of 160,401 acres in Montgomery, San Jacinto, and Walker counties. Lake Conroe, with 18,000 surface acres, offers swimming, fishing, and water sports. Within the forest, areas are designated specifically for off-road vehicles and for hiking.

Big Creek Scenic Area, west of Shepherd on TX 150, is a beautiful day-use area on the western edge of the Big Thicket. The 1,130 acres include rolling hills of mixed woodlands as well as spring-fed streams and rich bottomlands. There are several loop trails in the unit, some connecting with the Lone Star Hiking Trail and Double Lake. In contrast with the rest of the national forests in Texas, the Big Creek Scenic Area is managed to preserve the wilderness setting—no logging is permitted. There are no camping or picnicking facilities, and there is no water.

Double Lake Recreation Area is located on a 20-acre lake surrounded by dense, picturesque forest. Picnicking, swimming, fishing, canoeing, and paddleboating are available. A picnic pavilion can be reserved. A self-guided nature trail, three-quarters of a mile long, leads hikers through the towering pines and hardwoods typical of the East Texas forest, and a 5-mile trail connects Double Lake with the Big Creek Scenic Area. Throughout the summer, ranger programs and a small concession are available.

Kelley Pond Campground provides no water; it has one chemical toilet. It is in a trail-bike area used extensively by bikers.

Stubblefield Lake Campground, on a shallow inlet of Lake Conroe, offers fishing and hiking through the pine-palmetto woodlands. The park is frequented by trail bikers who have scarred the Lone Star Hiking Trail and the surrounding forest with deep ruts and unsightly mud holes. Unfortunately, the forest district has too few rangers to adequately enforce the regulations controlling the use of off-road vehicles.

HIKING

The 140-mile Lone Star Hiking Trail winds through Sam Houston National Forest. Its western trailhead is on FM 149 west of Lake Conroe. The trail passes through Kelley Pond and Stubblefield Lake campgrounds, then travels north of Huntsville State Park. It continues eastward to Double Lake and Big Creek Scenic Area; the eastern terminus is north of Cleveland on FM 1725. The trail is restricted to foot travel; however, it is much abused by trail bikers.

There are primitive campgrounds along the trail. Potable water is available at Stubblefield Lake and Double Lake campgrounds. Contact the headquarters for a map of the trail and other information. The Houston Group of the Lone Star Chapter of the Sierra Club helped establish the trail. For further information, contact the Sierra Club, 1 Main St., Room 5106A, Houston, Texas 77002.

151. SAN ANGELO: SPRING CREEK MARINA PARK

Tom Green County: 6 miles southwest of San Angelo on FM 584 to Fisherman's Road, then west 1.5 miles; on Lake Nasworthy. Mailing address; City Parks, P.O. Box 1751, San Angelo, Texas 76902. Phone: 915-944-3850. Camping: 24 sites with water, electricity, sewage, primitive camping area, restrooms with showers, store. Fees charged, reservations accepted, 10:30 P.M. curfew. Recreation: lake swimming, fishing, boating (30 mph speed limit), boat rentals.

SAN ANGELO: STATE PARK

Tom Green County. 6 miles southwest of San Angelo on U.S. 67 on Twin Buttes Reservoir. Mailing address: 3900-2 Mercedes, San Angelo, Texas 76901. Phone: 915-949-4757. For all state park reservations, call 512-389-8900. Camping: 45 campsites with electricity, group camping area, 12 RV sites without hookups, primitive camping area, chemical toilets, trailer dump station. Recreation: picnic areas, fishing, boat ramp, pavilion, store.

152. SAN ANTONIO: BRAUNIG LAKE PARK

Bexar County. Exit 130 off IH-37, south of San Antonio. Mailing address: 17500 Donop Rd., San Antonio, Texas 78223. Phone: 210-635-8289. Camping: numerous primitive campsites along shaded shoreline with tables, water nearby, flush toilets. Recreation: fishing from bank, pier, boats, boat ramp, fish-cleaning station, bird-watching. Entrance and camping fees charged. Day use only December and January. Camping limited to 7 days per month. Built as a cooling lake for a power plant, the lake offers good fishing for largemouth and striped bass, red drum, crappie, and catfish. Numerous birds are attracted to the lake, including egrets, cormorants, pelicans, osprey, ducks, and other waterfowl.

SAN ANTONIO: CALAVERAS LAKE PARK

Bexar County. South of San Antonio on U.S. 181, 2 miles east on FM 1604. Mailing address: 12991 Bernhardt Rd., San Antonio, Texas 78220. Phone: 210-635-8359. Camping: primitive campsites with tables and water nearby, flush toilets. Recreation: fishing for bass, catfish, and red drum; lighted pier, fish-cleaning station, boat ramp, water-skiing, fishing boat rental, concession stand. Open all year. Entrance and camping fees charged.

152. SEA RIM STATE PARK

LOCATION
Jefferson County. 24 miles southwest of Port Arthur on TX 87. Mailing address: Box 1066, Sabine Pass, Texas 77655. Phone: 409-971-2559. For state park reservations, call 512-389-8900.

FACILITIES
Camping: primitive camping on beach, primitive camping on platforms in marsh accessible by boat, 20 RV sites with water and electricity, 10 tent sites with water, modern restrooms with showers, trailer dump station. Fees charged.

Recreation: picnicking, nature trail with trail-guide booklet, interpretive exhibits, observation blinds accessible by boat, swimming in the Gulf of Mexico, fishing and boating in the Gulf and marsh, hunting waterfowl in designated areas of the Marshlands Unit.

MAIN ATTRACTIONS
With 15,109 acres of sandy beaches and marshes, Sea Rim State park provides a variety of recreational opportunities for fishermen, hunters, boaters, and nature enthusiasts. The park's gently sloping beaches are a haven for lovers of sun, sand, and surf. One of the outstanding features of the park is the 3,640-foot-long elevated boardwalk, the Gambusia Trail, which juts into the marsh. A pamphlet describes the significance of the coastal wetlands, their vital importance to wildlife, and some of the plants and animals commonly seen along the boardwalk.

The park is separated into two distinct areas by TX 87. On the coastal side is the D. Roy Harrington Beach Unit, site of the park headquarters, campgrounds, marsh boardwalk, and 5.2 miles of beaches. The Marshlands Unit, comprising the major portion of the park, is accessible only by boat. There are four camping platforms and four wildlife observation blinds along the waterways dissecting the salt marsh.

Galveston Island State Park is on the west end of Galveston Island. Galveston Island, with its outstanding beaches, seafood restaurants, museums, and historic structures, is south on TX 87 via a free ferry across Galveston Bay. TX 87 has been closed from Sea Rim to High Island because of the hurricane damage. To reach Galveston via High Island, you have to return to Port Arthur and take TX 73 and TX 124 to High Island.

ECOLOGY

Sea Rim State Park preserves coastal marshlands and lakes, estuaries and mud flats, and the unique sea rim marsh from which the park derives its name. Silt and mud flowing from the Sabine River are deposited by Gulf currents onto the northernmost 2.2 miles of beach in the park. Marsh grasses extend into the surf zone, forming the sea rim marsh—an excellent habitat for many types of wildlife. The shoreline is swept by the tides, creating fertile nursery grounds for marine life. This type of habitat is essential for shrimp, blue crabs, redfish, menhaden, and other crustacean and fish species. Estuarine environments such as these are of vital importance to the overall fishing economy of the Texas coast.

The abundant microscopic zooplankton and decomposing organic matter in the marsh provide food for a complex web of life. Wading birds stalk across the marsh, hunting for small fish, and probe for tiny organisms in the mud flats. Herons and egrets are common, as are clapper rails, gulls, and mottled ducks. The dense stands of marsh grass provide an important nesting habitat for many birds and mammals.

More than 289 species of birds have been recorded in the park. The Texas coastal wetlands are the wintering grounds for 45 percent of the ducks and 90 percent of the geese along the Central Flyway. The shallow lakes, mud flats, marshlands, canebrakes, scattered shrubs, and isolated trees provide migrating birds a welcome respite from their long flight across the Gulf.

Mink are infrequently seen along the boardwalk, and alligators and otters inhabit the marshlands. Nutrias, rabbits, skunks, raccoons, and opossums are year-round residents of the park, as are mosquitoes. Infestations of those pesky insects occur periodically, making repellent and a bug-proof sleeping shelter absolute necessities.

HISTORY

The coastal marshlands have been of significant importance through the ages. Shell mounds left by prehistoric Indians may represent the ancestors of the Atakapa Indians, who lived in areas from Louisiana to Galveston before they were eliminated there in the 1800s. Pirates frequented the upper Texas coast in the early 1800s, including the colorful Jean Lafitte, who founded Galveston.

During the Civil War, Confederate forts guarded the Texas coast against Union invasion. The ruins of the earthen fortifications of Fort Manhassett may be seen at a historical marker on TX 87 near Sabine Pass. The Sabine Pass Battleground State Historical Park commemorates the battle at Fort Griffin where 46 Texans repelled the Union navy and protected the strategic port of Beaumont from invasion. It is 9 miles north on TX 87 and has picnic tables, a boat ramp, RV and tent campsites, restrooms, and a fish-cleaning station.

153. SEMINOLE CANYON STATE HISTORICAL PARK

LOCATION
Val Verde County. 42 miles northwest of Del Rio on U.S. 90, east of the Pecos River.
Mailing address: Box 820, Comstock, Texas 78837. Phone: 915-292-4464. For state park reservations, call 512-389-8900.

FACILITIES
Camping: 8 campsites with water only, 23 campsites with water and electricity, modern restrooms with showers, trailer dump station. Fees charged.

Recreation: picnicking, hiking trail, tours of the canyon, interpretive exhibits.

MAIN ATTRACTIONS
Seminole Canyon is in an area of West Texas characterized by rugged countryside, deep canyons, and sparse vegetation. In many of the canyons, millions of years of erosion have created massive rock overhangs that were used by Indians for shelter 9,000 to 12,000 years ago. The outstanding feature of the park is the impressive pictographs, paintings thousands of years old, found on the canyon walls.

The interpretive center has informative and dramatic displays describing the cultural history of the area. Beautiful dioramas and full-size models depict the life-styles of the inhabitants from perhaps 12,000 years ago through the ranching and railroad era of the last century. The history of the first trans-Texas railroad, which passed through the park and connected West Texas both culturally and economically with the rest of the state, is presented with period photographs and artifacts. The artwork and historical interpretation in the center are the best of any state park in Texas.

HIKING

Some of the most spectacular pictographs in the canyon are in Fate Bell Shelter immediately below the interpretive center. Access to that historic artwork is limited to tours led Wednesday through Sunday at 10 A.M. and 3 P.M. The trail is slightly over a mile long each way and is fairly steep. In addition to the tours, visitors can walk along a hiking trail leading to a scenic overlook 200 feet above the Rio Grande. That trail, 3.5 miles each way, is on level ground above the canyon.

ECOLOGY

Seminole Canyon lies close to the juncture of three major vegetation zones in Texas: the Trans-Pecos Chihuahuan Desert province, the Edwards Plateau oak-juniper association, and the South Texas brush country. In addition, the nearby 67,000-acre Amistad Reservoir creates an unusually humid habitat in an otherwise arid part of Texas. The combination of vegetation from those different regions provides a diversity of plant and animal life in the park.

Unusual birds of the Mexican borderland occur in the park, including the zone-tailed hawk, green kingfisher, black phoebe, and varied bunting. Scaled quail, verdins, pyrrhuloxias, and black-chinned sparrows are commonly seen grassland species. Sandpipers, other shorebirds, herons, and ducks frequent the backwaters of the lake in the canyons along the Rio Grande.

HISTORY

Seminole Canyon and Val Verde County are rich in history, with human artifacts dating back possibly 12,000 years. Some of the oldest pictographs in the United States are located in the park. The pictures, dating from historical times to approximately 2,000 to 8,000 years ago, were painted on the protected canyon walls using pigments mixed with animal fat. White, black, red, yellow, and orange pigments were made from complex mixtures of clay and minerals.

There are numerous shelters with pictographs in the area, some with murals up to a hundred feet long. The interpretation of the rock art can only be surmised from known meanings of similar motifs from contemporary Indians. Pictographs dating from various periods throughout the past several thousand years can be classified according to subject matter and style; Forrest Kirkland and W. W. Newcomb's *The Rock Art of Texas Indians* depicts the many types. The rock shelters also contain remnants of sandals, clothes, and baskets woven from yucca and sotol. Similar articles are still being made in Mexico today.

The canyon probably derived its name from displaced bands of Seminole Indians from Florida, who survived briefly in the arid terrain, or from the Seminole-Negroes who settled at Eagle Pass after 1870. Scouts from that group assisted in the government campaign to eradicate the Plains Indians in West Texas from 1874 to 1875.

In 1882, the Southern Pacific Railroad reached the area of the park. The route connecting San Antonio to El Paso had to cross the deep Pecos River gorge, a task that required blasting two 1,500-foot tunnels to reach the river level. The bridge was built at the confluence of the Rio Grande and the Pecos River, and the last spike completing the route was driven in 1883, three miles west of the Pecos River.

Frontier life west of the Pecos is epitomized by the Judge Roy Bean Visitor Center, 20 miles away in Langtry. The original Jersey Lilly Saloon, named for the actress Lilly Langtry, a beautiful cactus garden, and a tourist center with maps and information are open daily.

154. SHERMAN: HERMAN BAKER PARK

Grayson County. West of Sherman on TX 56. 49 acres on a small reservoir. Mailing address: Box 1106, Sherman, Texas 75090. Phone: 903-892-4545, extension 219. Camping: 10 free primitive campsites accessible on foot, chemical toilets. Reservations accepted. Recreation: picnic areas, 2-mile hiking trail, fishing, boating (no motorboats). Open all year.

155. SILVERTON: LAKE MACKENZIE PARK

Mackenzie Municipal Water Authority. Briscoe and Swisher counties. 50 miles south of Amarillo on IH-27 to Tulia, 24 miles east on TX 86, 7 miles north on TX 207, in Tule Canyon. Mailing address: Route 1, Box 14, Silverton, Texas 79257. Phone: 806-633-4318. Camping: primitive campsites with water, 38 RV sites with electricity and water, group trailer campgrounds with electricity, flush toilets, trailer dump station. Reservations not accepted. Fees charged. Recreation: picnic areas, hiking trails, swimming in lake, water-skiing, fishing, boat ramps, pavilion, store. Open all year. Poor facilities for camping.

156. SONORA: CAVERNS OF SONORA

LOCATION
Sutton County. 10 miles west of Sonora on IH-10, 6 miles south on RR 1989.
Mailing address: Box 1196, Sonora, Texas 76950. Phone: 915-387-3105. Fax: 915-387-6507.

FACILITIES
Camping: 16 campsites with tables, water, modern restrooms with showers, 32 pull-through RV sites, store, snack bar. Fees charged.

Recreation: tours of commercially operated cave with spectacular formations, .5-mile nature trail, picnicking, summer dinner theater on Friday and Saturday.

MAIN ATTRACTIONS
The Caverns of Sonora have some of the most beautiful formations of any cave in Texas, or in the United States. A past president of the National Speleological Society said that its beauty couldn't be exaggerated, even by Texans. The tour leads through chambers and passageways lined with soda straws, cave coral, popcorn, and cave crystals, including one that looks like a butterfly. The cave is open seven days a week.

157. SOUTH LLANO RIVER STATE PARK

LOCATION
Kimble County. 4 miles south of Junction on U.S. 377.
Mailing address: HC 15, Box 224, Junction, Texas 76849. Phone: 915-446-3994. For all state park reservations, call 512-389-8900.

FACILITIES
Camping: 57 campsites with water and electricity, 12 walk-in tent sites, restrooms, showers, trailer dump station; primitive camping area for backpacking. Fees charged.

Recreation: picnicking, hiking, river activities, tubing, canoeing, fishing, bird-watching, backpacking, mountain biking.

MAIN ATTRACTIONS
This 2,700-acre park on the south shore of the Llano River includes 2 miles of riverfront. About 440 acres of the 500-acre park are bottomland heavily wooded with pecan trees. Hundreds of turkeys

roost in the trees in the winter and feast on the pecans. Access to the roosting area, which includes much of the park, will be limited while the turkeys are present from October to March. The endangered black-capped vireo also nests in the park in the spring. The park contains 18 miles of hiking and biking trails, 20 wildlife observation blinds, and an oxbow lake for fishing. Portions of the adjacent 2,610-acre Walter Buck Wildlife Management Area are open for hiking and biking, except during hunting seasons.

158. SOUTH PADRE ISLAND: ANDY BOWIE PARK

Cameron County. On South Padre Island, 5 miles north of the causeway. Mailing address: Box 2106, South Padre Island, Texas 78597. Phone: 210-761-5493. Camping: free primitive camping on beach. Recreation: swimming, fishing. Open all year.

SOUTH PADRE ISLAND: ISLA BLANCA RV PARK

Cameron County. Several blocks south of the causeway on South Padre Island. Mailing address: Box 2106, South Padre Island, Texas 78597. Phone: 210-761-5493. Camping: 613 RV sites with water, electricity, and sewage hookups; tent camping in open area, flush toilets, showers, trailer dump station. Reservations accepted by mail only. Fees charged. Recreation: swimming, fishing, boating, jetty pier, beach front pavilions. Open all year. Crowded RV park. The Port Isabel lighthouse, on the mainland, is open for tours.

159. STEPHEN F. AUSTIN STATE HISTORICAL PARK

LOCATION
Austin County. 30 miles west of Houston on IH-10 to San Felipe exit, 7 miles north on FM 1458 to PR 38.
Mailing address: Box 125, San Felipe, Texas 77473. Phone: 409-885-3613. For all state park reservations, call 512-389-9000.

FACILITIES

Camping: 40 campsites with water only, 40 campsites with water, electricity, and sewage hookups; 20 screened shelters, modern restrooms with showers, trailer dump station. Fees charged.

Recreation: picnic areas and playgrounds, short hiking trail, historic structures, swimming pool (summer only), fishing in the Brazos River, 18-hole golf course, large screened shelter with kitchen, park store.

MAIN ATTRACTIONS

Stephen F. Austin State Historical Park, named after the "Father of Texas," is located on a scenic bend of the Brazos River. The densely wooded park is ideal for a leisurely holiday, since a variety of recreational activities are available. The historic San Felipe de Austin, the first settlement of Austin's colonists, is a short distance outside the campground entrance. Replicas of Austin's log cabin and of a general store (now housing a museum, a statue of Austin, and other memorabilia) mark the original town site and ferry crossing.

Situated in the rich bottomland of the Brazos River, the 664-acre park provides an excellent environment for a wide variety of wildlife. Deer, raccoons, skunks, armadillos, opossums, foxes, and squirrels live in the woodlands, as do many birds. Large elms, sycamores, pecans, hackberries, and a number of oak species provide food and shelter for wildlife and a shady, tranquil setting for humans.

HISTORY

The first Anglo colonists in Texas established their headquarters at San Felipe de Austin in 1823. Stephen Austin brought several hundred families to colonize Texas on acreage granted him by the Mexican government. San Felipe was the social, economic, and political center of the colony until the Revolution in 1836. It was the location of the conventions of 1832 and 1833 and of the Consultation of 1835, which led to the Revolution.

During the Revolution, the provisional government was centered in San Felipe. The first Texas newspaper was published in the town, and the Texas Rangers were organized there. The original town, known as the Cradle of Texas Liberty, was burned by its inhabitants when they fled the advancing Mexican army.

160. STEPHENVILLE CITY PARK

Erath County. 70 miles southwest of Fort Worth on U.S. 377 to Stephenville, 2 blocks north on TX 108. Mailing address: 378 W. Long St., Stephenville, Texas 76401. Phone: 817-965-3864. Camping: 10 RV campsites with water and electricity, 50 primitive campsites, flush toilets, showers, trailer dump station. Fees charged. Recreation: picnic areas and playgrounds, nature trail, bicycle paths, swimming pool, fishing in the Bosque River, tennis courts, softball field, pavilion, recreation hall. Open all year.

161. SWEETWATER: LAKE SWEETWATER MUNICIPAL PARK

Nolan County. 40 miles west of Abilene on IH-20 to FM 1856, 7 miles south to lake. Mailing address: Rt. 1, Box 91, Sweetwater, Texas 79556. Phone: 915-235-5191. Camping: 10 campsites with water and electricity, flush toilets, trailer dump station. Fees charged. Recreation: picnic areas and playgrounds, swimming beach, fishing, boat ramp, golf course, store. Open all year.

162. TYLER STATE PARK

LOCATION
Smith County. 8 miles north of Tyler on FM 14.
Mailing address: 789 Park Rd. 16, Tyler, Texas 75706-9141. Phone: 214-597-5338. For all state park reservations, call 512-389-8900.

FACILITIES
Camping: 42 campsites with water only, 38 campsites with water and electricity, 39 campsites with water, electricity, and sewage hookups; 30 group trailer sites with electricity, 35 screened shelters, day-use group shelter with kitchen and dining facilities for 100 people, modern restrooms with showers, trailer dump station. Fees charged.

Recreation: picnic areas and playgrounds, hiking and nature trails with trail-guide booklet, minibike trail, interpretive exhibits, swimming in lake, fishing pier, boating, paddleboat rentals (summer only), store (weekends and summer only).

MAIN ATTRACTIONS

The beauty of the aromatic East Texas Piney Woods in this 985-acre park is accented by a picturesque 65-acre lake. Stocked with channel catfish and black bass, the lake is circled on one side by a hiking trail. Bicyclists will enjoy the undulating road through the park.

Nearby Tyler is famous for its beautiful roses and azaleas. The town hosts the annual Azalea and Spring Flower Trail, a route through the most colorful and historic sections of Tyler, during the last week in March. The Texas Rose Festival is scheduled in mid October.

Another area attraction, the Governor Hogg Shrine State Historical Park, a day-use area, is in Quitman, 37 miles north of Tyler.

HIKING/BIKING

The Whispering Pines Nature Trail winds through the forest of tall pines between the park headquarters and the group camping area. A pamphlet identifies many of the plants and describes the different vegetation communities along the trail. Mountain bikers can enjoy the 4.5-mile loop and a 2.25-loop trail.

ECOLOGY

Tyler State Park preserves a good example of the mixed hardwood-pine forest that once covered East Texas. The fast-draining ridgetops and the moist bottomlands are covered with a wide variety of trees, shrubs, and flowers. The drier uplands are forested with loblolly and shortleaf pines, hickories, post and blackjack oaks, and eastern red cedars, while sweetgums, elms, red oaks, and American holly trees dominate the lowlands.

A number of smaller trees and shrubs grow in the shaded forest. Sassafras with three shapes of leaves, rusty blackhaw, sumac, farkleberry, and other shade-tolerant plants form a diverse understory of vegetation.

In the spring, dogwood and redbud trees burst into bloom, patches of mayapples cover the woodland floor and perfume the air, and delicate shield ferns grow along the creek banks. The red flowers of the trumpet honeysuckle vine dangle from pine trees, complementing the snow-white flowers of the dogwoods.

The park woods are active with gray squirrels feeding on acorns and birds singing high in the trees. After sunset, raccoons and opossums patrol the campground, investigating trash cans, and armadillos root through the leaves covering the forest floor.

163. VICTORIA: COLETO CREEK REGIONAL PARK

Guadalupe-Blanco River Authority. Goliad County. 15 miles southwest of Victoria on U.S. 59. 190 acres on 3,100-acre Coleto Creek Reservoir. Mailing address: P.O. Box 68, Fannin, Texas 77960. Phone: 512-575-6366. Camping: 60 campsites with water and electricity, flush toilets, showers, trailer dump station. Reservations accepted. Fees charged. Recreation: picnic areas, half-mile nature trail, swimming in reservoir, fishing, 200-foot lighted pier, water-skiing, boat ramp, pavilion, park store (April–September). Open all year. Good facilities. The Fannin Battlegrounds are 5 miles southwest on U.S. 59.

VICTORIA RV PARK

City Parks Department: Victoria County. 2200 Vine Street, adjacent to Riverside Park; from U.S. 87, take Red River Street approximately 0.2 mile west to intersection of Vine Street. Mailing address: Box 1758, Victoria, Texas 77902-1758. Phone: 512-573-2401. Camping: 10 acres; 18 sites with water, electricity, sewage; dump station; water available but no restrooms or tables in camping area. Fees charged, no reservations. Open all year. Recreation: adjacent to Riverside Park with sports field, golf, playgrounds, hike and bike trails, fishing in Guadalupe River, and the Texas Zoo, an outstanding zoo featuring animals indigenous to Texas.

164. VIDOR: CLAIBORNE WEST PARK

Orange County. 11 miles east of Beaumont on IH-10, eastern city limits of Vidor. 453 acres of woodlands, swamps, and meadows. Mailing address; 4105 North St., Vidor, Texas 77662. Phone: 409-745-2255. Camping: 15 primitive campsites with water nearby, flush toilets. Reservations accepted. Fees charged. Recreation: picnic areas and playgrounds, 6 miles of nature trails, fishing, canoeing on Cow Bayou, softball field, amphitheater for public use, group picnic shelters. Open all year. The combination of diverse facilities, excellent playgrounds, and a pleasant natural environment makes this one of the better county parks in Texas.

165. VILLAGE CREEK STATE PARK

LOCATION
Hardin County. In Lumberton turn east off U.S. 96 on Alma Dr. Mailing address: P.O. Box 8575, Lumberton, Texas 75677. Phone: 409-755-7322. For all state park reservations, call 512-389-8900.

FACILITIES
Camping: 25 campsites with water and electricity, 17 walk-in tent sites, 1 group shelter for 20 people, primitive camping on backpack trail, restrooms, showers, trailer dump station.

Recreation: picnicking, canoeing, hiking, swimming on sandbar, bike trails, group facility with kitchen.

MAIN ATTRACTIONS
The scenic Village Creek winds through 2 miles of this 942-acre park. Only 44 acres are developed, leaving the remainder for exploring and nature study, bird-watching, and photography. Backpackers can camp in designated areas along a 7.2-mile trail, and hikers can also enjoy a 1.3-mile nature trail. River birch, cypress, and tupelo trees line the white sandbars of the tranquil creek, and a diversity of plant and wildlife call this portion of the Big Thicket home. See the Big Thicket National Preserve description for more information on the ecology of this area.

166. WACO: FORT FISHER PARK

McLennan County. In Waco off IH-35, Exit 335B, south side of Brazos River Bridge. Mailing address: Box 2570, Waco, Texas 76702-2570. Phone: 800-922-6386 or 817-750-5989. Camping: tent sites, RV campsites with water, electricity, and sewage hookups; screened shelters, flush toilets, showers, trailer dump station. Fees charged. Recreation: Texas Ranger Hall of Fame and Museum. Open all year.

167. WELLINGTON: COLLINGSWORTH COUNTY PIONEER PARK

Collingsworth County. 37 miles north of Childress on U.S. 83 through Wellington. Mailing address: County Courthouse, Wellington, Texas 79095. Phone: 806-447-5408. On Salt Fork of the Red River. Camping: 24 campsites with water and electricity, group camping area, flush toilets, trailer dump station. Fees charged. Recreation: picnic areas and playgrounds. Open all year.

168. YOAKUM COUNTY PARK

Yoakum County. 7 miles north of Denver City on TX 214. Mailing address: P.O. Box 438, Denver City, Texas 79323. Phone 806-592-3166. Facilities: 10 sites with electricity, flush toilets, dump station, walk-in primitive camping; no water or tables at sites. Picnic area, playgrounds. Fees charged, reservations accepted. Open all year.

State and National Historical and Day-Use Parks Without Camping

ADMIRAL NIMITZ MUSEUM AND HISTORICAL CENTER

Gillespie County. Downtown Fredericksburg on U.S. 290. Mailing address: Box 777, Fredericksburg, Texas 78624. Phone: 210-997-4379.

Located in the old Steamboat Hotel in downtown Fredericksburg, this museum and Peace Gardens are dedicated to the soldiers on both sides of the conflict who died in the Pacific during World War II. As commander in chief of the Pacific, Admiral Chester W. Nimitz, a native of Fredericksburg, commanded more men and military power than anyone in history. After the war, Admiral Nimitz honored the Japanese by returning Admiral Togo's samurai swords and initiating a fund drive to restore his flagship, the *Mikasa*, now a Japanese national memorial. In an act of friendship, the Japanese built the Garden of Peace in the museum incorporating classic Japanese architecture.

The museum includes a self-guided "History Walk of the Pacific War" with an extensive collection of war relics. On display are various American and Japanese attack planes and dive bombers, tanks, artillery weapons, bombs, and amphibious vehicles. Admission charged. Enchanted Rock State Natural Area is 18 miles north on FM 965.

THE ALAMO

San Antonio. Alamo Plaza, downtown. Mailing address: Alamo Plaza, San Antonio, Texas 78205. Phone: 210-225-1391.

This famous Texas shrine to freedom was established in 1718 and known as Mission San Antonio de Valero. In 1836, 187 Texas volunteers held off thousands of Mexican soldiers for 13 days. They all were killed, but the cry, "Remember the Alamo," became the motto for the revolution. Sam Houston defeated the Mexican forces a month later and gained independence for Texas. The Alamo and adjacent museum are open 9 A.M. to 5:30 P.M. weekdays and Saturday, 10 A.M. to 5:30 P.M. on Sundays. Admission free.

THE BATTLESHIP TEXAS

Harris County. From Houston, east on La Porte Freeway, TX 225, north on Battleground Rd., TX 134. Mailing address: 3527 Battleground Rd., La Porte, Texas 77571. Phone: 713-479-2411.

Once the most powerful weapon in the world, this battleship, or dreadnought as it was known, is now moored adjacent to the San Jacinto Battleground and Monument. Commissioned in 1914, it saw action for 32 years and is the only remaining ship that served in both world wars. It is longer than five football fields, had a crew of 1,800 men, and had a main battery of ten 45-caliber guns with a range of 12 miles. The ship is open daily, except Christmas, from 10 A.M. until 6 P.M. in the summer and 5 P.M. the rest of the year. Admission charged.

BIG SPRING STATE PARK

Howard County. Within city of Big Spring. Mailing address: #1 Scenic Drive, Big Spring, Texas 79720. Phone: 915-263-4931.

The 370-acre park is situated on Scenic Mountain, a 200-foot-high limestone mesa overlooking the city. Recreation includes picnic sites, pavilion, playground, restrooms, nature trail, scenic drive, and an interpretive center with Indian and natural history exhibits. Day use only, entrance fee.

CADDOAN MOUNDS STATE HISTORIC SITE

Houston County. 6 miles southwest of Alto on TX 21. Mailing address: Route 2, Box 85C, Alto, Texas 75925. Phone: 409-858-3218.

From 1000 B.C. to A.D. 1500, for 2,500 years, the Great Mound Builder culture thrived throughout the eastern woodlands of the United States. The Caddos were the westernmost group of Mound Builders. They had a complex cultural-economical-political system and for 500 years dominated East Texas and portions of Louisiana, Arkansas, and Oklahoma. The Caddos occupied this particular village site from A.D. 500 until the thirteenth century. The park includes a small museum with dioramas and artifacts and reconstructed Indian dwellings.

CONFEDERATE REUNION GROUNDS STATE HISTORICAL PARK

Limestone County. From Mexia take U.S. 84 west to FM 2705, then 3 miles south. Mailing address: Rt. 3, Box 95, Mexia, Texas 76667. Phone: 817-562-5751.

This small day-use park preserves an 1872 house, an 1893 dance pavilion, and a two-story log house. Besides shaded picnic tables and a pavilion, the park offers a hiking trail that leads alongside the Navasota River and Jacks Creek. Hours: winter, 8:00 A.M. to 5:00 P.M.; summer, 8:00 A.M. to 8:00 P.M. Entrance fee charged.

EISENHOWER BIRTHPLACE STATE HISTORICAL PARK

Grayson County. Located at 208 East Day Street, Denison, Texas 75020. Phone: 903-465-8908.

The park surrounds the two-story, frame house where Dwight Eisenhower was born on October 14, 1890. The house is furnished with Eisenhower family belongings and period antiques. Visitors can take an "Ike hike" through the wooded six acres surrounding the house and explore the woods, railroad tracks, and creeks where Ike grew up. The visitor's center includes a bookstore and a viewing library with videos depicting Ike's role in World War II and his presidency. Open 9:00 A.M. to 5:00 P.M. every day except Christmas, Thanksgiving, New Year's Day. Admission charged.

FORT LANCASTER STATE HISTORIC SITE

Crockett County. East of Sheffield on U.S. 290. Mailing address: Box 306, Sheffield, Texas 79781. Phone: 915-836-4391.

Operated from 1855 to 1861, this fort was one of the string of forts stretching across West Texas established to combat hostile Indians. It was near the Pecos River crossing on the road connecting El Paso and San Antonio. At its peak, the fort housed 72 soldiers in 25 stone and wooden buildings. Today, only a few of the hewn limestone chimneys remain. Open Wednesday through Sunday.

FORT LEATON STATE HISTORIC SITE

Presidio County. South of Presidio on TX 170. Mailing address: Box 1220, Presidio, Texas 79845. Phone: 915-229-3616.

This private fort was built by Benjamin Leaton on a bluff overlooking the Rio Grande in 1848. Leaton made his living collecting Indian scalps for bounty, terrorizing Mexican settlements, and operating a farming enterprise in the rich floodplains. The beautiful white-washed adobe structure with massive walls, 25 rooms, high ceilings, and vaulted doorways remains in excellent condition. It is on the scenic River Road that connects Presidio with Lajitas.

FORT MCKAVETT STATE HISTORIC SITE

Menard County. Mailing address: Box 867, Fort McKavett, Texas 76841. Phone: 915-396-2358.

Established on the San Saba River in 1852, this frontier fort was located on the Upper El Paso Road. It protected immigrants to the California goldfields and local settlers from hostile Indians. The fort was abandoned during the Civil War and reestablished in 1868 because of increased Indian warfare. Finally, it was no longer needed and was abandoned in 1883. Civilians moved in and lived in the fort, keeping the building in good condition. Today, 14 structures have been restored. The park also has interpretive exhibits and a self-guided trail.

FRANKLIN MOUNTAIN STATE PARK

El Paso County. In city limits: from IH-10, take Canutillo Exit (U.S. 54) north, west on Transmountain Road (TX 375) into park. Mailing address: Box 200, Canutillo, Texas 79835-9998. Phone: 915-566-6441.

This 23,810-acre undeveloped park preserves a section of the 3,500-foot-high mountain range overlooking El Paso. As a day-use park, no water or other facilities, except a picnic area, are provided. The park provides excellent opportunities for hiking, bird and wildlife watching, and experiencing the Chihuahuan Desert. Creosote bush, yuccas, cacti, agave, catclaw, and other thorny shrubs dominate the rocky limestone slopes, while hackberry, ash, and cottonwood trees seek the protection and moisture of canyon springs. Eight trails, varying from one to six miles long, lead to springs, crawl caves, and ridge tops with steep vertical drops. Hikers should come prepared for rough, rocky terrain, close encounters with thorny vegetation, and summer temperatures near 100°F. Bobcats, coyotes, mule deer, an occasional mountain lion, and a host of birds frequent the springs in the park.

FULTON MANSION STATE HISTORICAL PARK

Aransas County. North of Rockport, 3 miles on TX 35 to Fulton Beach Road, at intersection with Henderson Street. Mailing address: P.O. Box 1859, Fulton, Texas 78358. Phone: 512-729-0386.

Overlooking Aransas Bay, the Fulton Mansion recaptures the grandeur of the 1870s cattle barons. George Fulton came to Texas to fight for Texas independence and eventually amassed a 165,000-acre ranch in the coastal bend. He spared no expense in building his mansion in the French Second Empire style of architecture and incorporated the latest technology—gas light chandeliers and gravity fed water to flush toilets and bathtubs. Open for guided tours only, 9:00 to 11:30 A.M., 1:00 to 3:30 P.M. Wednesday through Sunday, closed Christmas. Admission charged, reservations recommended one month in advance. Nearby attractions include Goose Island State Park and Aransas National Wildlife Refuge.

JIM HOGG STATE HISTORICAL PARK

Cherokee County. 2 miles northeast of Rusk off U.S. 84. Mailing address: RR 5, Box 80, Rusk, Texas 75785. Phone: 903-683-4850.

This wooded 175-acre park preserves the homesite of the state's first native Texas governor. He was known as the people's governor and is considered, along with Stephen F. Austin, Sam Houston, and John H. Reagan, one of Texas' four greatest statesmen. He was one of the founders of Texaco. When he died in 1906, he told his daughter, Ima, that he desired no monument of stone. "Let my children plant at the head of my grave a pecan tree and at my feet an old-fashioned walnut. And when the trees shall bear, let the pecans and fruit be given out among the plain people so that they may plant them and make Texas a land of trees." The park includes a museum, historic structures, picnic tables, and nature trails through the scenic Piney Woods. The Governor Hogg Shrine State Historical Park in Quitman features the Governor's Honeymoon Cottage, another renovated home, and a museum.

LONGHORN CAVERNS STATE PARK

Burnet County. 6 miles south of Burnet on U.S. 281 to Park Road 4, then 6 miles west. Mailing address: Rt. 2, Box 23, Burnet, Texas 78611. Phone, tour information: 512-756-6976; business office: 512-756-4680.

Recreation: hourly cave tours, picnicking, nature trails, gift shop, snack bar. Indian artifacts indicate that human use of the extensive caverns beneath the 637-acre park dates back to prehistoric times. The Confederates stored gunpowder in the cave during the Civil War, and outlaws sought its darkness for safety. Later, local residents dined and danced in the cool, 64° Hall of Marble. Though not as decorated with flowstone formations as some central Texas caves, the huge rooms and sculpted hallways reflect the exquisite beauty of nature's handiwork. The labyrinth passageways reach 130 feet below the surface, making the cave one of the longest ever discovered. Admission charged. Open daily, except December 24 and 25.

LUBBOCK LAKE LANDMARK STATE HISTORICAL PARK

Lubbock County. Northwest Lubbock, near intersection of Loop 289 and Clovis Road (U.S. 84). Mailing address: 2202 Landmark Lane, Lubbock, Texas 79415. Phone: 806-765-0737; fax: 806-741-0306.

The perennial springs in Yellowhouse Draw have attracted humans for 12,000 years. When irrigation lowered the water table and decreased flow in the 1930s, the springs were dredged. Excavation revealed one of the richest archaeological sites in North America. The 336-acre site is the only location with artifacts from all the cultures known to have existed on the Southern Plains. Facilities include picnicking areas, an interpretive center and exhibit gallery, and a one-mile self-guided trail of the excavations with wayside exhibits. A four-mile trail through the natural area offers opportunities to see wildflowers, prairie dogs, burrowing owls, and small mammals such as foxes and coyotes. Open Tuesday through Saturday, 9:00 A.M. to 5:00 P.M., Sundays, 1:00 to 5:00 P.M. Admission charged.

LYNDON B. JOHNSON NATIONAL HISTORICAL PARK

Blanco County. In Johnson City. Mailing address: Johnson City, Texas 87636. Phone: 210-868-7128. Open daily except Christmas and New Year's Day.

This park preserves the boyhood home and mementos from the early life of President Johnson and gives a perspective on the roots that influenced him. In addition, it includes a living-history pioneer ranch with exhibits, a longhorn herd, log cabin, rock barn, and a museum documenting the rise to glory of the cowboy and trail drive.

LYNDON B. JOHNSON STATE HISTORICAL PARK

Gillespie County. 14 miles west of Johnson City on U.S. 290. Mailing address: Box 238, Stonewall, Texas 78671. Phone: 210-644-2252.

Created in honor of President Johnson and located across the Pedernales River from the president's ranch, the state park includes a visitor center with films, memorabilia, and exhibits, a bus tour of the LBJ Ranch, restored log houses, swimming pool, picnic areas, exhibition longhorns, bison and other native animals, nature trail, and a living-history farm depicting life in 1918. In the spring, the wildflowers make this one of the most beautiful regions of the state.

MONUMENT HILL AND KREISCHE BREWERY STATE HISTORIC SITE

Fayette County. 1 mile south of La Grange on U.S. 77, west on Spur 92. Mailing address: 414 State Loop 92, La Grange, Texas 78945-5733. Phone: 409-968-5658. Recreation: picnicking, interpretive and nature trails, historic buildings.

Twice in 1842, six years after Texas won its independence from Mexico, Mexican forces captured and looted San Antonio. After the second attack, a group of volunteers originating in La Grange marched toward San Antonio. The group intercepted the Mexican army, and after a hard battle, the fifteen surviving Texans were taken to Mexico. An army was raised to rescue the prisoners, but they too were captured and taken into Mexico. As punishment for an attempted escape, one prisoner in ten was shot. The men drew beans from a pot, with a black bean meaning death and a white bean meaning life. After the United States defeated Mexico in 1847, the bones of the slain prisoners were returned and interred at Monument Hill.

In 1849, Heinrich Kreisch purchased the property and constructed the first brewery in the state. His descendants lived in his original stone house until 1952. Guided tours of the brewery and home are on Saturdays and Sundays at 2:00 and 3:30 P.M. Admission charged.

PORT ISABEL LIGHTHOUSE STATE HISTORIC STRUCTURE

Cameron County. In Port Isabel near the South Padre Island Causeway. Mailing address: Box 863, Port Isabel, Texas 78578. Phone: 210-943-1172.

This 60-foot lighthouse was constructed in 1853 to aid navigation to the army facilities at Point Isabel. The light could be seen for 16 miles. Except for a few years of disuse, the light guided ships until 1905. The facility is open from 10 A.M. until 5 P.M. daily. Admission charged.

SAN ANTONIO MISSIONS NATIONAL HISTORICAL PARK

San Antonio. Mailing address: 2202 Roosevelt, San Antonio, Texas 78210. Phone: 210-229-5701.

Four missions built by Franciscan friars in the early 1700s. Admission charged. All the missions are open daily 9 A.M. to 6 P.M., April 1 to October; 8 A.M. to 5 P.M., October to March.

Mission Nuestra Senora de la Purisima Concepcion, 807 Mission Rd. Oldest unrestored stone church still in use in the United States, and the best preserved. Some original frescoes still can be seen.

Mission San Francisco de la Espada, 10040 Espada. Has an ornate triple bell tower and is still used as a church.

Mission San José y San Miguel de Agauyo, 6539 San Jose Dr. at Mission Rd. The entire compound of this "Queen of the Missions" has been restored. Some original art remains, including the famous Rose Window. The chapel is still used for church services.

Mission San Juan Capistrano, 9101 Graf Rd. off Mission Rd. The small chapel is still used as a church.

SAN JACINTO BATTLEGROUND STATE HISTORICAL PARK

Harris County. From Houston, east on La Porte Freeway, TX 225, north on Battleground Rd. Mailing address: 3523 Highway 134, La Porte, Texas 77571. Phone: 713-479-2431.

On April 21, 1836, Sam Houston and a ragtag group of 927 Texans surprised and attacked the Mexican General Santa Anna and his army of 1,600 soldiers. Hemmed in by waterways, the Mexicans suffered 630 casualties and 208 wounded and surrendered in 18 minutes. The Texans lost 9 men. After numerous defeats, the Texans finally won their independence and became a sovereign republic with Sam Houston as the first president. The 570-foot monument, 15 feet taller than the Washington Monument, was opened in 1939 to commemorate the battle. The monument and museum as its base are open daily from 9 A.M. to 6 P.M. Admission is free, but a fee is charged to ride the elevator to the top, or you can walk.

VARNER-HOGG STATE HISTORICAL PARK

Brazoria County. From Angleton, 15 miles west on TX 35 to West Columbia, north on FM 2852. Mailing address: P.O. Box 696, West Columbia, Texas 77486. Phone: 409-345-4656.

The first native-born governor of Texas, James Hogg, purchased the land and two-story plantation home in 1901. As one of the founders of Texaco, he believed oil lay under the property. His conviction proved true. After his death the West Columbia oil field was discovered. Hogg's daughter and renowned philanthropist, Ima, filled the mansion with antebellum furnishings in the Empire and Rococo Revival style. She donated the mansion and accompanying buildings to the state in 1958. Day use only, scheduled guided tours daily except Mondays and Tuesdays. Picnic areas, restrooms. Admission fee.

WASHINGTON-ON-THE-BRAZOS STATE HISTORICAL PARK

Washington County. 21 miles northeast of Brenham on TX 105, northeast on FM 1155. Mailing address: Box 305, Washington, Texas 77880. Phone: 409-878-2214.

On March 2, 1836, while the Alamo was under siege, representatives from across Texas met in the town of Washington to declare Texas free from Mexico. They wrote a constitution and established an interim government. Then they fled from the advancing Mexican army. After San Antonio was invaded by Mexico, President Sam Houston moved the capital from Austin to Washington, where it remained until 1845. Today, the 154-acre park on the banks of the Brazos River includes the reconstructed Independence Hall; the residence of Anson Jones, the fourth and last president of Texas; and the Star of Texas Museum, with slide presentations and exhibits relating to Texas history. Picnic areas, an amphitheater, and auditorium with kitchen facilities are also in the park.

Appendix 1

PARKS WITH CABINS, SHELTERS, OR MOTELS

In addition, private concessionaires at many Corps of Engineers reservoirs operate motels and cabins.

CABINS
Bastrop State Park
Big Bend State Natural Area
Black Kettle National Grassland
Bridgeport: Wise County Park
Caddo Lake State Park
Caddo National Grasslands
Daingerfield State Park
Garner State Park
Lake Brownwood State Park
Lake Sam Rayburn
   Shirley Creek Park
   Powell Park
Lake Tawakoni: Wind Point Park
Lake Texoma
   Big Mineral Park
   Cedar Mills Park
   Paw Paw Park
   Preston Fishing Camp
   Rock Creek Park
   Walnut Creek Park
Possum Kingdom State Park

MOTELS
Balmorhea State Park
Big Bend National Park
Davis Mountains State Park

PARKS WITH SCREENED SHELTERS
Abilene State Park
Blanco State Park
Brazos Bend State Park
Buescher State Park
Caddo Lake State Park
Choke Canyon State Park
Cleburne State Park
Eisenhower State Park
Falcon State Park
Fort Griffin State Historical Park
Fort Parker State Park
Fort Richardson State Park
Galveston: Fort Travis Seashore Park
Galveston Island State Park
Garner State Park
Goliad State Park
Huntsville State Park
Inks Lake State Park
Kerrville-Schreiner State Park
Lake Bastrop North Shore Recreation Area
Lake Bob Sandlin State Park
Lake Brownwood State Park
Lake Casa Blanca State Park
Lake Corpus Christi State Park
Lake Cypress Springs, Walleye Park
Lake Hords Creek
Lake Jacksonville Park
Lake Lewisville State Park
Lake Livingston State Park
Lake Mineral Wells State Park
Lake Tawakoni, Wind Point Park
Lake Whitney State Park
Martin Creek Lake State Park
Martin Dies, Jr. State Park
McKinney Falls State Park
Meridian State Park
Stephen F. Austin State Park
Tyler State Park

Appendix 2

PARKS WITH GROUP FACILITIES

GROUP TRAILER CAMPGROUNDS WITH HOOKUPS
Abilene State Park
Eisenhower State Park
Freeport: Quintana Beach County Park
Galveston Island State Park
Goliad State Park
Lake Livingston State Park
Lake Somerville State Park, Birch Creek Unit
Lake Texana: Brackenridge Plantation Campground
Perryton, Wolf Creek Park
Rusk-Palestine State Park, Rusk Unit
Silverton: Lake Mackenzie Park
Tyler State Park

PARKS WITH KITCHENS, BUNKHOUSES, OR DINING HALLS
Abilene State Park
Bastrop State Park
Big Bend Ranch State Natural Area
Bonham State Park
Buescher State Park
Caddo Lake State Park
Cleburne State Park
Daingerfield State Park
Devils River State Park
Eisenhower State Park
Fort Parker State Park
Garner State Park
Goose Island State Park
Kickapoo Cavern State Park
Kerrville-Schreiner State Park

Lake Brownwood State Park
Lake Colorado City State Park
Lake Lewisville State Park
Lake Mineral Wells State Park
Lake Somerville State Park, Birch Creek Unit
Lake Tawakoni, Wind Point Park
Lake Whitney State Park
Martin Dies, Jr. State Park
McKinney Falls State Park
Meridian State Park
Monahans Sandhills State Park
Rusk-Palestine State Park
Stephen F. Austin State Historical Park
Tyler State Park
Village Creek State Park

Appendix 3

PARKS WITH BICYCLE AND HORSE TRAILS

PARKS WITH BICYCLE TRAILS

Many parks have old roads that are suitable for mountain biking.
The parks listed here have maintained trails.

Bastrop State Park
Big Bend National Park
Brazos Bend State Park
Bridgeport: Wise County Park
Caprock Canyon State Park
Cedar Hill State Park
Colorado Bend State Park
Davy Crockett National Forest
Devils River State Park
Dinosaur Valley State Park
Eisenhower State Park
Enchanted Rock State Natural Area
Garner State Park
Hill Country State Natural Area
Huntsville State Park
Joe Pool Lake, Loyd Park
Kerrville-Schreiner State Park
Lake Benbrook, Holiday Park
Lake Grapevine, Rockledge-Twin Coves
Lake Houston State Park
Lake Livingston State Park
Lake Mineral Wells State Park
Lake O.C. Fisher, Red Arroyo Park
Lake Rita Blanca State Park
Lake Somerville State Park
Lost Maples State Natural Area

Lyndon B. Johnson National Grassland
Martin Creek Lake State Park
McKinney Falls State Park
Palo Duro Canyon State Park
Pedernales Falls State Park
Ray Roberts Lake State Park
San Angelo State Park
Seminole Canyon State Park
South Llano River State Park
Tyler State Park
Village Creek State Park

PARKS WITH EQUESTRIAN TRAILS
Big Bend National Park
Big Bend Ranch State Natural Area
Caprock Canyon State Park
Copper Breaks State Park
Dinosaur Valley State Park
Hill Country State Natural Area
Lake Arrowhead State Park
Lake Benbrook, Holiday Park
Lake Grapevine
Lake Houston State Park
Lake Lavon
Lake Lewisville
Lake Livingston State Park
Lake Mineral Wells State Park
Lake Rita Blanca State Park
Lake Somerville State Park
Lubbock: Buffalo Springs Lake Park
Lyndon B. Johnson National Grassland
Monahans Sandhills State Park
Palo Duro Canyon State Park
Pedernales Falls State Park
Ray Roberts Lake State Park, Isle du Bois Unit

Appendix 4

STATE PARK REGULATIONS

The state park regulations, available from any state park headquarters, should be carefully read. The following is an abbreviated
list of the major items:

1. Unauthorized removal of rock, earth, or other materials con-
   stitutes theft.
2. Archaeological sites, features, and artifacts are protected.
3. Wildlife may not be harmed, captured, or harassed.
4. Firewood may not be gathered. All plants, trees, and dead-
   wood are protected.
5. Fires may be built only in camp stoves or designated fireplaces.
6. Pets must be kept on leash and attended at all times.
7. No alcoholic beverages may be consumed in any place to
   which the public has access.
8. Noise may not be broadcast into the camp of another visitor
   between 10 P.M. and 6 A.M.
9. Trash and sewage must be disposed of properly.
10. Two- and three-wheeled vehicles must be equipped with
    street-legal muffler and spark arrester-exhaust system. They
    may be operated only in areas designated for their use.
11. Use of motor vehicle or bicycle on a pedestrian trail is pro-
    hibited.
12. Campers must obtain a camping permit.
13. Camping is limited to 14 consecutive days and 2 vehicles and
    8 people per site.
14. Waste water or sewage may not be deposited on the surface of
    the ground or in bodies of water.

Bibliography

Abbott, Tucker R. 1968. *Seashells of North America*. New York: Golden Press.

Ajilvsgi, Geyata. 1979. *Wild Flowers of the Big Thicket, East Texas, and Western Louisiana*. College Station: Texas A&M University Press.

—1984. *Wildflowers of Texas*. Bryan, Texas: Shearer Publishing.

Correll, D. S., and M. C. Johnston. 1970. *Manual of the Vascular Plants of Texas*. Renner: Texas Research Foundation.

Cox, Paul, and Patty Leslie. 1988. *Texas Trees, a Friendly Guide*. San Antonio, Texas: Corona Publishing Company.

Enquist, Marshall. 1987. *Wildflowers of the Texas Hill Country*. Austin: Lone Star Botanical.

Garrett, Judith M., and David G. Barker. 1987. *A Field Guide to Reptiles and Amphibians of Texas*. Austin: Texas Monthly Press.

Girard, Roselle M. 1964. *Texas Rocks and Minerals*. Austin: Bureau of Economic Geology, University of Texas.

Kutac, Edward A. 1989. *Birder's Guide to Texas*. Houston: Gulf Publishing.

Loughmiller, Campbell, and Lynn Loughmiller. 1984. *Texas Wildflowers*. Austin: University of Texas Press.

Maxwell, Ross A. 1971. *The Big Bend of the Rio Grande*. Austin: Bureau of Economic Geology, University of Texas.

—1970. *Geologic and Historic Guide to State Parks of Texas*. Austin: Bureau of Economic Geology, University of Texas.

Maxwell, William H. 1960. *Texas Fossils*. Austin: Bureau of Economic Geology, University of Texas.

Miller, George O. 1986. *Texas Photo Safaris*. Austin: Texas Monthly Press. 1991. Texas Hill Country: Voyageur Press.

—1988. *A Field Guide to Wildlife in Texas and the Southwest*. Austin: Texas Monthly Press.

Peterson, Roger Tory. 1963. *A Field Guide to the Birds of Texas and Adjacent States*. Boston: Houghton Mifflin.

Powell, Michael A. 1988. *Trees and Shrubs of the Trans-Pecos*. Big Bend National Park: Big Bend Natural History Association.

Robbins, Chandler S., Bertel Bruun, and Herbert S. Zim. 1983. *A Field Guide to the Birds of North America*. New York: Golden Press.

Rose, Francis L., and Russell W. Strandtmann. 1986. *Wildflowers of the Llano Estacado.* Dallas: Taylor Publishing.

Sheldon, Robert A. 1979. *Roadside Geology of Texas.* Missoula, Montana: Mountain Press.

Simpson, Benny J. 1988. *A Field Guide to Texas Trees.* Austin: Texas Monthly Press.

Tennant, Alan. 1985. *A Field Guide to Texas Snakes.* Austin: Texas Monthly Press.

Tennant, Alan, and Michael Allender. 1980. *The Guadalupe Mountains of Texas.* Austin: University of Texas Press.

Tull, Delena. 1987. *A Practical Guide to Edible and Useful Plants.* Austin: Texas Monthly Press.

—and George O. Miller. 1990. *A Field Guide to Wildflowers, Trees, and Shrubs of Texas.* Austin: Texas Monthly Press.

Vines, Robert A. 1984. *Trees of Central Texas.* Austin: University of Texas Press.

—1982. *Trees of North Texas.* Austin: University of Texas Press.

—1977. *Trees of East Texas.* Austin: University of Texas Press.

—1960. *Trees, Shrubs, and Woody Vines of the Southwest.* Austin: University of Texas Press.

Warnock, Barton H. 1970. *Wildflowers of the Big Bend Country, Texas.* Alpine, Texas: Sul Ross University.

—1974. *Wildflowers of the Guadalupe Mountains and the Sand Dune Country, Texas.* Alpine, Texas: Sul Ross University.

—1977. *Wildflowers of the Davis Mountains and Marathon Basin, Texas.* Alpine, Texas: Sul Ross University.

Weniger, Del. 1984. *Cacti of Texas and Neighboring States.* Austin: University of Texas Press.

Woodall's Campground Directory. Lake Bluff, Illinois: Woodall Publishing, published annually.

Index

238

240